# Advanced Generalist Practice

With an International Perspective

# Maria O'Neil McMahon

*East Carolina University*

c 1994

Prentice Hall, Englewood Cliffs, New Jersey 07632

**Library of Congress Cataloging-in-Publication Data**

McMahon, Maria O'Neil
   Advanced generalist practice : with an international perspective /
Maria O'Neil McMahon.
     p.  cm.
   Includes bibliographical references and index.
   ISBN 0–13–120635–4
   1. Social work education.  2. Social service.  I. Title.
   HV11.M373  1994
   361.3′2—dc20                     93–39940
                                            CIP

Acquisitions editor: Nancy Roberts
Editorial assistant: Pat Naturale
Editorial/production supervision and
  interior design: P. M. Gordon Associates
Cover design: Design Source
Production coordinator: Mary Ann Gloriande

© 1994 by Prentice-Hall, Inc.
A Paramount Communications Company
Englewood Cliffs, New Jersey 07632

Printed in the United States of America
10  9  8  7  6  5  4  3  2  1

ISBN 0-13-120635-4

Prentice-Hall International (UK) Limited, *London*
Prentice-Hall of Australia Pty. Limited, *Sydney*
Prentice-Hall Canada Inc., *Toronto*
Prentice-Hall Hispanoamericana, S.A., *Mexico*
Prentice-Hall of India Private Limited, *New Delhi*
Prentice-Hall of Japan, Inc., *Tokyo*
Simon & Schuster Asia Pte. Ltd., *Singapore*
Editora Prentice-Hall do Brasil, Ltda., *Rio de Janeiro*

Dedicated to Social Workers everywhere
as they respond to their call
to solidarity with people in need

# CONTENTS

# 2

# INTERNATIONAL PERSPECTIVE OF ADVANCED GENERALIST PRACTICE  20

# 3

# VALUES AND ETHICS IN ADVANCED GENERALIST PRACTICE    47

# 4

# KNOWLEDGE FOR ADVANCED GENERALIST PRACTICE    80

# 5

## THE METHODOLOGY OF ADVANCED GENERALISTS    107

# 6

## THE ADVANCED GENERALIST ADMINISTRATOR    128

### SARAH A. DELANCEY AND NANCY M. HALL

# 7

# RESEARCH AND TECHNOLOGY FOR ADVANCED GENERALIST PRACTICE 152

**LINNER WARD GRIFFIN**

# 8

## SOCIAL POLICY FOR ADVANCED GENERALIST PRACTICE   184

**ELBERT SIEGEL**

# 9

## THE FIELD OF ADVANCED GENERALIST PRACTICE: CHANGING PRACTICE NEEDS   208

**MARILYN A. BIGGERSTAFF, FRANK R. BASKIND, AND CARY JENSEN**

# 10

## ADVANCED GENERALIST PRACTITIONERS: RESPONDING TO CHANGING PRACTICE NEEDS  226

# PREFACE

The meaning of "generalist practice" in social work was clarified in the United States as the need for baccalaureate-level education for beginning professional social work practice became recognized by both the National Council on Social Work Education and the National Association of Social Workers in the 1970s. The need for the development and understanding of "advanced generalist practice" persists in the 1990s. Just as generalist practice developed due to changes and demands in the social and professional environment, advanced generalist practice is finding its identity in response to emerging needs and demands within the profession and within the social, national, and international environments. It took 10 to 15 years of searching and refining before a general consensus became apparent among social workers as to the meaning of generalist practice. Struggles and debates on the subject included (1) definition (generic versus generalist), (2) scope (public versus private agencies, mental health settings versus social service settings), (3) method (problem-solving process versus casework, group work, community organization), and

(4) theoretical orientation (selected theoretical perspective or eclectic use of multiple theories).

Although little debate or resistance remains regarding these topics for generalist practice, the search for understanding and agreement at the advanced generalist level continues. For example, the term "advanced generalist practice" may be called "generalist practice at the advanced level" or "advanced practice from a generalist perspective." Debate continues regarding the appropriateness of advanced generalists' engaging in clinical practice in mental health settings or in private clinical practice. It may be argued, too, that certain theories or interventions (models or methods) are too specialized for advanced generalists to demonstrate with competence. The relationship between generalist and advanced generalist practice is also a question in need of clarification.

This text is an attempt to further the dialogue and offer a guiding model that is in step with contemporary needs and developments within the profession and the extended social environment. It provides answers to the what, where, how, and why of advanced generalist practice. The interrelationship between generalist and advanced generalist practice as kindred and progressively connected practice models is emphasized. Without losing the basic characteristics of generalist practice, which is primarily a direct practice model, advanced generalist practice is presented as an integrated practice model that uses key concepts and processes in direct and indirect practice roles. Building on the direct practice model of generalist practice, emphasis is given to indirect practice roles for holistic advanced generalist practice. Several examples offered throughout the text were given by advanced generalists practicing or teaching in different countries.

A reader of this text would benefit from having first read my book, *The General Method of Social Work Practice: A Problem-Solving Approach* (Prentice-Hall, 1990). It was first published in 1984 in response to the need for a guide for action and integration of the various dimensions of generalist practice for entry-level workers as they problem solved with diverse systems. This author sees a need today for a sequel to respond to a current need in social work education and practice for guidance and integration in advanced generalist practice. The model of advanced generalist practice presented in this book responds to a need for practitioners with a global awareness in an increasingly technological postmodern environment.

# ACKNOWLEDGMENTS

The author wishes to express gratitude to all who helped to make this book a reality, particularly those colleagues who contributed to the chapters of the book, including Sarah DeLancey, Nancy M. Hall, Linner Ward Griffin, Elbert (Al) Siegel, Marilyn A. Biggerstaff, Frank R. Baskind, and Cary Jensen.

Sarah DeLancey is the Regional Director of the North Carolina Division of Social Services. She administers the delivery of social services in 33 county departments in eastern North Carolina. Her professional background includes experience as manager, consultant, supervisor, teacher, and direct service provider. She has served as an adjunct faculty member in the East Carolina University School of Social Work. Nancy Hall is a Regional Trainer for the North Carolina Division of Social Services. She coordinates and arranges training for all employees of 16 county departments of social services. Her prior roles in the Division of Social Services have included Director of Social Services, Staff Developer, Coordinator, and Assistant Program Director. She has also been a faculty member in the School of Social Work at the University of North Carolina at Chapel Hill. Throughout the state of North Carolina, all new employees

of the Division of Social Services receive an orientation in which they are introduced to generalist practice as presented in Chapter 1 of this text. In Chapter
6, Sarah DeLancey and Nancy Hall discuss the various roles of the advanced
generalist administrator, offering numerous firsthand examples from their
years of experience in public social services.

Linner Ward Griffin is the lead Professor of the Health/Aging Sequence
in the Masters of Social Work program at East Carolina University's School of
Social Work. Her research, publications, and teaching are primarily in the
areas of health, mental health, research, policy, practice, and gerontology. She
is the author of the ten volume practice monograph series called *A Guide to
Adult Protective Services,* 1990. In Chapter 7, Dr. Griffin gives a thorough overview of contemporary research with emphasis on research and technology for
advanced generalist practice.

Elbert (Al) Siegel is the Director of the Social Work Program in the
School of Social Work and Human Services at Southern Connecticut State
University. His practice experience has included working in Jewish community
centers and the field of psychiatry, and directing a resettlement agency for
immigrants in Israel. Case examples in Chapters 2 and 8 of this text reflect
some of his experiences while practicing in Israel. Currently, Dr. Siegel's research and publications are in the areas of resettlement, acculturation, and
orientation processes of larger organizations. In Chapter 8, he contributes
valuable insight and information for understanding and integrating social policy into the advanced generalist perspective.

Marilyn A. Biggerstaff is Professor of Social Work at Virginia Commonwealth University. She received her Doctorate in Social Work from the University of Southern California. Dr. Biggerstaff teaches research and social work
practice and conducts research in the practice of social work and the legal
regulation of the profession. She is in private practice in Williamsburg, Virginia. Frank R. Baskind is Professor and Dean of the School of Social Work at
Virginia Commonwealth University. He previously served as Dean of the
School of Social Work and Human Services at Southern Connecticut State
University and Director of the Undergraduate Social Work Program at the
University of Tennessee, Knoxville. Dr. Baskind conducts research in generalist social work practice. Cary Jensen received his Master of Social Work Degree
from Virginia Commonwealth University. He has been a practicing clinical social worker for 10 years and is currently on the clinical staff at the Virginia
Treatment Center for Children, Medical College of Virginia Hospital. In addition, he is a social work doctoral student at Virginia Commonwealth University. In Chapter 9, Marilyn Biggerstaff, Frank Baskind, and Cary Jensen share
results of a study they conducted using 14 focus groups of practicing social
workers. Their findings communicate changing practice needs of particular
relevance to advanced generalist practice.

I am deeply grateful to Sister Mary Joan Cook of Saint Joseph College in
West Hartford, Connecticut, for her review of the manuscript and helpful edi-

torial comments, and to my graduate assistants, Jennifer Wilson and Dorothy Sinclair Burd, and Dorothy's husband, John, for their help with data collection and graphics.

The enthusiastic reception of my first book, and the continued requests and support I have received from so many others, especially my friends in the Scandinavian countries, greatly contributed to my perseverance in writing this sequel. Special gratitude goes to Cecilie Pedersen and the faculty, students, and administrators of the Sosialhogskolen (School of Social Work) in Stavanger, Norway, for their inspiration and kind hospitality. Several people assisted also with the translations of the questionnaires sent to different countries, and social workers from a variety of countries provided me with case examples used in the text. Without their help, the information presented could not have been obtained. Finally, I wish to thank my husband, Dennis, for his humor and patience throughout the process.

*Maria O'Neil McMahon*

# 1

# Advanced Generalist Practice

## THE FOUNDATION

In 1958, the National Association of Social Workers identified a "Working Definition of Social Work Practice" to be used for developing a "common base" for practice.[1] The base for social work is a generic foundation consisting of five components that are found at the roots of any profession. They are purpose, sanction, values, knowledge, and method (Diagram 1–1). Social work educators and practitioners have identified specific content in each of these five areas to distinguish social work from other professions (Diagram 1–2). All accredited social work education programs teach the generic foundation of social work.

Basically, the primary *purpose* of social work is to enhance social functioning. Social workers develop the capacities of individuals and the resources of society to achieve the highest quality of life for both the individual and society. *Sanction* is defined as "authoritative permission."[2] Sanction to practice social work comes from a variety of sources, including governmental or voluntary

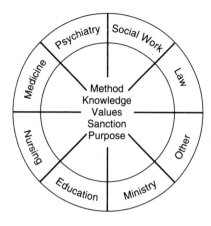

**DIAGRAM 1–1**
Foundation Components of a Profession

agencies, the organized profession, professional licensing, and the clients served.

The foundation *knowledge* for social work is primarily directed toward an understanding of human need, behavior, and diversity within the context of the social environment. Social work knowledge includes study of human biology, psychology, sociology, political science, economics, and social welfare policy and services.

The fundamental *values* of the profession are rooted in a belief in the dignity and worth of every human being and in a recognized need for a democratic, caring society. Flowing from these two basic values are the profession's Code of Ethics and identified Practice Principles which guide the actions of social workers in all areas of human service.[3]

The *method* of social work refers to "an orderly systematic mode of procedure."[4] It includes the techniques, skills, and processes used in practice. The original "mode of procedure" used in social work was patterned after the medical model of study, diagnosis, and treatment. As the profession developed, the three traditional methods of casework, group work, and community organization emerged. Today, the practice of social work "embraces multiple methods and models, including generalist practice."[5] In the generic foundation of so-

**DIAGRAM 1–2**
Foundation Components of Social Work

cial work, an overview of methods is presented and various techniques and skills are developed as central to forming helping relationships with individuals, groups, families, and communities. Foundation skills include interviewing, recording, and research skills.

As pointed out by Max Siporin, "In social work, there was from the beginning of the profession a concern for character and circumstance, for people and environment."[6] Mary Richmond stressed the psychosocial nature of the person in her noted book, *Social Diagnosis* (1917). She described "forces" and "resources" internal and external to a family.[7] The "person in environment" perspective continues to be generic to social work practice.

At the foundation of social work, therefore, there are the basic components of purpose, sanction, value, knowledge, and method carried out within the overriding perspective of person(s) in environment. An integration of the components and perspective of the social work foundation may be pictured through the use of a conoid (Diagram 1–3).

## GENERALIST PRACTICE

Generalist social work is a recognized model of practice in the profession.[8] Although it became institutionalized primarily as a focus in undergraduate social work education, generalist practice is also found as a common focus in first year graduate programs. When a social work curriculum clearly states that it prepares students for generalist practice, the basic components of knowledge, values, and method of the generic foundation of social work are expanded and augmented with key elements that are essential to generalist practice (Diagram 1–4). Knowledge development is centrally focused around systems theory and how it applies to person and environment. The study of values is expanded primarily in the area of social justice and human rights. Method and skills de-

**DIAGRAM 1–3**
The Generic Foundation of Social Work

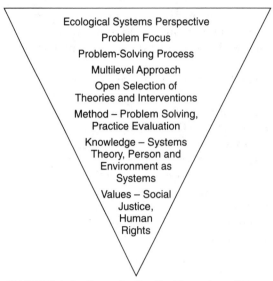

Ecological Systems Perspective

Problem Focus

Problem-Solving Process

Multilevel Approach

Open Selection of
Theories and Interventions

Method – Problem Solving,
Practice Evaluation

Knowledge – Systems
Theory, Person and
Environment as
Systems

Values – Social
Justice,
Human
Rights

**DIAGRAM 1–4**   Generalist Practice Elements and Extended Foundation Components

velopment is mainly in the areas of problem solving and practice evaluation. As these basic components are expanded, the following five essential elements are integrated throughout a generalist curriculum:

1. An ecological systems perspective
2. A problem focus
3. A problem-solving process
4. A multilevel approach
5. An open selection of theories and interventions

An *ecological systems perspective* builds on general and social systems theory with major emphasis on the concept of person (organism) in environment and the transactions that take place at the boundary where person and environment meet. The perception of person and environment includes an awareness of the various components (parts) within each system (person and environment). For example, the perception of person is developed to include the social, spiritual, educational, economic, political, psychological, physical, and sexual dimensions of self. The environment of the person is seen from the dual perspective of nurturing and sustaining systems.[9] The nurturing system includes family, friends, significant others, community, and culture. The sustaining system is composed of the institutions, organizations, and services found in the society of the person (Diagram 1–5).[10]

The *problem focus* of generalist practice refers to centering on whatever problem, need, question, or issue may be presented at a particular time. This

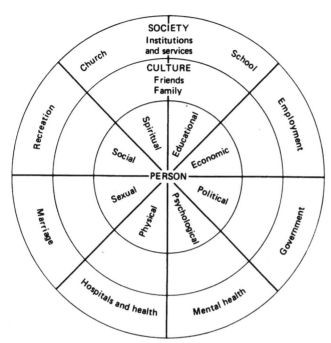

**DIAGRAM 1–5**   An Ecological Systems Perspective of Person in Environment

is in contrast with practice where the focus is on the client or one specialized problem area or system. The *problem-solving process* of generalist practice is a "multi-level problem-solving methodology."[11] It is a six-stage process, called a "general method," that guides the actions of the generalist. The stages are (1) engagement, (2) data collection, (3) assessment, (4) intervention, (5) evaluation, and (6) termination (Diagram 1–6).[12] There may be overlap and interchange among the stages depending on emerging circumstances. The process is not linear but cyclical and dynamic. It may take a short period of time, a month, or years to complete the process.

The *multilevel approach* refers, in part, to the fact that generalists may work with various sized systems, such as individuals, groups, families, or communities. It may refer also to their working with these systems individually, sequentially, or concurrently. An *open selection* of theories and interventions means that the generalist is not constricted in assessment or intervention by an area of specialization. The particular problem of focus directs the worker's use of theory and interventive strategies. The generalist frequently refers clients to specialists or uses teamwork when it becomes apparent that the intervention needed is beyond the competence of the generalist.

Basically, generalist practice is in itself a perspective. It is a way of viewing the art of helping holistically. The components of the generic foundation and

**DIAGRAM 1–6**  The General Method

I.   Engagement
    a. Problems
    b. Feelings
    c. Goals
II.  Data Collection
    a. Problems
    b. Persons
    c. Environment
III. Assessment
    a. Assessment statements
    b. Problem prioritization
    c. Contracting (plan)
IV.  Intervention
    a. Direct
    b. Indirect
    c. Teamwork
    d. Referral
V.   Evaluation
    a. Goal analysis
    b. Contract review
    c. Contract reformulation
VI.  Termination
    a. Decision: transfer, refer, terminate
    b. Plan: timing, follow-up
    c. Termination: feelings, life-cycle approach

the key elements of generalist practice are executed through an ecological systems perspective, as depicted in Diagram 1–7. The scope of attention or intervention may extend from the person to society at large. While focusing on the problem within the context of the person in environment, the whole range of possible causes and solutions is perceived as interrelated. The generalist perspective does not call for the worker to have great depth of understanding or specialized competence in one theory or model for understanding and intervention. It challenges the worker to have the ability to think with conceptual complexity, to pinpoint the particular system or point of interface in need of attention, and to mobilize whatever theory or intervention is needed.

## ADVANCED GENERALIST PRACTICE

Advanced generalists are expected to have the competence to practice independently in complex systems with a variety of problems and populations. In advanced generalist practice, identified foundation components and generalist practice elements are extended for greater breadth and depth, as outlined

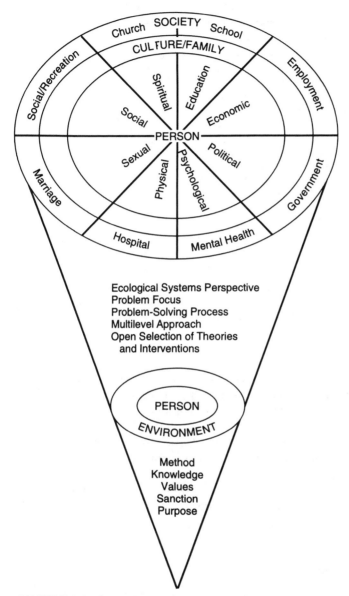

**DIAGRAM 1–7** Generalist Practice

in Diagram 1–8. Central concepts that characterize advanced generalist practice according to the model presented in this book include ethical decision making, international social work and welfare, advanced theories and interventive models, advanced general method, advanced research and technology, and advanced ecological systems perspective.

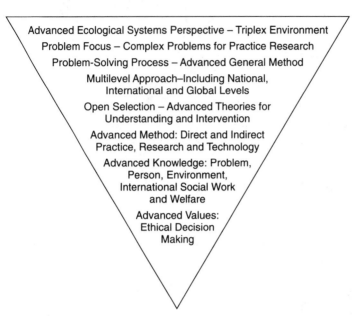

Advanced Ecological Systems Perspective – Triplex Environment

Problem Focus – Complex Problems for Practice Research

Problem-Solving Process – Advanced General Method

Multilevel Approach–Including National,
International and Global Levels

Open Selection – Advanced Theories for
Understanding and Intervention

Advanced Method: Direct and Indirect
Practice, Research and Technology

Advanced Knowledge: Problem,
Person, Environment,
International Social Work
and Welfare

Advanced Values:
Ethical Decision
Making

**DIAGRAM 1–8**   Extended Elements and Components for Advanced Generalist Practice

### Values and Ethics

In addition to demonstrating a commitment to the fundamental values and practice principles identified for generalist practice, the advanced generalist is able to demonstrate commitment and competence in complex situations calling for ethical decision making and resolution of ethical dilemmas. Working within complex systems may include multinational situations. The advanced generalist is sensitive and knowledgeable, with an ability to recognize cross-cultural conflict in norms and values. For example, an American advanced generalist working for the military in a foreign country with people of different nationalities may need to face issues involving conflicting parental roles, legal rights, and service opportunities.

### Advanced Knowledge

The advanced generalist calls upon more extensive personality, political, and practice theory than the beginning generalist. Theories to explain causes of personal and social problems and theories to direct practice interventions are studied with greater breadth and depth. The advanced generalist has enhanced knowledge of persons and their environments. Advanced study may be selected in such areas as psychopathology, drug addiction, learning styles, spirituality, advanced economics, law, complex organizations and bureaucracies, and international social work. Specific advanced content to be studied depends on what each student needs according to an individualized assessment for advanced practice with persons and environments.

### An International Perspective

Knowledge of environment at the advanced level extends outside the boundary of society to the world sphere of nations. The dual perspective of the environment becomes a triplex perspective of nurturing, sustaining, and international systems. The third dimension is a global awareness built on knowledge of national and international problems, policies, and programs. Systems theory is used to study the distinctiveness and interdependence of nations and to analyze and compare their welfare policies and services. In addition, knowledge of problems includes an ability to recognize universal problems, such as mental illness and drug addiction, and more distinctively national problems, such as racial discrimination and abject poverty. Advanced generalists may practice at any pinpointed area of this advanced ecological systems perspective of person and environment (Diagram 1–9).

### Skills and Methodology

The advanced generalist brings a problem focus and a problem-solving process to work with multiple systems and cultures. Because the nature of the work is advanced and complex, the practitioner is expected to have the competence to practice with little or no supervision and with a broad range of skills and interventions based on diverse practice theories.

The skill level of the advanced generalist is developed to work with a variety of systems, particularly in the area of indirect practice, while the entry-level generalist is prepared primarily for direct practice with individuals, groups, families, and communities. All of the key characteristics of generalist practice are called upon as the advanced worker interacts with complex client systems, supervisees, employees, administrators, or public and national representatives.

### The Advanced General Method

The problem-solving process called *the general method of social work practice* (see Diagram 1–6) is an essential element in both the entry and advanced levels of generalist practice. At the advanced level, the process may be called the *advanced general method*. It does not exclude the use of other methods or interventions.

Within the profession of social work, there appears to be some confusion regarding the words "method" and "intervention." According to the NASW "working definition," method means "an orderly systematic mode of procedure."[13] As stated earlier, generalist practice has a six-stage method that is a

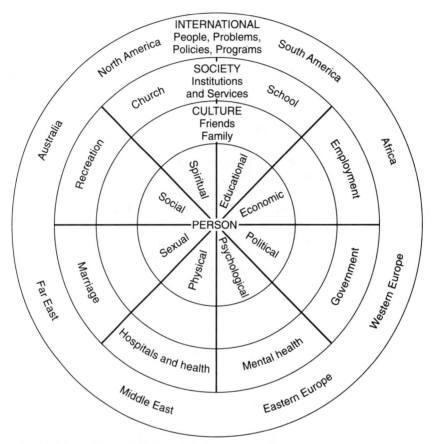

**DIAGRAM 1–9**    Advanced Ecological Systems Perspective

"mode of procedure" known as a problem-solving process. The fourth stage is called "intervention." It refers to the planned roles, tasks, and activities selected by the worker to address the identified problem. The problem-solving process called the general method or the advanced general method does not exclude the use of various theories, modes, or methods of intervention. Rather, the general method calls upon various modes, models, or methods as the process is executed during the fourth stage. Interventions at both entry and advanced levels of generalist practice differ according to the specific problem, need, or circumstances of attention at any given time. The advanced generalist, however, is expected to have greater breadth and depth in knowledge and selection of diverse interventions.

The advanced general method differs from the general method primarily in its application to indirect practice situations. Both advanced generalists and generalists use the six-stage process as they practice directly as line workers. At the advanced level, however, advanced generalists use the process also as they practice indirectly as supervisors, managers, administrators, advanced researchers, or social planners.

### Advanced Research

Research in advanced generalist practice goes beyond the ability to evaluate one's own practice or to conduct traditional research studies. A key expectation of the advanced generalist is to be able to evaluate and compare problems, populations, programs, and policies in order to understand and select the most appropriate plan for a particular problem or need. Comparative or evaluative studies of a broad range of systems, including those of a global nature, are appropriately found in the research of advanced generalist practitioners.

In addition, advanced generalists are expected to be able to manage complex data through enhanced skills in the use of computer technology. They use computer-operated statistical packages to compare and analyze data. The advanced practitioner, therefore, will need to have the knowledge and skills to take advantage of available software and equipment for data processing and analysis.

### The Advanced Generalist Perspective

Diagram 1–10 illustrates the perspective of advanced generalist practice. This model of practice is rooted in the generic foundation of social work. It integrates a generalist practice perspective with advanced knowledge of persons and environments, advanced values and ethics, and advanced skills and methodology for direct and indirect problem solving, from an advanced ecological systems perspective (triplex environmental perspective). The culminating characteristics of advanced generalist practice are identified in tier three of Diagram 1–10.

## PREPARATION FOR ADVANCED GENERALIST PRACTICE

Studies have shown that contemporary graduates of MSW programs are moving into indirect practice roles within one year after graduation. Approximately 40% of the work time of new graduates is spent in teaching, supervision, and management. They have reported strong feelings of insecurity in these roles because they received little or no preparation while in their MSW programs.[14] In an effort to respond to the emerging needs of students today, some MSW programs across the country have begun to offer a concentration to prepare students for practice at all four levels of line worker, supervisor, program

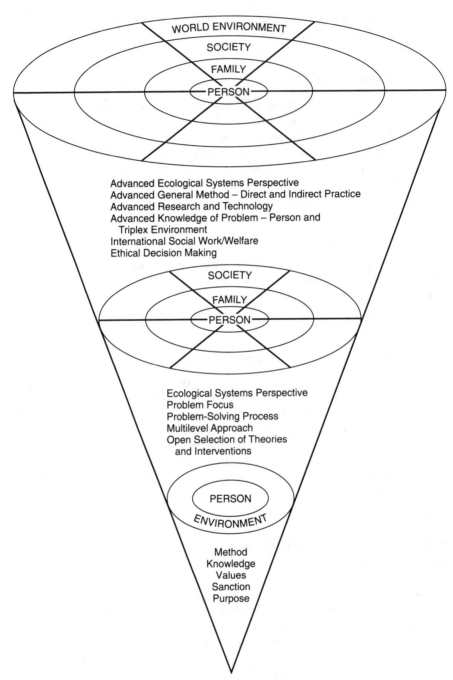

**DIAGRAM 1–10**   Advanced Generalist Practice Perspective

manager, and agency administrator. This curriculum may be identified as a "concentration" in advanced generalist practice.

Every accredited graduate social work program must offer one or more "concentrations." There are several practice dimensions that could be used to organize concentrations. These include fields of practice, method, population, or problem. As pointed out by Patricia Ewalt, "No single organzing dimension for concentrations has yet been adopted by social work education or practice."[15] Required content to be found in each concentration is described in the *Curriculum Policy for the Master's Degree* as follows:

> Included in each concentration should be relevant content in each of the following areas: social policy and legislation, existing and potential service strategies from prevention to treatment, and relevant practice theories, methodologies, and research. Other frameworks for organizing concentrations are also possible, as in a concentration of knowledge and skill leading to advanced generalist practice.[16]

A major question under study today in social work education is, What should be included in an advanced generalist "concentration of knowledge and skill"? Related questions for consideration are the following: What is currently being offered in educational programs identified as having advanced generalist practice concentrations? Are the five essential elements of generalist practice described earlier (i.e., ecological systems perspective, problem focus, problem-solving process, multilevel approach, open selection) common threads interwoven throughout each program? Do the concentrations include advanced knowledge, values, and skills built on these generalist elements and the generic foundation of social work? Are the competencies of the generalist extended for both direct and indirect practice? How is the ecological systems perspective advanced in programs offering "a concentration of knowledge and skills leading to advanced generalist practice?"

In the 1989 *Summary Information on Master of Social Work Programs* (CSWE), ten graduate programs indicate an offering of a concentration in advanced generalist practice.[17] Two of the ten use the word "generic" instead of "generalist,"[18] and one calls the concentration "advanced practice in the generalist perspective."[19] One of the programs requires students in the advanced generalist track to study beyond the usual two years for an MSW degree program.[20]

In reviewing catalogues and literature from each of the ten schools with advanced generalist concentrations, it becomes apparent that the general elements of problem focus, problem solving, ecological systems perspective, multilevel approach, and open selection of theories and interventions are present in all of the programs. There is clear indication that all the programs prepare students to work with more complex systems and problems than would be expected of entry level generalists. All ten schools indicate that they prepare students for both direct and indirect practice. With some variation, the indirect practice roles identified include administrator, supervisor, manager, consultant, staff developer, grants writer, program and resource developer, social activist, and professional leader.

In the area of research, only four of the programs describe their advanced research as including evaluative research of macro systems and programs. Only three of the programs clearly indicate a requirement to enhance skills in computer technology. None of the programs describes any content on comparative research of an international nature.

Two of the advanced generalist programs require courses in advanced ethics and two require courses in psychopathology. Some of the programs offer elective courses in the areas of law (4 programs), drug/alcohol addiction (3), and human sexuality (1).

There is no indication that any advanced generalist curriculum requires content on international social welfare or social work. One program offers an elective course called "Comparative Social Welfare Policies and Services." Although the programs use an ecological systems perspective in advanced generalist practice, the perspective is not extended to include an awareness of the needs, problems, programs, and policies of other nations. In one catalogue, however, the Dean of the school writes:

> As our world moves into the 21st Century many new challenges, problems and opportunities await us all. What is being touted as a globally based information driven world will gradually, and inexorably, replace the industrially based world we now know. The practice of social work will be affected by the many forces which move us through the 1990s. In my opinion, the person-in-situation perspective of social work will serve our profession and our clients well in our new social environment.[21]

The question may be raised as to whether content on the "globally based information driven world" should be included in all programs preparing students for advanced generalist practice in the 21st century? Advanced generalist practice is on the cutting edge of what is needed for contemporary and futuristic professional service "in our new social environment." Further study and development are needed for clarification and consistency in offering advanced generalist concentrations. In response to this felt need, an advanced ecological generalist model of practice is presented in this text.

## THE ADVANCED ECOLOGICAL GENERALIST

The advanced ecological generalist is one of the newest practitioners in the profession of social work. As illustrated in Diagram 1–11, there are three levels of preparation for this practitioner. Advanced ecological generalists acquire all three levels of preparation and hold Master of Social Work degrees.

In the field of social work education there are, at a pre-professional level,

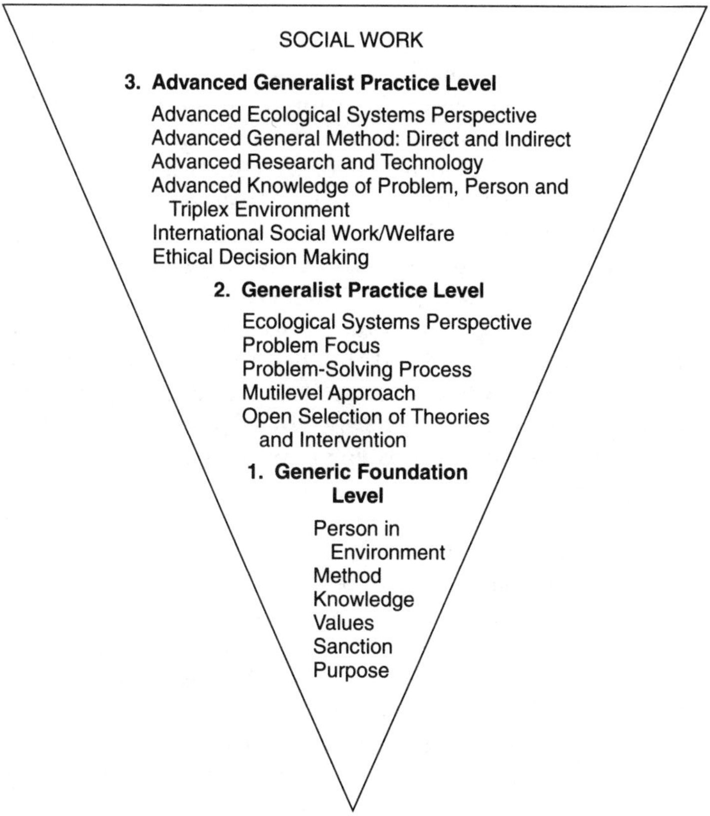

SOCIAL WORK

**3. Advanced Generalist Practice Level**

Advanced Ecological Systems Perspective
Advanced General Method: Direct and Indirect
Advanced Research and Technology
Advanced Knowledge of Problem, Person and
    Triplex Environment
International Social Work/Welfare
Ethical Decision Making

**2. Generalist Practice Level**

Ecological Systems Perspective
Problem Focus
Problem-Solving Process
Mutilevel Approach
Open Selection of Theories
    and Intervention

**1. Generic Foundation
    Level**

Person in
    Environment
Method
Knowledge
Values
Sanction
Purpose

**DIAGRAM 1–11**    Three Levels of Preparation for Advanced Generalist Practice in Social Work

social work associates from two-year college programs. They are expected to have the social work generic foundation if they are to call themselves "social work" associates. They serve in helping, supportive roles throughout the field of human services.

At the entry level of professional practice, social workers have baccalaureate degrees in which they acquire the generic foundation and generalist practice knowledge and competence. At the Master's level, all social workers build on the generic foundation and acquire preparation for a concentration. Generalist practice is the foundation for a concentration in advanced generalist practice. It may serve also as the foundation for a number of other concentrations in MSW programs. Some MSW students develop generalist practice competence in the first year of graduate education and select a concentration in a particular field, problem, population, or method in their second year. MSW students selecting an advanced generalist practice concentration move along the continuum of generic foundation to generalist practice to advanced generalist practice throughout their graduate curriculum (Diagram 1–12).

As professions age and social problems multiply, there is an apparent merging of disciplines and overlapping of services. The "turf protection" or "pure discipline" of the past is becoming increasingly obsolete. It is essential that each discipline and each practitioner has a clear identity in order to make a valid and clear contribution to a helping team or situation. There is a strong need for new, emerging practitioners, such as advanced generalists, to be able to articulate who they are and what they have to bring to the field of human services.

A central, distinguishing characteristic of all social work practitioners is the "person in environment" perspective, which is found at the roots of the profession. This perspective is nurtured and enriched through ecological systems theory, which is pervasive throughout generalist and advanced generalist practice. The advanced ecological systems perspective of person and environment (see Diagram 1–10) provides an overriding framework and force for the identification of the advanced ecological generalist.

The major challenge and contribution of advanced ecological generalists is their holistic perception and understanding of phenomena. They bring to any practice situation their advanced ability to perceive the whole. Holistic theory stresses that the whole is greater than the sum of its parts.[22] Advanced ecological generalists enrich human services as they work in concert with other social workers and professionals from other disciplines. They contribute a keen ability to see the interrelationship of parts as well as the potential of the whole.

An inmate in a maximum security prison asked a church volunteer, "What color is God?" The inmate was a husky, 19-year-old black male who had

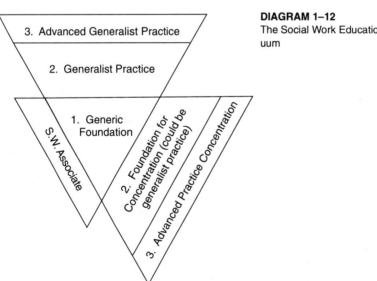

**DIAGRAM 1–12**
The Social Work Education Continuum

been in correctional institutions since he was 14. The volunteer was a 35-year-old white nun who visited the prison with a church group once a month for a prayer service with the inmates. She responded, "Norberto, I think God is golden." He looked at her in dismay, and said, "Say what?" She said, "I think God is golden because when you unite the four races of the world, the red, yellow, black, and white, I think you come up with a brilliant gold color." Norberto was speechless. The nun saw things holistically. She was able to see that the whole was indeed greater than the sum of its parts. Advanced ecological generalists have a holistic perspective that enables them to understand and respond to the persons and environments of the world in an enlightened process for becoming whole.

Advanced generalists working as direct practitioners, managers, administrators, and educators in a variety of countries have provided case examples that are used throughout this book. In the following case example, a generalist and an advanced generalist work together to provide joint service for a mother and daughter living in Paris, France. The entry-level generalist serves the clients directly as case manager. The advanced generalist provides direct treatment for one of the clients and serves as supervisor for the generalist and manager of the counseling program.

## CASE EXAMPLE: JOINT SERVICE—GENERALIST AND ADVANCED GENERALIST

Evelene M. is a 32-year-old single parent. She works as a receptionist in a military hotel in Paris, France. Her daughter, Marie, is 13 years old. Evelene sought help from the Social Service Department because she was unable to cope with her daughter's defiance toward her. She believed that her daughter was getting into drugs and failing in school. She saw a poster in her Church announcing counseling services for parents of teen-agers with problems.

Jon Wolfe conducted the initial interview. He is an entry-level generalist social worker who recently graduated from the École de Service Social de l'Assistance Publique. His supervisor, Leslie R., has been practicing in the Department for ten years. She serves as an advanced generalist. In addition to supervising entry-level workers, she is the manager of the counseling service program of the Department. During intake, Jon listened to Ms. M. and encouraged her to bring her daughter to the next interview. He collected data regarding person(s), problem(s), and environment(s). As he identified needs, he gathered information about possible resources available for the family. Marie said that her mother was always picking on her and that she did not like her new school. With supervision from his supervisor, John developed a social history and a case assessment, and, in dialogue with Evelene and her daughter, he completed a service plan.

Jon worked primarily as the case manager for the family. He networked with other local agencies and programs to provide supplemental services for mother and daughter. Marie joined a youth group and her mother attended a parenting skills class. Both the youth group and the parenting classes were offered by a social worker, called "an education specialist" in France. The classes and group were held at a branch office of the department in the section of the city where Evelene and her daughter lived. Leslie, Jon's supervisor, provided individual casework for Evelene, who was assessed as depressed with occasional alcohol abuse problems. Evelene wondered if she had made the right decision to have a child and not marry. She feared that she was going to lose her job because she did not have the computer skills needed. She did not have the money to attend classes and her employer was not willing to cover the cost for training employees. Leslie R. met with the department's chief administrator and advocated for parents at risk of having to go on public assistance to be allowed to receive job training along with those receiving assistance.

Both Jon and Leslie met regularly to review planned interventions and case progress. After a year of service, Evelene started to feel better about herself and improved communication with her daughter. Marie was not presenting any major problems at home or at school. The joint service offered by a generalist and an advanced generalist was apparently providing the scope, depth, and coordination of services needed to effectively maintain the family.

## SUMMARY

Social work educators are being called upon to identify and refine the meaning of generalist and advanced generalist practice for greater consistency and unanimity. In this chapter, a three-level model has been presented to describe the dimensions, content, sequence, and boundaries of advanced generalist practice. Brief descriptions of the generic foundation of practice, the key elements of generalist practice, and the central components of advanced generalist practice have been offered. A case example was given to demonstrate how a generalist and an advanced generalist could complement each other in joint service for a client system.

The results of a survey of existing Master of Social Work programs with concentrations in advanced generalist practice have been reviewed in light of the model presented in this text. Although all programs were consistent in addressing the key elements of generalist practice, there was an apparent need for further clarification and development in the advanced practice area. The model of advanced generalist practice proposed in this chapter challenges and encourages graduate programs to demonstrate vision and provide students with content that expands the boundaries of practice to encompass a global perspective of "our new social environment."[23]

In the following chapters, focus will be given to those key concepts that have been identified as characteristic of the advanced level of generalist practice. An effort will be made to provide case examples of advanced generalist practice with diverse problems, roles, and geographic locations.

In summary, a perspective of advanced generalist practice consists of foundation, generalist, and advanced generalist components. It is a perspective with a process and focus that are problem oriented and problem pervasive. The holistic perspective of advanced generalist practice extends from the person to the global environment. Advanced generalist practice is an exciting, challenging addition to the social work profession. It brings hope and growth to those who enter its boundaries and struggle with the call to explore its unknown potential.

## NOTES

1. Commission on Social Work Practice, NASW, "Working Definition of Social Work Practice," quoted in Harriet M. Bartlett, *The Common Base of Social Work Practice* (New York: National Association of Social Workers, 1970), pp. 221–224.

2. Ibid., p. 222.

3. National Association of Social Workers, *Code of Ethics,* as adopted by the 1979 NASW Delegate Assembly, effective July 1, 1980; Felix P. Biestek, S.J., *The Casework Relationship* (Chicago: Loyola University Press, 1957).

4. Commission on Social Work Practice, NASW, "Working Definition," p. 223.

5. Council on Social Work Education, *Curriculum Policy for the Master's Degree and Baccalaureate Degree Programs in Social Work Education,* adopted by the Board of Directors 1982, effective July 1, 1983, p. 11.

6. Max Siporin, "Ecological Systems Theory in Social Work," *Journal of Sociology and Social Welfare* 7 (1980): 508.

7. Mary E. Richmond, *The Long View* (New York: Russell Sage Foundation, 1930), pp. 186–202.

8. National Association of Social Workers, *Encyclopedia of Social Work,* 1987, p. 663.

9. Dolores G. Norton, *The Dual Perspective: Inclusion of Ethnic Minority Content in the Social Work Curriculum* (New York: Council on Social Work Education, 1978), p. 5.

10. Maria O'Neil McMahon, *The General Method of Social Work Practice: A Problem-Solving Approach,* 2nd ed. (Englewood Cliffs, N.J.: Prentice-Hall, 1990), p. 5.

11. Group for the Study of Generalist and Advanced Generalist Practice, Colorado Meeting, 1988.

12. McMahon, *The General Method,* p. 339.

13. Commission on Social Work Practice, NASW, "Working Definition," p. 223.

14. S. Maria Joan O'Neil, R.S.M., "A comparative study of Quality Practice of Social Workers from One and Two Year Graduate Social Work Programs, Utilizing an Ecological Perspective of Professional Competence." Unpublished Dissertation, National Catholic School of Social Service of the Catholic University of America, Washington, D.C., 1977.

15. Patricia L. Ewalt, *Curriculum Design and Development for Graduate Social Work Education* (New York: Council on Social Work Education, 1983), p. 23.

16. Council on Social Work Education, *Curriculum Policy Statement,* p. 13.

17. Council on Social Work Education, *Summary Information on Master of Social Work Education Programs* (Alexandria, Va.: Council on Social Work Education, 1990).

18. Ibid., pp. 13 and 25.

19. Ibid., p. 75.

20. Ibid., p. 24.

21. Dean Donald R. Bardill, *School of Social Work, Florida State University* (Catalogue), p. 1.

22. Jan C. Smuts, *Holism and Evolution* (New York: W. W. Norton, 1939).

23. Bardill, *State University,* p. 1.

# 2

# International Perspective of Advanced Generalist Practice

## *INTRODUCTION*

Social workers value human diversity. The social work profession is committed to preparing students to understand and appreciate the uniqueness of each person and the distinctiveness of cultures. In advanced generalist practice, this understanding and appreciation are enhanced through the development of an international perspective of social work practice.

Students in undergraduate programs learning to be generalists are prepared to practice as social workers in a variety of social service programs in their own country. They learn about different people, particularly populations-at-risk. They study human oppression and the meaning of social justice.[1] In advanced generalist education, the focus broadens to populations in different countries and their diverse needs. Advanced generalists learn about the practice of social work and social services offered around the world. They develop skills for detecting similarities and differences among peoples and practices to make sound professional judgments for selecting interventions appropriate to person and place.

## THE INTERNATIONAL PERSPECTIVE

The person in environment perspective of the foundation of social work and the ecological systems perspective of generalist practice are extended in advanced generalist practice to an international perspective of social work practice (see Diagram 1–10). The advanced generalist develops an awareness of the interdependence of a person's nurturing and sustaining environment with the international macro system or world environment. Applying systems theory, which presents every system as a subsystem of a larger system,[2] advanced generalists recognize such realities as economic, physical, psychological, and social effects on local people and societies due to international conflict or shifts in the balance of power or resources. The Gulf Crisis of 1991, for example, had a major impact on individuals, families, communities, human service programs, and countries around the world.

The international perspective of advanced generalist practice, therefore, is a global awareness that includes a sensitivity to the uniqueness of countries as well as to the universality of humankind. While seeing each country as a distinct system with multiple dimensions, the advanced generalist recognizes the interface and interdependence of countries with each other and of each country with the world system as a whole.

## INTERNATIONAL SOCIAL WORK

With today's mobility and easy access to distant places, advanced generalists and the people they serve often move in and out of different locations, countries, cultures, and environments. Advanced generalists are exceptionally well prepared for international social work. The term "international social work" may refer to social welfare services provided by international agencies, such as the World Health Organization or the Save the Children Federation.[3] It may refer also to exchanges that take place between social work teachers, practitioners, and students from different countries.[4] A social worker from one country who is practicing in another country may be described as an "international social worker."

The education and experience of advanced generalists foster their capability to practice in international agencies and social work settings in various countries. They are prepared to work with a broad range of problems and diverse populations in direct and indirect practice roles. This preparation is complemented by their advanced ecological perspective, which includes knowledge of international social work and social services.

In this chapter, information is provided about the people, problems, programs, and practice of social work in countries around the world. Data were collected primarily through literature search, questionnaire (see Appendix A), and personal interviews with practicing social work educators, practitioners, and students of different nations. The topics addressed include (1) social work (definition, education, and practice), (2) social services (public and private), and (3) the problems of people coming to the attention of social workers (pervasive problems, emerging needs). The countries identified were selected because they represent a cross-section of the globe and because they have social work programs with individuals who responded to the questionnaire or personal interview. Advanced generalist students are encouraged to individualize their learning needs and to give those countries they know the least about their particular attention.

## SOCIAL WORK IN DIFFERENT COUNTRIES

Is social work universal? Is it the same in Africa as it is in England? What type of social services is available in Japan as compared to Germany or the United States? Is there a common, universal foundation of social work? Are the social work values, knowledge, and skills taught in educational programs in different countries the same? Are social workers around the world facing similar social problems or individual needs? Are there generalists and advanced generalists in other countries?

In response to these questions, an attempt will be made to briefly describe twenty countries and to identify the meaning of social work, social services, and the problems brought to the attention of social workers in these diverse geographic locations. The descriptions relating to social work were provided primarily by social work educators and practitioners in the countries identified. Data about population and geography were found mainly in the *World Atlas* 1990–1991.[5]

### North America

*Canada:* Canada is slightly larger (3,851,788 square miles) than the United States. The country is divided into ten provinces and two territories. In 1990, the population was 26,510,000, with 76.5% living in urban areas. Forty percent of the population are of British Isles origin, 27% of French origin, and 1.5% of indigenous Indian and Eskimo ethnicity. There is a recent influx of people from the Caribbean and Asia into Canada. English and French are the official languages of the country.

Social work is a recognized profession in Canada, requiring BSW (minimum of four years) and MSW (additional year) university degrees. Social workers can be found working in private and public agencies and in private practice. They practice in schools, hospitals, and other institutions. Their duties include counseling, family therapy, home visits, community organization, administration, and policy development. Major problems presented to social workers include child neglect and abuse, poverty, care of the elderly and handicapped, work with minorities, substance abuse, family breakdown, and lack of access to needed services.

Canada has a public social welfare program organized at a provincial level that offers financial support and other services such as child, family, elderly, and handicapped services, universal health care, and drug/alcohol programs. Child care services are delivered by child care workers. Most other services are offered by social workers. In 1962, the Canadian Association of Social Workers was founded. Each province and the territories have at least one school of social work and an affiliated association with CASW.

*USA:* The United States of America extends for 3,618,765 square miles and includes fifty states and the District of Columbia. It is one third the size of Africa and one half the size of South America. The population in 1990 was 251,398,000, with 73.7% of the population living in urban areas. The language of the country is predominantly English, with a growing Spanish minority.

In the United States, social work is a recognized profession at both the baccalaureate and master's degree levels. Baccalaureate social workers are identified as "generalists." Master level workers are called "advanced practitioners" with a concentration in an area of practice, which may be according to field (e.g., health, education, etc.), problem (e.g., drug addiction, mental illness, etc.), or methodology (e.g., micro, macro, advanced generalist practice, etc.).

There is a public welfare system in the United States at the federal, state, and local levels. Services include financial aid for basic needs, medical care, and social services. The majority of "social workers" in public social services do not have professional social work degrees. Social workers are employed in public and private agencies and in private practice. In addition to public welfare, there are private networks of sectarian agencies (Jewish, Catholic, Lutheran, and others), and a national network of family service agencies. Major problems brought to the attention of social workers in the United States include substance abuse, health care costs, homelessness, marital discord, and structural inequalities.

### South America

*Peru:* Peru covers 496,223 square miles and is slightly smaller than Alaska. In 1990, the population in Peru was 21,906,000, with 68.8% living in urban areas. Forty-five percent of the population are Indian, and 37% are of mixed Indian and European ancestry. The official languages of the country are Spanish and Quechua.

Social work in Peru has been recognized by law since 1936, with courses offered at universities since 1979. There are thirteen universities in Peru (six state and seven private) that offer the five-year bachelor degree in social work. The majority of social workers in Peru work for state agencies. Their duties include individual and family counseling, education, organization, administration, and investigation of abuse. They also offer services in the areas of health, housing, social security, minority assistance, and justice issues.

Over the last fifteen years, social services in Peru have increased in the number of available service organizations, including international centers and church organizations. Major problems in Peru as identified by social workers are poverty, hunger, malnutrition, premature death, unemployment, poor working conditions, violence, abandoned infants, and political/economic issues.

### Africa/South Africa

*Egypt:* Egypt covers 386,660 square miles, with a population of 54,706,000. The percentage of people living in rural areas is 54.2%. Ninety percent of the population are of Eastern Hamitic ethnicity, and 10% are of Greek, Italian, or Syro-Lebanese background. The official language is Arabic, with English and French widely spoken.

Social work in Egypt has been a recognized profession since the 1940s, requiring a university degree in social work (BA or BSW), which includes four years of academic studies and practical training after high school. Social work education is available also at the MSW and PhD levels. The majority of social workers are employed by public agencies. Private practice has recently developed. Social workers are engaged in community organization and development, group work, policy development, and counseling. Major problems they encounter include a lack of participation of citizens in problem solving, extended families with low income, drastic changes in family life, and inability of parents to meet the changing needs of their children and youth.

Egypt has a public welfare program that offers public assistance, family planning, youth programs, services for the aged, family and children services, and services for the handicapped. Social services are also delivered by social workers in schools and universities, underdeveloped urban and rural areas, the armed forces, and religious institutions.

*Kenya:* The land area of Kenya covers 224,961 square miles, with some dispute over land boundaries with Sudan and Somalia. Kenya is one of Africa's most successful agricultural production regions. The population in 1990 was 24,639,000, with 80.3% living in rural areas. There are ten identifiable ethnic divisions in Kenya, with the Kikuyu (21%) being the largest. The primary languages of Kenya are Swahili (official) and English.

Efforts to have social work become a recognized profession in Kenya have largely been fruitless. Social work is seen primarily as volunteer work involving delivery of services to the poor. The educational background of social workers is varied, from no formal education, to diplomas from government training institutions, to degrees from universities with three years of training after advanced level high school.

Kenya has a public welfare program in the form of subsidized essential services, such as health and education, delivered by the government. There are also a number of nongovernmental service agencies, which include private agencies, religious agencies, and private practice. Work activities of social workers in Kenya include family counseling, home visits, community organization, policy formulation, and administration. Major problems brought to the attention of social workers are general poverty, health problems, school-related expenses, and family conflict.

*South Africa:* The total land area of South Africa included 471,444 square miles, slightly less than twice the size of Texas. The population in 1990 was 39,550,000, with 55.9% living in urban areas. The percentage of blacks in South Africa is 73.8%, with 14.3% white, 9.1% colored, and 2.8% Indian. The official language of South Africa is English. Afrikaans and many other vernacular languages (Zulu, Xhosa, North and South Sotho, Tswana, and others) are also spoken.

In South Africa, social work is a recognized profession requiring a minimum of four years of training at a university. The degree received is a BASW. Social workers may be found in public and private agencies and in private practice. Their duties cover a range of services, including counseling and community organization. The public welfare system provides poor relief and social pensions. Services include statutory work involving juvenile offences, probation, and casework to families on relief. Although the normal caseload in public welfare service is 60 cases, some workers carry 120 cases. Major problems seen by social workers in South Africa are poverty, lack of adequate housing, unemployment, and family breakdown.

### Europe

*Finland:* Finland covers 130,127 square miles, with a population of 4,984,000 people. Approximately 61.8% of the population live in urban areas. The official languages of the land are Finnish (93.5%) and Swedish (6.3%). There are small numbers of Lapp and Russian-speaking minorities in Finland.

Although social work is a recognized profession in Finland, it is often called a semi-profession because it is seen as not having a theory of its own. Social workers may have a master's degree, a bachelor's degree, or a Diploma from a Qualification Program after extensive work in the practice field.

Most social workers are employed in public agencies. Their practice is mainly individual counseling or administration. Some social workers practice in prisons, refugee centers, hospitals, schools, and rehabilitation centers. Primary problems brought to the attention of social workers are income/unemployment, alcohol abuse, relationship problems, child welfare, needs of the elderly, and problems with self-esteem.

Finland has a highly developed model for public social welfare and health care. Services include financial assistance, homemaker help for families and the elderly, child welfare, services for the handicapped, and counseling for individuals and families. There are some emerging private agencies that attempt to offer people an alternative to public services.

*France:*   France extends for 211,208 square miles and is the largest country in western Europe. The population of France in 1990 was 56,367,000, with 73.4% residing in urban areas. Approximately 7% of the population are recent immigrants from such countries as Algeria, Morocco, Tunisia, Portugal, Italy, Spain, Turkey, and Indochina. French is the official language of the country.

Social work is a recognized profession in France. Preparation requires the passage of a social work entrance exam followed by three years at a university and one year of field placement. In some public and private agencies, social workers are appointed and the agency has the responsibility for the preparation of its workers. Each societal institution (e.g., armed forces, railways, agriculture, etc.) is free to develop its own social services. The government is attempting to supplement the efforts of institutions by having a family social worker available for each geographic area of 5000 people. Public, semi-public, and private agencies are recognized and often funded by the government.

France has a family allowance policy that provides benefits to any mother with children regardless of marital status or occupation. The social insurance program provides benefits for the salaried and the nonsalaried. Farmers' or farm workers' social needs are supported fully by the government. The government subsidizes housing by giving money directly to pay rent or by offering to build homes. Eighty percent of the hospitals in France are publicly owned. In both public and private hospitals, patients are reimbursed 65% to 100% of their health costs. Approximately half of the social workers in France work in public services, with one fourth in semi-public (partially subsidized) and one-fourth in private agencies. Major problems brought to their attention are family breakdown, unemployment of women, adolescent youth problems, and drug addiction.

*Germany:*   Germany (East and West) covers 137,803 square miles. The total population is 79,544,000, with over 85% of the people living in urban areas. The language of the land is German, with some diversity in dialects.

In Germany, as in other European countries, social work is seen as a profession, but separate from the university for educational preparation. The social worker is educated in the Fachhochschule, which is a technical professional college, rather than the Universitaet, which is a place for research and science. There are two models of social work education, both taking four years for completion. In the "one-phase" model, the third year is a guided fieldwork experience; in the "two-phase" model, the field practicum is in the fourth year. Social workers are prepared to practice in the areas of (1) youth work, youth education, adult education; (2) elementary and preschool education and special education; (3) youth welfare service, family assistance, and help for the elderly; (4) Re-socialization and rehabilitation; and (5) social welfare administration and social planning.

The German social welfare system consists of public assistance, private welfare, and publicly sponsored insurance. Emphasis is placed on a public-private partnership in human services. It is based on a subsidiary principle that holds that if private organizations are available, they should be supported rather than forming a state monopoly. Financial assistance is available for anyone who falls below a guaranteed standard of living. Housing in Germany is often built and supported by federal money. Rent is income based. Social workers practice in both public and private agencies, and work with individuals, families, groups, and communities. They frequently make house calls and write letters to officials about emerging needs. They also work as supervisors, administrators, and consultants. Major problems brought to their attention include money management, home care for the elderly, and discrimination toward those needing financial assistance and toward immigrants.

*Ireland:*   Ireland extends for 27,135 square miles. It is slightly larger than the state of West Virginia. The population of Ireland in 1990 was 3,538,000, with 56.4% of the people living in urban areas. The main language used in Ireland is English, with Gaelic spoken in a few areas.

Social work is a recognized profession in Ireland. In addition to a degree or diploma, individuals in professional social work courses are awarded a Certificate of Qualification in Social Work (CQSW). Social workers work in both public and private agencies and institutions and also in private practice. They perform a variety of duties, including home visiting, counseling, community organization, family therapy, policy development, and administration.

There is a public welfare program in Ireland that offers extensive services, including contributory social insurance, means-tested supplementary welfare allowances, and children's allowances. The government offers housing grants as incentives to encourage citizens to modernize their dwellings, particularly for improved plumbing and electricity. In addition, there are extensive religious agencies and services available.

*Netherlands:*   The Netherlands covers 14,398 square miles and has 14,886,000 inhabitants. Eighty-eight and one-half percent of the population live in urban areas. The language of the land is Dutch.

Social work in the Netherlands is seen as both a recognized profession and as volunteer work in human service. The educational background required for professional social work is the completion of high school and a four year professional education. Students may specialize in cultural social work, personnel social work, residential social work, or in community work.

Social workers practice in general public welfare, therapeutic communities, regional organizations for the ambulatory mentally ill, re-education programs for offenders, public agencies for youth and family treatment, hospitals, psychiatric hospitals, AIDS programs, child care, alcohol and drug organizations, and elsewhere. Their duties include investigations, supervision, prevention projects, home visits, family therapy, management, and administration. Frequent problems identified by social workers are child abuse and neglect, unemployment, alcohol abuse, financial problems, and multiproblem families.

The Netherlands has a public social welfare system that is extremely complex. Services are delivered by the Ministry of Welfare, Health, and Culture. Major services include financing the unemployed (each citizen given the right to $300 per month), financial assistance for the physically or mentally ill, and financing cultural development on both the micro and macro levels. The average workload of social workers in the Netherlands is twenty to forty clients.

*Norway:*   Norway covers 125,181 square miles and is slightly larger than the state of New Mexico. Of the 4,247,00 people living in Norway, 70.7% live in urban areas. The official language is Norwegian, with a small Lapp- and Finnish-speaking population (approximately 20,000).

Social work is a recognized profession in Norway but may be seen as including some volunteer work by nonprofessionals. The requirement for professional social work education is three years of school after the gymnasium (which is the regular twelve years of education). Social workers practice primarily in public agencies, with some in private agencies and very few in private practice. Their duties include counseling, family therapy, home visits, community organization, policy development, and administration. They work primarily with such problems as unemployment, depression, criminality, and child welfare issues.

Norway has a public social welfare program that offers a wide range of services delivered by social workers and other professionals. As a result of a recent influx of immigrants, there has been a drain on social resources, and a cut-back in available services for individuals and families.

*Sweden:*   Extending for 173,730 square miles, Sweden is slightly larger than the state of California. Eighty-three percent of the 8,527,000 population of Sweden live in urban areas. Approximately 12% of the population are foreign born or first-generation immigrants. The official language is Swedish, with a small minority speaking Lapp or Finnish.

In Sweden, social work is seen as an applied social science, directed at the study and solution of social problems through such methods as research, social planning, social services, and community work. It has been a recognized profession for the past thirty years. Sweden has six state schools and one private school that have Schools of Social Work offering three and one-half years of study with a diploma of socionom (BSSW). Eighty to ninety percent of Swedish social workers are employed by the communities (municipal government), county councils, or the state. There are very few voluntary social service agencies in Sweden. There are private organizations for particular groups (e.g., the handicapped, mentally ill, epileptics, etc.), which may employ social workers and are run by parents of the group members. Social workers may work in a variety of institutions run by the municipality receiving financial help from the local government and under their control. These include schools, hospitals, child guidance clinics, programs for drug and alcohol abusers, family counseling agencies, and treatment homes for children. The main problems identified by social workers are unemployment, drug abuse, and family problems.

Over 15% of the national income of Sweden is devoted to social welfare. The social welfare programs and insurances of the country include general child allowances, national health insurance, old-age pensions, and unemployment benefits. Allowances come from the government, the county, and the municipality. Housing supplements, for example, are available from the municipality. Social services include the providing of information, counseling, and support services for families and for people with drug and alcohol problems.

*United Kingdom:*  The United Kingdom claims 94,525 square miles of land. Currently, it is facing several land boundary disputes with such countries as Ireland, Spain, Argentina, Denmark, and Iceland. In 1990, the population of the United Kingdom was 57,410,000. The urban population constitutes 89.6%. The primary languages spoken in the United Kingdom are English, Welsh, and Scottish.

Social work is recognized professionally and used extensively in Britain to carry out the country's comprehensive, universal social services. The education of social workers may vary from a two-year nongraduate to a two-year postgraduate program, all needing approval from the Central Council for Education and Training in Social Work. The Council awards the Certificate of Qualification in Social Work (CQSW), the national qualification required for all social work positions in Britain. In 1971, consolidated social service departments were created by local governments and located in district offices. A full range of services for all populations is offered, including financial assistance, social care of the elderly and handicapped in their homes, emergency aid, shelter, and day care. The government frequently uses voluntary agencies and institutions for particular services, such as institutional care for children and the aged.

Social service departments in the United Kingdom commonly have social work teams who work together on case assessments, treatment or service delivery, and follow up. Social workers may engage in facilitation of mutual aid systems, and are beginning to get more involved in community social work. They may be assigned also as hospital or school social workers. Predominant problems or needs confronting social workers are child abuse, frail aged in need of care, mental illness, and unemployment.

*Yugoslavia-Croatia:* Yugoslavia was a country covering 98,764 square miles with a population of 23,842,000. Following the dissolution of USSR control, the country experienced major conflict and change. A response to the international questionnaire about social work was received from a social worker in "Croatia," a newly formed country located in north-western Yugoslavia.

In Yugoslavia/Croatia, social workers are seen as professionals with a four-year, university level education. They practice primarily in public agencies, with some in private agencies. They perform a variety of professional functions, including research, planning, group and family therapy, home visits, and social advocacy. A social worker in a family agency may work with up to 1000 families under such special conditions as war. Major problems presented to social workers include alcoholism, health problems, poverty, and problems connected with adjustment to changes in society (unemployment, placement of refugees).

There is a public social welfare program that delivers professional services in a variety of social agencies and organizations, covering such fields as school social work, gerontological social work, psychiatric social work, health care, industrial social work, child welfare, and work with families. Additional human services are offered through private and religious agencies, self-help groups, and support groups.

### Middle East

*Israel:* Israel covers 8,019 square miles, with the West Bank and Gaza Strip under dispute. The population in 1990 was 4,586,000. Approximately 90% of the inhabitants live in urban areas. Eighty-three percent of the population are Jewish, and 17% are mostly Arab. The official language of the land is Hebrew with Arabic used officially for the Arab minority.

In Israel, social work is a recognized profession, requiring a BA degree in Social Work, with an increasing demand for the MSW. Social workers work mainly in local and central governmental agencies. Some are employed in volunteer agencies, and some engage in private practice. The duties of social workers include counseling, community organization, family therapy, and administration. The major problems they work with are inadequate income, unemployment, inter-family conflicts, and problems with the law.

Israel has a public welfare program that offers income maintenance, counseling, community development, probation, and rehabilitation services. These services are delivered by public welfare departments of local governments and local branches of central government offices. There is a Ministry of Immigrant Resettlement that employs over one hundred social workers. Social services are available also within their highly developed programs for the elderly and in well-baby clinics.

*Jordan:* Jordan extends for 35,475 square miles, with the land of the West Bank and the Gaza Strip under dispute. The population of Jordan is 4,123,000. The urban population is 64.4%. The ethnic divisions of the land are 98% Rab, 1% Circassian, and 1% Armenian. The official language of the land is Arabic, with English widely understood and spoken.

Social work is a recognized profession in Jordan, requiring either a Diploma or a Bachelor's degree in social work. Social workers practice in public and private agencies and in private practice. Their activities cover a full range of direct and indirect practice roles, including counseling, home visits, community development and administration of social agencies. The major problems brought to the attention of social workers in Jordan are the needs of orphans, widows, broken families, and delinquent children.

Jordan has a public social welfare program that offers such services as general assistance, medical aid for the poor and elderly, and boarding houses for orphans and deviant children. These services are delivered by a Ministry of Social Development and private social agencies, including religious sectarian agencies.

### Far East

*India:* India covers 1,269,338 square miles and is slightly more than one third the size of the United States. The country has land and water disputes with Bangladesh and Pakistan. The population of India is 853,373,000, with 74.2% of its people living in rural areas. In India, Hindu, English, and fourteen other official languages are spoken.

Although social work is a recognized profession in India, there is a general tendency toward thinking that any help given to anyone may be identified as social work. Professional social workers are expected to have a baccalaureate degree in social work, which calls for three years of university studies, or a master's degree in social work, which requires two years of study after the baccalaureate. Some agencies employ untrained persons as social workers. The type of work performed by social workers in India includes medical and psychiatric social work, counseling, family therapy, community development, school social work, and labor welfare in industries. Social workers practice in public and private agencies. Major problems they encounter include poverty, alcoholism, unemployment, delinquency, and marital problems.

India has a public welfare program offering limited services in such areas as integrated child welfare, health and nutrition, and pre-primary education. Scholarships are offered for physically disabled persons and grants for some aged persons. In addition to these governmental services, other services in India include programs for the poor run by voluntary agencies such as religious organizations or committed citizens. These groups have to be registered with the government and may be entitled to receive grants.

*Japan:* Japan extends for 145,882 square miles. It is slightly smaller than the state of California and has approximately one half the number of inhabitants as the United States. The population of Japan in 1990 was 123,638,000, with 76.7% of the people living in urban areas. The language of the country is Japanese.

Japan has 30 undergraduate and 6 graduate schools of social work. Social services are provided by several ministries of the government. Social workers practice in the fields of general assistance, social security, medical and psychiatric services, child welfare, youth groups, older citizens services, family and marital counseling, and services for the blind and disabled.

Social welfare is handled by the Social Affairs Bureau and Children and Families Bureau of the Ministry of Health and Welfare. Other programs in the Ministry include Health Programs and Services, Health Insurance, Employee Pension Insurance, and Pharmaceutical Affairs. There are also welfare programs in the Home Affairs, Education, Labor and Justice Ministries. The people of Japan continue to see asking for help as somewhat shameful, believing that problems should be solved by the individual and family. Major problems brought to the attention of social workers include depression and suicide, stress, alcoholism, and substance abuse.

### Australia

Australia covers 2,967,893 square miles and is slightly smaller than the United States. It consists of six states. Its population is 17,083,000, with 85.7% living in urban areas. The majority live on the coast in six state capital cities and surrounding towns. Ninety-five percent of its inhabitants are Caucasian, 4% are Asian, and 1% are Aboriginal or of other ethnicity. The language spoken in the country is English, with some additional native languages. The English is frequently spoken with a dialect called "strine," which is the condensing of groups of words with idioms somewhat similar to cockney English.

In Australia, a social worker is seen as a professional, usually with a four-year baccalaureate degree. Social workers may be found working in federal, state, local government agencies and in voluntary agencies. A few may be found in industry and private practice. The activities of a social worker may include street youth work, research, home visiting, family therapy, migrant integration, probation and parole work, community organization, policy development, social gerontology, and statutory responsibilities related to areas such as child protection.

Public Welfare programs are provided through federal and state departments. Services offered include income support (solely federal), child protection, family counseling, youth work, housing, medical care, rehabilitation, and community care. Major problems brought to the attention of social workers in Australia are alcoholism, unemployment, mental illness, and family violence. Work with ethnic communities is predominant in the large cities, such as Sydney and Melbourne.

## COMMONALITY AND CONTRAST

Through studying social work in various countries, it becomes apparent that there is great commonality in the meaning and practice of social work around the world. Generally, it appears that the more northern countries of the world have comprehensive national social services, with extensive use of public social workers. The more southern countries appear to have fewer public social services, with greater dependence on private or informal sources to meet human needs. Whether northern or southern, in oppressed countries, such as Latvia, there may be no professional social work or social work education and little available private social services.[6]

While the values and purpose of social work are commonly understood, there is a difference in emphases or focus in practice, depending on the prevailing social circumstances. For example, in third world countries where there is great need for social development and human rights, focus is placed heavily on the development and support of social movements and social action. In more affluent countries, direct or clinical practice is the predominent mode of social work practice.

Social work education programs vary in years of study, location of program, and type of recognition (e.g., degree, diploma, or certificate). A constant in programs around the world is field experience under supervision.[7] The need for social workers to stand in solidarity with the oppressed and to advocate for social justice is commonly understood as fundamental to social work but difficult to demonstrate in countries where oppression, apartheid, or caste systems exist. Although not always identified by name, it appears that there are social workers who practice as generalists and as advanced generalists throughout the world. In Europe, as found in the study edited by Hans-Jochen Brauns and David Kramer, 17 of the 21 European countries surveyed indicated a movement from specialization to greater generalization in social work education to prepare workers for "the wide range of social work practice."[8] There is also an increasing commonality in the types of problems clients of social workers around the world are facing. Such universal problems include unemployment, family breakdown, addictions, and the needs of refugees for assistance in their adjustment and resettlement.

## *THE PROCESS OF INTERCULTURAL LEARNING*

A basic goal of social work education is growth in self-awareness. A particular need of practitioners is awareness of one's prejudices and negative feelings or assumptions about any group or class of people. Acquired feelings of fear or hostility toward a group or groups different from one's own may become strong barriers to impede progress in practice. At the entry level, generalists study human diversity and become aware of and appreciative of the differences of others. The advanced generalist builds on this foundation insight and grows in knowledge of self and others for greater effectiveness in cross-cultural and multicultural practice.

### *Definition of Terms*

"Culture" is a concept that is used generally to refer to the values, beliefs, language, thought processes, and behaviors of groups that are learned through the socialization process within their social environments. In addition to the basic characteristics of culture identified in this traditional definition, there are numerous hidden dimensions that make culture "an irrational force" that impacts the thoughts, actions, and very existence of people.[9] According to E. T. Hall, such dimensions include culture as time and space, rhythm and body movement, imagery, memory, extensions of self in one's environment, contexting of language, base for learning, self-identification, and expected sequences of events when people interact, called "action chains."[10] To truly understand and fit into a foreign culture is extremely difficult. As Hall states:

> A given culture cannot be understood simply in terms of content or parts. One has to know how the whole system is put together, how the major systems and dynamisms function, and how they are interrelated. This brings us to a remarkable position; namely, that it is not possible to adequately describe a culture from the inside or from the outside without reference to the other. Bicultural people and culture-contact situations enhance the opportunity for comparison.[11]

The need for advanced generalists to find opportunities to communicate with people who are "bicultural" (having two cultures) and to experience situations where they come in direct contact with other cultures ("culture-contact situations") is emphasized in this chapter.

"Cross-cultural practice" is a term used when the cultural background of a worker is different from the cultural background of a client system. This term is frequently used in the context of international social work. "Multicultural practice" is used when a practitioner is working with client systems from two or more different cultures. This term is used mainly to refer to practice in one country. However, the two terms are closely related and often used interchangeably. As stated by James Midgley:

> Also, multicultural social work has been almost exclusively concerned with the United States, paying little attention to issues of cultural diversity in the international context. Although an international focus might more appropriately be categorized as cross-cultural social work, the two should not be separated.[12]

He points to the fact that many ethnic minorities in America retain such close ties with their countries of origin that their communities represent "third world cultures," and therefore, working with them could be called "cross-cultural practice."[13] In this text, the term "cross-cultural" will be used when a worker is working nationally or internationally with a system of a culture different from that of the worker.

The terms "culture," "race," and "ethnicity" are often used together. According to James W. Green:

> "Races" exist only to the degree that phenotypic characteristics of individuals, such as skin color or hair form, are given prominence as criteria for allocating or withholding social and economic benefits. . . . [I]t serves no purpose other than to make and justify invidious distinctions between groups of people.[14]

"Ethnicity" is a term that has been used to categorize groups according to their common past and distinctive traits. From a transactional perspective, "ethnicity" refers to the values, behaviors, beliefs, and traits that are maintained during cross-cultural encounters.[15] Such values, behaviors, beliefs and traits are referred to as "boundary maintenance activity."[16] For "ethnic competence," social workers must have the skill to analyze the "boundary maintenance" of individuals and groups and to interact with them in a manner that is not in conflict with the expectations or acceptable behaviors of those they serve.[17]

### Advanced Generalists: Intercultural Practitioners

Advanced generalists develop the "ethnic competence" to engage comfortably in cross-cultural and multicultural practice. Communities, groups, and individuals of diverse ethnic backgrounds are able to maintain their cultural distinctiveness as they communicate and interact with them. Prior to meeting with systems cross-culturally, advanced generalists study ethnographic data about the culture and interview bicultural people who can assist by sharing personal experience and information relating to the culture. Visits to communities of the culture provide the worker with opportunity to observe, experience, and reflect on distinctive customs, behaviors, resources, patterns, and processes.

As a practitioner works with an individual system cross-culturally, an assessment is made to determine the degree to which the system is committed to its culture. With knowledge and sensitivity, the worker becomes aware of the cultural boundaries and expectations of the particular system. There is an openness and respect apparent in the words and actions of the worker. Each transaction is seen as an opportunity for learning and growth for the worker as well as for the system of contact. The advanced generalist recognizes and welcomes the distinctive ways in which people communicate, interact, and display their identity. To arrive at this level of competence, each individual professional needs to enter into an intercultural process of becoming.

### The Intercultural Process

It is natural to see one's own nurturing system as reflecting the primary and most desirable culture. The unknown is often berated, feared, or avoided, especially if it has been described by significant others as undesirable. Believing that one's culture is superior to others is referred to as "ethnocentrism." Before understanding or appreciating other cultures, an individual may need to go through a sequence of stages for de-ethnocentrism based on study and experience.

During the professional socialization of advanced generalists, they are guided through a process of self-awareness and growth for effective work with individuals of other cultures and countries. David S. Hoopes has identified a seven-stage "Intercultural Learning Process" which may be used as a framework for studying movement from ethnocentrism to multiculturalism. The stages are: Ethnocentrism, Awareness, Understanding, Acceptance/Respect (tolerance), Appreciating/Valuing, Selective Adoption, and Multiculturalism.[18] Each stage, as described in Diagram 2–1, refers to how an individual perceives or relates to any one culture or group of diverse cultures. The term "multiculturalism" in this context means the same as "interculturalism." Hoopes writes,

> Thus, multiculturalism is that state in which one has mastered the knowledge and developed the skills necessary to feel comfortable and communicate effectively (1) with people of any culture encountered and (2) in any situation involving a group of people of diverse cultural backgrounds.[19]

Through study, supervision, self-examination, and commitment, advanced generalists are able to advance through the intercultural process. They attain the ability to enter into different cultures and environments with comfort and confidence, maintaining their own unique identity while, at the same time, sharing and growing through communication and transactions with others. They begin by accepting who they are and where they are in the intercultural learning process. Sometimes, it is only with resistance and painful growth that they are able to advance to the point of "multiculturalism" and begin to practice as intercultural social workers. An "intercultural social worker" is able to engage in cross-cultural

**DIAGRAM 2–1**  Stages of Intercultural Learning

| 0 | +1 | +2 | +3 | +4 | +5 | +6 |
|---|----|----|----|----|----|----|
| Ethno-centrism | Aware-ness | Under-standing | Accep-tance/ Respect | Apprecia-tion/ Valuing | Selective Adoption | Multi-cultural-ism |

0 = Ethnocentrism: Believing that one's culture is superior to others; the right way; need to defend and impose one's culture on others

+1 = Awareness: Acknowledging that other cultures exist; aware of different cultural groups, not necessarily enemies

+2 = Understanding: Acquiring understanding of other cultures; cognitive growth in knowledge of different groups

+3 = Acceptance/Respect: Accepting the validity of other cultures without judging or comparing; respecting differences

+4 = Appreciation/Valuing: Appreciating specific aspects of other cultures; more subjective consideration and valuing of strengths of others

+5 = Selective Adoption: Adopting new attitudes and behaviors toward others; recognizing and using desirable aspects of other cultures

+6 = Multiculturalism: Learning the art of intercultural communication and interaction; knowledge and skill to relate comfortably with people of any culture or groups of people of different cultures

and multicultural practice with comfort and ethnic competence. The intercultural process is an on-going, life-long process of becoming whole.

### The General Method in Intercultural Practice

As stated earlier, the problem-solving process, called the General Method (see Diagram 1–6), is an integral component of generalist and advanced generalist practice. With flexibility and innovation, the advanced generalist uses the General Method as a guiding framework for intercultural practice. Paralleling the intercultural process, which helps prepare workers for multicultural practice in general, the advanced generalist may cross over into a specific culture of a client system by applying the stages of the problem-solving process to self. The first three stages are seen as a type of "homework" prior to contact, as the worker tries to understand the *home* or *culture* of the client system in relation to his or her own home or culture.

In *engagement*, in which the three key elements are *problem, feelings,* and *goal,* the worker engages self with the culture by identifying the problem/need in terms of the worker's need for, lack of knowledge about, or experience with the particular culture. The feelings relate to a self-exploration of the worker's feelings toward the culture. And the goal is for the worker to acquire the ability to work effectively with members of the culture.

As the worker explores his or her feelings toward the culture, a prejudice may be uncovered that needs attention. One way to recognize the degree of a prejudice is to consider one's actions or words whenever members of the particular cultural group are discussed or present. Gordon W. Allport has developed a five-point scale to identify degrees of acting out prejudice. The five major headings are: (1) antilocution, (2) avoidance, (3) discrimination, (4) physical attack, and (5) extermination. Descriptive criteria for each of these subheadings may be found in Diagram 2–2.[20]

During the data collection stage, the worker collects data on the *problem, persons,* and *environment.* The problem as stated is the worker's lack of knowledge and experience. To acquire this information, the worker studies written data, interviews and consults with knowledgeable people, and visits the community of the culture for observation and possible participation.

Data collected include information about the history, values, norms, roles, behaviors, customs, expectations, and boundaries of the culture. Also included are reflection on one's own history, values, and experiences and a consideration of why the worker may have negative feelings or actions toward members of the culture. The worker begins to identify possible areas of commonality or conflict for the *persons* (worker and cultural system) when they interact with each other. The study of *resources* focuses on how the members of the culture receive help formally and informally. This includes not only a study of what resources are available but also in what manner they are most appropriately delivered.

In the *assessment* stage, the worker assesses his or her readiness to begin to interact with the system cross-culturally. A plan for initiating contact is developed. This plan may be reviewed with resource people of the culture prior to its initiation.

During *intervention,* the worker actually begins contact and goes through the problem-solving process with the system cross-culturally. As depicted in Diagram 2–3, cross-cultural practice is a dual problem-solving process. The worker is applying the process to self for effective cross-cultural interaction while, at the

**DIAGRAM 2–2**   Degrees of Acting Out Prejudice

| −5 | −4 | −3 | −2 | −1 |
|---|---|---|---|---|
| Extermination | Physical attack | Discrimination | Avoidance | Antilocution |

−1 = Antilocution: Talking negatively about individuals of a particular group

−2 = Avoidance: Avoiding, or withdrawing from, members of a particular group

−3 = Discrimination: Excluding, or segregating, members of a group; showing preference for others

−4 = Physical attack: Performing acts of destruction, violence, or semi-violence toward persons or property of a particular group

−5 = Extermination: Engaging in massacres, lynchings, genocide; ultimate expression of prejudice

Engagement

Data Collection

Assessment

Intervention
B

Evaluation

Termination

A = Self/Culture Problem-Solving Process

B = Worker/Client Problem-Solving Process

**DIAGRAM 2–3**   Dual Problem Solving in Cross-Cultural Practice

same time, going through the process with the client system for problem resolution. The A line is the process of self/culture problem solving, and the B line is the general problem solving process of work with a client system.

As the advanced generalist goes through the process with the cross-cultural system, the focus is not only the problem or need that first brought the system to the attention of the worker for professional intervention. The worker gives special attention to the system's degree of identification with the culture and tries to respect and maintain cultural boundaries.

While working with the client system, the worker takes time for on-going evaluation of his or her growth in understanding the culture of the client system. The worker knows that there are various subcultures in each cultural group and that there are levels or degrees of identification with a culture by any individual, group, or family. For example, 14 distinguishable subcultures have been found within the African American culture,[21] 98 in the American Indian culture,[22] 23 in the Asian-Pacific group,[23] and 5 within the Hispanic culture.[24] During the evaluation stage, workers continue to seek greater refinement in understanding the particular culture or subculture of the client system.

In addition, workers continue to evaluate their understanding of the boundary or degree of identification and commitment the client system has to the particular culture. Individuals may behave according to their culture while within their cultural environment but act differently when removed from their community. Culture is not an absolute but instead may be situational and transitional.[25]

Besides refinement in knowledge about the culture and the client's identification with the culture, advanced generalists extend on-going evaluation to include a monitoring of their own growth in feelings and behavior toward the culture and client system. In assessing growth or regression in attitude or actions, a scale may be used which juxtaposes the intercultural learning process stages of Hoopes and the degree of acting out prejudice stages of Allport (see Diagram 2–4). Although the distance between intervals may not be measured as exactly equal in significance, the scale serves as a general guide for evaluating movement. Recognizing where one was prior to working with the client system during the engagement stage of problem solving with self, workers evaluate their progress (or regression) in acceptance of and comfort with the culture and in movement toward the state of "multiculturalism."

Upon termination with the client system, the worker considers "termination" in terms of self and the particular culture under study. In developing a termination plan, the worker identifies what problems or gaps in knowledge about the culture or skills in communication may persist and need attention for more effective cross-cultural practice in the future.

Thus, advanced generalists apply the key components of generalist practice, such as the general method (problem-solving process), with greater complexity in cross-cultural practice. The international perspective of advanced generalists, their growth in self-awareness, and their flexibility in use of knowledge and skills enable them to practice as competent, intercultural social workers.

**DIAGRAM 2–4**  Intercultural Evaluation Scale

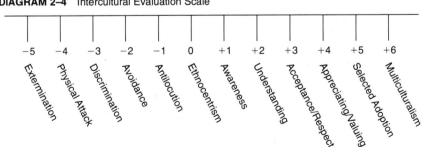

### Case Examples

The case examples that follow demonstrate cross-cultural, multicultural, and intercultural practice. The worker in Case 1 is an American advanced generalist who is employed by the U.S. Army and working with the schools on an Army base in Germany. Dependents of military personnel stationed overseas attend schools operated by the Department of Defense (DoDDS). Social services are provided through the military's Exceptional Family Members Services. The schools have Host Nation Teachers who help students and teachers understand the culture, laws, policies, and programs of Germany. The client system in this case consists of a Spanish mother, an African-American father, and their two children. American and German resources are used to assist the family.

In Cases 2 and 3, a District Director of the Social Service Division of the Ministry of Immigrant Absorption in Israel is working with immigrants from the former Soviet Union. According to law in Israel, each immigrant may receive up to three years of privileges, which include access to health care, housing subsidies, day care, reduced tax obligations, language classes, occupational counseling or retraining, and cash or in-kind services until appropriate employment may be found. The social workers in this Ministry utilize a generalist model of practice because client problems are so varied. A primary goal is to assist clients in their transition to the "mainstream" as quickly as possible. The workers engage in multiculturalism in their daily practice. Most of the practitioners in the Ministry either are native born Israelis or migrated at an early age from such countries as the United States, Argentina, Morocco, England, or Canada. Few of them speak Russian, Yiddish, or the local languages of the immigrants they serve. Paraprofessionals have to be employed frequently to serve as translators. The American-born District Director in Cases 2 and 3 learned to speak Yiddish and Hebrew as a child. He worked as the District Director of the Social Service Division during a period of high emigration from the Soviet Union.

## CASE EXAMPLE 1: AMERICAN ADVANCED GENERALIST
## WORKING IN EXCEPTIONAL FAMILY MEMBERS SERVICES
## ON A MILITARY BASE IN GERMANY

Mrs. Carmen A. is 28 years old. She was born in Spain where she met and married her husband, Robert, a sergeant in the U.S. Army. Mr. A. is African-American, 32 years old, and was born in New York. He joined the military when he was 18 years old. He fathered a child from a previous relationship who was adopted by the A's shortly after they were married. Their adopted daughter, Rosamaria, is 6 years old. The A's also have a son named Jason who is 3 years old.

Shortly after being stationed in Germany, Rosamaria was entered into the special class for exceptional children at the Department of Defense Dependents School (DODDS) on base. She was unable to talk and had trouble walking. After testing by the school psychologist, Rosamaria was diagnosed as "autistic." At a school case study meeting, the social worker who serviced the school from the Military Exceptional Family Members Services learned from the child's teacher that there was another child (Jason) in the A. family who appeared to have special problems also. Since Mrs. A. spoke very little English and was new to the area, she had difficulty communicating the needs of this child to anyone. Fortunately, Rosamaria's teacher was Spanish and had begun to develop a positive relationship with Mrs. A. The social worker, Cathy B., arranged to meet with Mrs. A. and her son along with the special education teacher, who would assist with translation.

Before meeting with Mrs. A., Cathy engaged in preliminary "homework," which included (1) communicating with an African-American colleague and the Hispanic special education teacher who served as knowledgeable resources and (2) reflecting on her attitudes and behaviors toward the cultures represented in the family. After study and self-assessment, Cathy B. decided that she was ready to begin contact. During the interview with Mrs. A., her son, and the special education teacher, the social worker noticed that 3-year-old Jason was developmentally delayed in speech and motor development. With the help of the teacher, the worker learned that the child had recently begun to have epileptic seizures at home. Mrs. A. was encouraged to express her feelings of fear and helplessness. Her husband had been sent to the field and was not expected back for a month. Mrs. A. said that she could see that both her children were in need of special help. She was hesitant to agree to take her son for an evaluation until her husband returned from the field. She said that she was doing the best that she could and didn't want her husband to be upset with her. She feared that God was punishing them through the problems of their children. She also said that she had no means of transportation. Mrs. A. agreed to have the social worker try to contact Sergeant A. to inform him of his son's problem and to discuss a plan for his son to get the help he needed. Sergeant A. was located, and he called in to the social worker. He said that he would be grateful for any help Mrs. B. could arrange for his family. Mrs. A. was relieved to hear that her husband had been informed about Jason and that he approved of the idea of her taking him for help.

As the worker, the client system, and the special education teacher moved through the six-stage problem-solving process, a number of resources had to be mobilized, crossing over from military services to local German resources (Diagram 2–5). The medical clinic on base said that Jason needed to be referred for a neurological assessment at a German medical center. Because of the nature of Jason's illness, he was placed in a German Kinder Care Clinic where he could get the proper medical attention. The problem of no transportation for Mrs. A. to take Jason for his appointments was resolved by the worker's activating the Chain of Concern on base. This is a group of spouses of the military in the unit. With Mrs. A.'s permission, the worker notified the group or Mrs. A.'s situation. They immediately responded and offered Mrs. A. support and transportation. Rosamaria was referred to the physical therapist on base for help with walking. Mrs. A. expressed a desire to improve her English. She was informed about language classes offered on base. Eventually, she signed up to take a class. The Chain of Concern continued to be a support system for Mrs. A. and the family. Upon Sergeant A.'s return, he met with the worker and agreed to work with her and his wife as they tried to cope with their problems and adjust to their new environment. He was not of the same cultural background as his wife, and it became apparent that he welcomed any help his wife could get to become more independent.

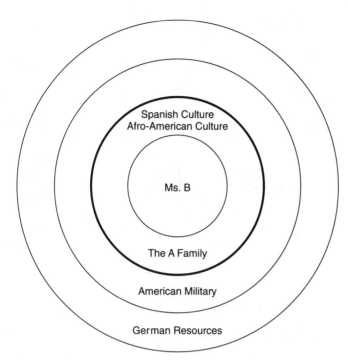

**DIAGRAM 2–5** Ecological Perspective: The A Family

Throughout the process of helping, Cathy B. evaluated her own progress in understanding and communicating with the multicultural family system. After regular contact was terminated with the family, she developed a plan for herself to acquire further knowledge of Spanish subcultures, particularly regarding their religious beliefs and practices.

In this case, the worker engaged in cross-cultural, multicultural, and intercultural practice as she worked with American, Spanish, African-American, and German clients and resources. She recognized the needs of Mrs. A. and her children and found ways to understand and respond to them by mobilizing multiple American and German resources. Mrs. A.'s need to have her husband in the role of decision maker for her children was respected. Her obvious dependence on her husband, her need for transportation, and her limitations in verbal communication were addressed in a sensitive and satisfying manner. The worker demonstrated particular skill in working with both Mr. and Mrs. A. together as they represented two different cultures.

CASE EXAMPLE 2: DISTRICT DIRECTOR OF THE SOCIAL SERVICE DIVISION OF THE MINISTRY OF IMMIGRANT ABSORPTION IN ISRAEL WORKING WITH RUSSIAN IMMIGRANT FAMILY WITH HOUSING PROBLEM

When it was difficult to find housing for an immigrant family, the Ministry of Immigrant Absorption would often rent vacant apartments from private owners to house the family until permanent housing could be found. In this case, the District Director of the

Social Service Division received a phone call from an owner-resident of a fashionable apartment building. The individual complained about a Russian family who had been placed there through the Ministry of Housing. Without any permission from the owner of the building, the family members had ripped out part of the flower garden on the grounds of the building and planted potatoes.

A social worker was sent to assess the situation. The father claimed that he needed to do this because he did not have enough money to feed his five children. It was cheaper to grow his own food. He did not believe that he was doing anything wrong. The family had not been urban dwellers in the Soviet Union, and they could not understand why people were complaining since flowers and grass were so much more impractical than growing food. The father began to badger the worker to get him a goat to keep in the back yard so that he could provide the family with milk.

The Director and worker decided to find another apartment for the family in a geographic area closer to people of their same cultural background. In addition, educational and orientation services were provided to help them understand why their behavior was not acceptable to local norms and laws. The Director and worker recognized how cultural and ethnic differentials can impede practice plans and goals.

## CASE EXAMPLE 3: DISTRICT DIRECTOR AND LOCAL AGENCY SOCIAL WORKER OF THE MINISTRY OF IMMIGRANT ABSORPTION DOING OUTREACH WORK TO HELP WOMAN WITH HEALTH PROBLEM

A family of four children, ranging in ages from 14 to 31, and their elderly parents emigrated to Israel and settled in an area populated by people from their same place of origin in the USSR. It was a mountainous section of Bukhara near the Caspian Sea. The couple's age was estimated to be in the late 50s. The family was very religious with little, if any, formal education.

The husband was a robust, striking-looking man, with a respectable reputation as a wise elder in their community. His wife was a frail, simple-looking woman who took care of household manners in a very traditional manner. The mother of the family was referred to the local agency social worker by the outreach worker of the Ministry of Housing who managed the apartment building where the family lived. The social worker was told that the woman had a growth on the left side of her forehead as large as an orange. When the worker tried to visit the family, she was informed by other building residents that the husband would not allow her to talk with him because a man of his honor and respect would only speak to somebody in authority. At this point, the worker asked the District Director to accompany her on a home visit to speak with the husband.

Upon entering the apartment, the Director and worker met the husband, the wife, the children, and some neighbors and relatives. There were oriental carpets on the floors of the modestly furnished apartment. A table was set with fruit, vegetables, drinks, and bread. A neighbor translated for the family and told the Director and worker that it was customary to partake in the four types of food with the family before anything was discussed. To refuse was to show a lack of respect. After some blessings were said, they ate from all four types of food. The worker and Director then began to discuss the reasons for their visit. They said they were concerned for the wife because of the growth on her forehead. The wife was sitting with her face almost fully covered.

She showed the worker her forehead with the growth on it. She did not do this until her husband told her to do so, and she did not speak throughout the entire interview.

The Director and worker explained that such a growth was not usual and that it could result in a serious medical problem. The husband said that nothing happened until now and that nothing would if God did not want it to happen. He ruled out any medical assistance, stating that God would take care of everything, just as He did in bringing the family to Israel.

The Director and local social worker consulted with members of the Ministry and it was concluded that little could be done about the situation. Home visits would continue to note any changes in the wife's condition. The family was told that if they felt at a later time that the wife needed medical attention, the agency was prepared to assist.

In this example, culture served as a roadblock to receiving care. Limitations of professional social work services due to cultural variance were demonstrated. Although initial outreach efforts to provide health care were refused in this case, the Division of Social Service would continue efforts to build a positive relationship with family members and to grow in understanding their culture and boundary maintenance.

### SUMMARY

The international perspective of advanced generalist practice as presented in this chapter is an expansion of knowledge and skills for effective communication with people of multiple cultures and countries. The results of an international survey of social workers and educators reveal several ways in which the universality of social work can be understood along with identifiable characteristics that distinguish practice and education according to geographic location.

Advancing in self-awareness for effective intercultural practice is presented as a life-long process of growth. Recognizing one's own cultural boundaries as well as prejudices is a major first step in the process. The need for a worker to engage in homework prior to cross-cultural service is stressed as imperative for effective practice. A scale is constructed to assist workers as they monitor their growth in understanding, skill, and sensitivity toward other cultures (see Diagram 2–3).

Case examples offered in this chapter demonstrate how advanced generalists competently conduct cross-cultural, multicultural, and intercultural practice. The international perspective joined with the creative use of the problem-solving process of advanced generalist practice contribute to a high level of preparation and readiness of advanced generalists for international and intercultural practice.

### NOTES

1. *Curriculum Policy for the Master's Degree and Baccalaureate Degree Programs in Social Work Education,* found in Appendix I of *Handbook of Accreditation Standards and Procedures,* 1991 Ed. (Washington, D.C.: Council on Social Work Education, 1991), p. 111.

2. Margaret R. Rodway, "Systems Theory," in Francis J. Turner, ed., *Social Work Treatment; Interlocking Theoretical Approaches,* 3rd ed. (New York: The Free Press, 1986), p. 518.

3. Lynne M. Healy, "International Agencies as Social Work Settings: Opportunity, Capability, and Commitment," *Social Work* 32, no. 5 (September–October 1987): 405–409.

4. James Midgley, "International Social Work: Learning from the Third World," *Social Work* 35, no. 4 (July 1990): 295.

5. The Software Toolworks, *World Atlas,* Version 2.0. Copyright 1989–91. Electromap, Inc. All rights reserved.

6. Letter from Signe Dobelniece, University of Latvia, to Maria O'Neil McMahon, December 9, 1991.

7. Miriam Raskin, Louise Skolnik, and Julianne Wayne, "An International Perspective of Field Instruction," *Journal of Social Work Education* 27, no. 3 (Fall 1991): 258.

8. Hans-Jochen Brauns and David Kramer. eds., *Social Work Education in Europe: A Comprehensive Description of Social Work Education in 21 European Countries* (Frankfurt Main, Germany: Eigenveriag des Deutschen Vereins, 1986), pp. 7–8.

9. Edward T. Hall, *Beyond Culture* (Garden City, N.Y.: Anchor Press/Doubleday, 1976), p. 187.

10. Ibid., p. 124.

11. Ibid., p. 195.

12. James Midgley, "Social Development and Multicultural Social Work," *Journal of Multicultural Social Work* 1, no. 1 (1991): 86.

13. Ibid.

14. James W. Green, *Cultural Awareness in the Human Services* (Englewood Cliffs, N.J.: Prentice-Hall, 1982), p. 6.

15. Ibid., p. 12.

16. Frederick Barth, *Ethnic Groups and Boundaries* (Boston: Little, Brown, 1969), p. 11.

17. Ibid., p. 52.

18. David S. Hoopes, "Intercultural Communication Concepts and the Psychology of Intercultural Experience," in Margaret D. Pusch, ed., *Multicultural Education: A Cross Cultural Training Approach* (Yarmouth, ME: Intercultural Press, Inc., 1981), pp. 17–22.

19. Ibid., p. 21.

20. Gordon W. Allport, *The Nature of Prejudice* (Reading, Mass.: Addison-Wesley, 1989.), pp. 14–15. 25th Anniversary Edition. © 1979, by Addison-Wesley Publishing Company, Inc., 1989. Reprinted with permission of the publisher.

21. Charles Valentine, "Deficit, Difference and Bicultural Models of Afro-American Behavior," *Howard Education Review* 41, no. 2 (May 1971): 137–157.

22. Eddie F. Brown and Timothy F. Shaughnessy, eds., *Education for Social Work Practice with American Indian Families,* American Indian Projects for Community Development, Training and Research (Arizona School of Social Work, Arizona State University, 1979), cited in Jacquelyn Dupont-Walker, Region IX Child Welfare Training Center, University of California as Los Angeles, School of Social Welfare, *Ethnic Minority Cultures—Shades of Difference?* (Ann Arbor, Mich. National Child Welfare Center, 1982), p. 16.

23. Royal F. Morales et al., *Asian and Pacific American Curriculum on Social Work Education* (Los Angeles: Asian American Community Mental Health Training Center, 1976), p. 2.

24. Dupont-Walker *Ethnic Minority Cultures,* p. 2.

25. Green, *Cultural Awareness,* p. 13.

# 3
# Values and Ethics in Advanced Generalist Practice

## INTRODUCTION

Social work professionals, particularly those at the advanced level, are challenged daily with ethical decisions and dilemmas. Does an individual need to be removed from a home, placed in protective custody, or committed to a mental institution? Should a worker remain in an agency that clearly demonstrates values contrary to social work values? What about sharing confidential information for data processing or the computerization of human services? Where does the worker stand in the decision-making process regarding removal of life supports from a dying patient or in decisions regarding the distribution of scarce resources? Should a worker engage in social action in a risky environment? What if there is some question of manipulation rather than enhancement of a community, an organization, or another country? As pointed out by Thomas Holland and Allie Kilpatrick,

Little is known about how practitioners respond to moral and ethical issues, how they understand and cope with these aspects of their work, or what resources are used or needed for improving performance in this area.[1]

In this chapter, an effort will be made to identify a guiding framework to assist advanced generalists as they recognize and respond to ethical issues and dilemmas in their practice.

### Definitions

*Ethics* are standards, statements, or principles that guide actions in terms of right or wrong decisions and behaviors. The terms "ethics" and "morals" are often used interchangeably. *Morals* are fundamental principles that usually relate to an individual's personal or religious beliefs in terms of good or evil. Ethics build on values. A *value* is a desired outcome, standard, or quality held in high esteem. Ethics differ from values in that ethics refer to what is seen as correct and values to what is seen as desirable. Ethics direct the means, whereas values identify the end. An *ethical dilemma* is an apparent conflict between ethical principles concerning the choice of the right course of action in a particular situation.[2]

A branch of philosophy that is concerned with the conduct of professionals is called professional ethics. It includes micro ethics (direct practice) and macro ethics (social ethics). *Micro ethics* refers to behaviors and decisions of professionals while engaging in direct practice with clients or patients. *Macro ethics* deals with the ethics of groups and organizations in societies and with the values and ethics reflected in social policies.[3]

### Social Work Ethics

Social workers and the profession of social work emphasize micro ethics in their Code of Ethics and in professional literature.[4] The prevailing ethical focus found in the field of practice is that of micro ethics also. In professional socialization programs, however, social work students are encouraged to embrace both a concern for individuals and a commitment to social reform and social change for the common good. Although both micro and macro levels of ethical commitment are stressed in professional social work programs, the commitment to macro ethics is often reduced as social workers practice in the field. In a study conducted by David Wagner, he discovered reasons for the decline in focus. He writes,

> Commitment to social work professionalism and radical change is found to be strongest at the point of entry into the field and while undergoing professional training. Difficulties experienced in social work positions as well as the lure of positions outside of the field and the experience of upward mobility all serve to fragment the marriage of idealism and professionalism.[5]

Generalist practitioners, according to their nature as generalists and the scope of their workloads, have a shared interest and commitment to both macro and micro ethics. This is particularly true at the advanced level where professionals often meet daily challenges as advanced direct service providers as well as policy makers and program administrators.

### Team Ethics

Social workers frequently engage in shared ethical decision making as they serve on ethics committees or as members of treatment teams. To make a valuable contribution to these groups, social workers must understand ethical dilemmas and the process of ethical decision making. It is not enough for them to be able to articulate the values and ethics of their profession. They need to demonstrate the ability to see the conflict or congruence of their values with those of other professionals and to be able to activate a plan and process for reaching a group decision. The holistic perspective of a generalist social worker, particularly an advanced generalist, prepares the worker to function effectively within complex groups facing serious ethical choices.

## ETHICS IN GENERALIST PRACTICE

In preparing generalists, as stated earlier, the basic values and ethics identified in the foundation of social work are augmented with particular emphasis on the macro values of social justice and human rights. The preparation of advanced generalists builds on the values and ethics of the social work foundation and the macro values of generalist practice, and emphasizes the development of a deeper understanding of professional ethics and the process of ethical decision making at both the micro and macro levels.

### Foundation Ethics

The two fundamental values found in the profession of social work relate directly to the "person in environment" perspective of the social work foundation. Social workers value "individual worth and human dignity."[6] The profession is founded on a belief in the potential for human growth and the realization of human potential. Every person of any age, limitation, or diversity is valued because he or she is a human being. This value of person leads to a commitment to human rights and equal opportunity for everyone.

The second fundamental value of the profession of social work relates directly to the social environment. Social workers value a caring, participatory society that gives priority to the general welfare of its members. As stated in the *Curriculum Policy Statement* of the Council on Social Work Education:

Social workers hold that people should have equal access to resources, services, and opportunities for the accomplishment of life tasks, the alleviation of distress, and the realization of their aspirations and values in relation to themselves, the rights of others, the general welfare, and social justice.[7]

These two fundamental values provide the basic foundation for a Code of Ethics for the profession. The Code is a collection of standards describing how social workers "should" behave to demonstrate their ethical responsibility to clients, colleagues, employers and employing organizations, the profession, and society. The Code of Ethics of the American National Association of Social Workers and the International Code of Ethics of the International Federation of Social Workers may be found in Appendix B of this text.

In addition to the two foundation values and the Codes of Ethics, central concepts have been deduced from these fundamental references to provide basic practice principles to guide further the actions of workers. The following practice principles are often included in any study of foundation values and ethics in social work:

1. Individualization: Recognize that every client system is unique and deserving of consideration and respect.
2. Purposeful expression of feelings: Understand the human need to express one's feelings and the value in this expression as a means of fostering growth.
3. Controlled emotional involvement: Use one's feelings and emotions appropriately for the service of others.
4. Acceptance: Demonstrate that human beings have a right to be accepted as they are.
5. Nonjudgmental attitude: Avoid passing judgments on people.
6. Self-determination: Respect the right of clients to choose for themselves as much as possible.
7. Confidentiality: Keep information obtained from or about clients confidential.[8]

### Ethical Emphases in Generalist Practice

Building on foundation values and ethics, the macro values of social justice and equal rights are emphasized in generalist practice. Social justice is highly valued as a desired outcome for society. In studying social justice in a particular environment, society, or country, the values and ethics that underlie and guide its social policies are highlighted. Focus is on the theories and principles that are used to identify the obligations of the society and to guide the distribution of its resources. In effectively promoting social justice, generalists often need to address such social issues as poverty, homelessness, hunger, segregation, racism, exploitation, and inequality.

The concepts of human rights, social rights and development, and empowerment are key components of social justice. *Human rights* are fundamental freedoms inherent in our nature to develop fully. In 1948, the United Nations General Assembly adopted a Universal Declaration of Human Rights (Appendix B). *Social rights* refer to that which is due to individuals as a just claim because they are members of the social group or society. Social rights may include freedom from arbitrary arrest and imprisonment, a right to a fair public trial, civil and political liberties, and freedom of thought, speech, and assembly.

*Social development* is a goal and a process aimed at the welfare of people through the creation or modification of institutions in society to meet human needs and improve the relationships of people with the social institutions.[9] *Empowerment* is a term that describes the actions and processes used to increase the power held by a person or persons, thereby enabling them to achieve greater control over their own destinies.

The issues and problems that call for macro ethics impact the individuals and families found in the caseloads of social workers. Societies, institutions, and professional providers tend to perceive the problems and people they serve as unique. Generalists are encouraged to see the connections and dynamics that interrelate micro and macro problems.

The boundary of social concern for social workers should not be limited to American society. Kenneth Hermann Jr., states:

> Social workers' ethical obligations to improve social conditions, choice, and opportunity; eliminate discrimination; and promote social justice demand a look not just beyond one's own agency but also beyond national borders.[10]

Advanced generalists build on the knowledge acquired as generalists about macro and micro ethical issues and extend their awareness and skills to a more complex, global framework for effective, holistic practice. They see the interrelatedness of social needs and problems in different countries. Their advanced ecological systems perspective extends their environmental awareness and ethical commitment to world justice and global needs.

## ETHICS IN ADVANCED GENERALIST PRACTICE

In addition to generic and generalist values and ethics, advanced generalists have knowledge and skills to recognize and respond to ethical dilemmas. They use their advanced ecological perspective and problem-solving process to ascertain the multiple factors involved in a dilemma and to prioritize options for the most satisfactory ethical decision.

### Ethical Decision Making

How should a professional helper proceed when faced with an ethical problem in need of attention? What philosophical theories or approaches are useful to the process of making ethical judgments? When there are several options, how does a practitioner prioritize to make the most correct choice or decision? More specifically, what theory and process would an advanced generalist use when there is need for an ethical decision to be made regarding a particular client or situation?

### Theoretical Approaches

When human service professionals have to make ethical judgments, they may call upon various theories and approaches to direct their perception of facts, principles, and circumstances leading to ethical choices. The approaches used generally fall under the following categories:

1. Principle approach: using a set of rules, laws, or standards given by God, society, profession, or other authority
2. Casuistry approach: locating a similar case and patterning decision after resolution in the precedent case
3. Metaethical approach: using logic and reason to direct the decision after consideration of the facts in the context of the individual situation
4. Female/male approach (gender impact): relational, caring, connectedness approach of females influenced by values of relationship and responsibility; abstract, discrete unit approach of males based on values of rights, success, and justice.

More fundamentally, ethical judgments or decisions may stem from basic teleological or deontologic philosophical theories.[11] The teleological theories focus on consequences and context. They constitute a relative philosophy that stresses a consideration of individual circumstances and probable results of each option as central to making a decision. Within this theoretical category, there are different outcomes seen as desirable, ranging from the good of the individual to the good for the greatest number.

In the deontologic philosophic category of theories, there are absolutes or fixed moral rules. These rules or principles may be seen as coming from various sources, ranging from human-made rules to Divine Rule. It is the rule that dictates the decision.

Rather than select one approach or philosophical theory, the advanced generalist uses a holistic perspective and strives to respect the values and standards of both person and environment. At the same time, the worker calls upon the practice principles of individualization and self-determination as the circumstances of the situation and possible environmental results for each optional decision are considered.

### Process Models

Various helping disciplines have suggested procedures to assist professionals in their efforts to choose the most effective course of action when confronted with an ethical issue or dilemma. In reviewing models from different disciplines, one sees that there are key concepts and stages that emerge as central and basic to any process of ethical decision making. The problem-solving process, called the General Method in generalist practice, may be adapted to include these concepts and stages and serve as a guiding framework in the process of ethical decision making for the advanced generalist.

*Nursing*   In the field of nursing, a six-stage process called a Method for Resolving Nursing Ethics Problems has been developed. The stages are identified as:

1. Identify the problem
2. Gather data
3. Identify options
4. Think the ethical problem through
5. Make a decision
6. Act and assess[12]

In addition, the following five-stage shared nurse-patient decision-making process has been formulated to be used when the ethical problem involves the health of a patient:

1. The nurse and patient develop a dialogue in which they interact about the patient's health concerns and problems and in which the nurse helps frame a therapeutic setting showing concern.
2. The nurse makes data evident to the patient.
3. The nurse presents proposed alternatives and consequences of the patient's health problems in discussion with the patient and in conjunction with physicians and relevant others.
4. The dialogue between patient and nurse includes discussion of the implementation of treatment alternatives with consideration of costs, risks, and benefits.
5. Finally, the nurse encourages the patient to come to the best possible resolution and accommodation to the patient's health care situation.[13]

*Medicine*   In the field of medicine, a four-part system of decision making has been introduced to assist physicians in resolving clinical-ethical quandaries. The method is a systematic approach used to identify and organize the most relevant facts in a case. It is a four-step process that usually gets resolved with steps 1 and 2. In situations where patients are unable to express a preference regarding medical treatment and in which the medical indications are limited, steps 3 and 4 are invoked. The four steps consist of the following categories of consideration:

1. Medical indications: diagnosis, prognosis, therapeutic alternatives, clinical strategy
2. Patient preferences: informed consent or refusal of patient

3. Quality-of-life considerations: subjective evaluation of the value of prolonging or preserving a life
4. External factors: wishes and needs of patient's family, costs of medical care, allocation of limited medical resources, research and teaching needs of medicine, safety and well-being of society[14]

Also in the field of medicine, a six-stage formal process of moral reasoning is used to teach ethics to students in health sciences. It was designed to provide a sense of discipline and continuity for medical professionals in their efforts to make ethical decisions. The six stages are:

1. Collect the medical facts.
2. Determine the relevant human factors: clinical context, patient and family obligations and rights.
3. Extrapolate the values involved in the situation: patient, physician, hospital administration, patient's family, and so on.
4. Distinguish class or type of case and clashes of values, i.e., case of consent, experimentation, right to treatment, truth-telling vs. benevolence, patient rights vs. principle of doing no harm, rights of children vs. rights of parents, and so on.
5. Make an ethical judgment about the ranking of goods from alternatives. Reasoning: Why are these choices good?
6. Make medical decision: What is the right thing to do? Identify criteria.[15]

*Social Work*   In the profession of social work, a number of ethical decision-making models have appeared to guide the actions of social workers. M. Vincentia Joseph proposed a five-step model that uses ethical principles in a rational decision-making process. It is a collaborative approach that allows for considering different views before arriving at an ethical position. The five steps in the model are:

1. Attain a clear understanding and description of the practice situation and a precise identification of the ethical dilemma.
2. Gather the background information on the issues's varying positions: ethical principles justifying various positions.
3. Identify the values intrinsic to the situation and prioritize.
4. Formulate the alternatives for action and logically consider and present the reasons (values and principles) justifying each option available for action.
5. Choose an ethical position after reviewing the data, reflecting on the values, and analyzing the options.[16]

Frank Loewenberg and Ralph Dolgoff proposed an eleven-step General Decision-Making Model to guide social workers in making ethical decisions. In addition to identifying the problem, values, goals, and alternatives, they include steps to identify specifically the persons and institutions involved in the problem and those who should be involved in the decision making. They also have steps for monitoring the implementation of the selected strategy and for the evaluation of the results and identification of any additional problems.[17] To assist workers in their selection from alternatives, they developed a priority screen of ethical principles to be used if the social work Code of Ethics does not give sufficient guidance to address the particular problem or if the Code rules appeared to be in conflict with each other. The screen consists of the following seven prioritized principles:

Ethical Principle 1: Principle of the protection of life
Ethical Principle 2: Principle of equality and inequality
Ethical Principle 3: Principle of autonomy and freedom
Ethical Principle 4: Principle of least harm
Ethical Principle 5: Principle of quality of life
Ethical Principle 6: Principle of privacy and confidentiality
Ethical Principle 7: Principle of truthfulness and full disclosure[18]

In a study conducted by Thomas P. Holland and Allie C. Kilpatrick, practicing social workers were interviewed and asked questions about situations that involved ethical questions. Three bipolar value dimensions of ethical judgment used by social workers were identified. The three dimensions were seen as basic ways or patterns used by social workers when dealing with ethical issues or dilemmas. Holland and Kilpatrick suggest that the three dimensions when considered simultaneously could contribute to a more comprehensive analysis of the actions and decisions made by social workers in ethical situations. They write:

> The first dimension is the focus of decisions, which ranged from an emphasis on the ends or goals sought to an emphasis on the means or principles by which one decides. A second dimension was the interpersonal orientation, ranging from priority on individual client autonomy and freedom to priority on mutual responsibility and benevolence even at the cost of some individual liberty. A third dimension involved the locus or source of decision-making authority, ranging from reliance on internal or individual judgment to compliance with external rules, norms, or laws.[19]

### The Ethical Decision-making Process for Advanced Generalists

Obviously, there are numerous factors that should and do influence professionals as they undertake ethical decisions. Efforts continue to be made to formulate processes and frameworks that reflect a comprehensive and integrated approach to ethical problem resolution. The ecological systems theory and general method of generalist practice provide a perspective and process that greatly assist advanced generalists as they engage in a holistic approach to ethical decision making. Diagram 3–1 illustrates the multiple systems that

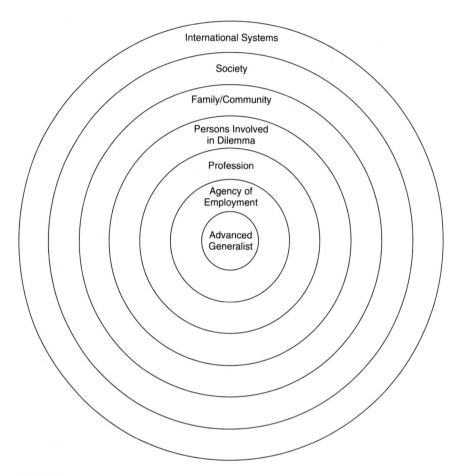

**DIAGRAM 3–1**   Multiple Systems in Ethical Decison Making

often need to be considered in the process. Using this advanced ecological systems perspective, the worker proceeds through the six-stage general method.

As outlined in Diagram 1–6 of Chapter 1, the General Method of generalist practice consists of the following six stages:

1. Engagement—problem, feelings, goals
2. Data collection—problem, person(s), environment
3. Assessment—assessment statement, problem prioritization, planning, contracting
4. Intervention—direct, indirect, teamwork, referral
5. Evaluation—goal analysis, contract review, goal reformulation
6. Termination—decision, plan, termination[20]

In social work, it has been found that prior to collecting hard factual data, time is needed to first listen and sense what is going on. Engagement in ethical decision making would begin also with a stage where the worker hears what is said or felt about the problem. The "problem" here refers to the question, issue, difficulty, or need that calls for an ethical decision. The worker's empathic skills are used to tune into what is perceived by others as the problem, feelings, and goals in the ethical situation.

In the data collection stage, the information collected would be not only about the problem but, more specifically, about the values and ethical principles underlying the problem. In collecting information about person(s), the question would center on the value stance of the person(s) involved and on the impact of the dilemma on the life and well-being of the person(s). Data about the environment would extend to a study of the values and ethics that underlie existing laws, rules, policies, and expectations in the environment that surrounds the ethical situation. Inquiry would extend also to the impact of the dilemma on the life and well-being of the environment.

The assessment stage would be the time to consider options in decision making and to prioritize them. The information collected would assist the worker in recognizing conflicting ethical principles or values. The ecological systems perspective of generalists promotes sensitization to the simultaneous impact of each possible decision on both the person(s) and the environment involved in the ethical situation. Through a careful study of outcomes, the worker would prioritize and select the decision of choice. The assessment statement would provide a clear rationale based on sound ethics and values to justify the decision made. If others are involved directly in the ethical situation, they would share in the decision-making process. The decision would be followed by a step-by-step plan for implementation. If the decision involves the life space or future of others, the worker may move into contracting with those involved. This would necessitate a clear articulation of responsibilities in the step-by-step strategy for implementing the decision of choice.

The intervention stage of the process takes place as the planned decision is implemented. Each step of the decision is monitored as it is executed. The results of the decision are carefully studied as the worker moves into the evaluation stage.

During evaluation, the worker would follow up to see if the expected outcome of the decision was in fact happening. If the goals were not achieved, the plan would need to be reconsidered and reformulated. Even when it appears that the goals have been achieved, the worker would take time before terminating or moving on to other matters to make sure that the outcome of the decision had been stabilized. If additional resources or actions are needed for the goals to be sustained, the worker would make a referral or transfer for supplemental support during the termination stage of the process.

### Ethical Dilemma Prioritization

When faced with an ethical dilemma, advanced generalists recognize the different options and ethical principles that relate to the particular situation. Options are studied to answer the question, What ought to be done about this? The prioritization instrument used during assessment in generalist practice may be adapted for use by advanced practitioners as they make a holistic assessment and selected response to the ethical dilemma.[21]

Rather than focus on one or a few dimensions of the dilemma, advanced generalists bring together their findings and professional judgment regarding both norms and circumstances, the absolute and relative, decisions and outcomes, means and ends, and the person(s) and environment. The instrument they may use requires first a clear articulation of the dilemma. They begin with the question, "What ought to be done about_____?" Next, the practitioner proceeds to making a list of the options that may be used to answer the question (Diagram 3–2). With each option, the worker indicates the probable outcome or impact the outcome will have on others. This is followed with a list of the philosophical or ethical principles, values, or norms that are called into play with each option under consideration. These may include such principles as equality, self-determination, privacy, confidentiality, autonomy, freedom, protection of human life, nonmaleficence (no harm), beneficence, utilitarian concern with the good for the greatest number, or the egalitarian justice principle that stresses the needs of the most disadvantaged. Often, each option may reflect more than one principle, making a selection of an option based solely on principle difficult. If ethical principles are not easily identifiable for an option, the apparent values underlying the option (e.g., family, parent-child relationship, money, and so on) may be listed. The conflicting values or principles that are causing the dilemma are debated according to the options that reflect them. In addition, each option is considered in terms of its impacting outcome on persons and environment.

**DIAGRAM 3–2**   Ethical Dilemma Prioritization Instrument

QUESTION: What ought to be done about _____ ?

| OPTIONS | | |
|---|---|---|
| Decision (choice, action, means) | Outcome (results, consequence, end) | Principles (values, norms, laws) |
| 1. | 1. | 1. |
| 2. | 2. | 2. |
| 3. | 3. | 3. |
| 4. | 4. | 4. |
| . | . | . |
| . | . | . |
| . | . | . |

**DIAGRAM 3–3**   Ethical Dilemma Prioritization Scale.

```
 ┬────┬────┬────┬────┬────┬────┬────┬────┬────┬────
 0    1    2    3    4    5    6    7    8    9    10
No posi-          Some      Average        Much       Maximum
tive out-                                             positive
come                                                  outcome
```

The advanced generalist then gives consideration to each option and makes a professional judgment using a scale of 0 to 10. The most positive or fulfilling probable outcome receives a rating of 10. If there would probably be no positive or fulfilling outcome as a result of a decision, it would receive a rating of 0. The assessment could be any number between 0 and 10, indicating points on or between the descriptive criteria range of no, some, average, much or maximum (Diagram 3–3).

The scale is used as each outcome listed in Diagram 3–2 is juxtaposed with four factors indicating the outcome's relationship to the person(s) factors and the environment factors of the situation. The "person(s)" refers to the person or persons directly involved in the ethical dilemma. The "environment" refers to those systems in the extended life space of the person(s) of the dilemma and may include community, society, or country.

The person factors and the environment factors under consideration are divided into a teleological and a deontological assessment. The impact of the outcome on the values/norms of the person and of the values/norms of the extended environment are assessed along with the impact of the outcome on the life circumstances (human life and quality of life) of the person(s) and on the life circumstances (human life and quality of life) of the environment (Diagram 3–4).

As each option is considered, the worker reflects on the decision, outcome, and principles of the option first in relation to the values of the person(s) involved in the dilemma, asking: On a scale of 0 to 10, would this option be in concert with the values of the person(s)? More specifically, one asks: To

**DIAGRAM 3–4**   Ethical Dilemma Prioritization Instrument

| QUESTION: What ought to be done by _____ about _____ ? | | | | | | | | |
|---|---|---|---|---|---|---|---|---|
| OPTIONS | | | PERSON(S) | | ENVIRONMENT | | PRIORITY* | |
| DECISION | OUTCOME | PRINCIPLES | VALUES | LIFE | VALUES | LIFE | TOTALS | RANK |
| 1. | | | | | | | | |
| 2. | | | | | | | | |
| 3. | | | | | | | | |
| . | | | | | | | | |
| . | | | | | | | | |
| . | | | | | | | | |

*Option in conflict with ethics (personal or professional) of worker

what extent is there congruence between the values and principles reflected in this choice with the values and principles of the person(s)? If there is congruence rather than conflict, the worker predicts from this matching that the option is positive to the degree assessed. If there is not congruence in the values reflected in the option with those of the person(s) involved, it is expected that there will be resistance from the person(s) involved and the option may not be effective in resolving the dilemma.

Next, the worker asks about the extent of relationship between the particular option and the life and well-being of the person(s) involved. The worker asks: On a scale of 0 to 10, would the results of this option contribute positively to the life of the person(s)? This consideration uses a holistic perspective of "life," meaning the physical, psychological, social, spiritual, intellectual, political, and economic well-being of the person(s) involved in the dilemma. To the extent that the option will be detrimental to the life of the person(s) involved, it is seen as an undesirable low-priority option. This consideration is based on the fundamental natural, spiritual, professional, and societal value of human life.

Similar assessments are made between the option and the values and principles of the person's(s') environment and the life of the environment. The following questions are raised: On a scale of 0 to 10, to what extent is there a positive correlation between the values and principles reflected in this option and the values and principles of the environment (family, community, and society) of the person(s)? And, to what extent does this option have positive results for the life (physical, social, psychological, economic, and so on) of the environment of the person(s) involved in the dilemma? If more than one system is involved in the choice or the outcome, and they have differing values or expected life outcomes, the worker needs to weigh the two and include both in the total of 10. For example, if both mother and father are involved, the total of 10 may be divided into 5 and 5. If the mother is rated 3 and the father 5, the total placed in the column would be an 8.

After numbers are given for each dimensional assessment, they are totaled across each option line. The totals are then prioritized. The option with the highest probable fulfillment for enhancing life and promoting value/norm congruence rather than conflict for person(s) and environment is given top priority. If extenuating circumstances enter the picture and prevent the worker from actualizing the option given top priority, the second highest priority may need to be the one decided upon.

At the far right of the instrument, there is a column with an asterisk. As advanced generalists review the ranked options of the prioritization, they reflect on each option in the light of their own personal and professional ethics. If an option is in conflict with the personal ethics of the professional, the agency of employment, or of the social work profession, an asterisk is placed at the end of the option line. If this option is selected by the person(s) or imposed by the environment of the person(s) involved in the dilemma, the practitioners would need to make it clear that the option is in conflict with their ethics (self, agency, or profession) and, therefore, it would not receive their support. A transfer, referral, or termination by a worker may be necessary. The ethical principles prioritized by Lowenberg and Dolgoff[22] and the National Association and International Federation of Social Workers' Codes of Ethics (see Appendix A) may serve as helpful guides in determining the profession's perspective on each option. When an option is prioritized highly in the person and environment assessment and it is congruent with a self/agency/profession assessment, the holistic perspective and process provides the advanced generalist with clear direction for decision making in an ethical dilemma.

The Ethical Dilemma Prioritization Instrument does not call for or produce purely scientific data that can be empirically verified. It is a tool for advanced generalists to make a generalized assessment and prioritization when faced with an intricate ethical situation. When the prioritization instrument is used repeatedly, it becomes an integral part of the skills and procedures of advanced generalists. Even if the worker does not write down the assessed scores, the instrument may be applied mentally. It is a valuable resource that provides a comprehensive perspective for practitioners confronted with ethical dilemmas in need of a response or decision.

### Case Examples

The following case examples will demonstrate the use of the ethical decision-making process and the Ethical Dilemma Prioritization Instrument by advanced generalists.

## CASE SUMMARIES

### Case 1: Advanced Generalist in a Public Social Service Agency in Norway Working with a Palestinian Mother, Father, and Son

Mr. A. has not been able to find employment in Norway. He plans to return to his native country next month. Mrs. A. does not wish to go with her husband. She knows that he intends to take a second wife when he returns. She is asking for a divorce and custody of her son. Mr. A. expects to take his son with him. In his country, the children belong to the father of the family and remain with him if there is any marital separation. The worker is expected to present the case in two weeks to the Magistrate with a case summary and recommendation regarding the future of the child.

### Case 2: Advanced Generalist Administrator of a Private, Church-Related Multiservice Agency Faced with a Need to Cut Programs

Ms. B. has recently been informed by the Bishop's financial officer that there will be a cutback in financial resources for the year ahead. Some of the programs will have to be cut or canceled. She needs to meet with the Finance Committee of the Board and present a proposed budget reflecting the reduced budget. The programs under consideration for reduction or deletion include premarital counseling, a group home for girls, direct assistance to the poor, and services for migrants and the elderly.

Case 3: A Social Work Educator Who Is an Advanced Generalist Recognizes a Past Client Who Escaped from Prison Ten Years Ago

While attending a conference in another state, Ms. C., an advanced generalist, is invited by a friend who lives in the area to a local neighborhood party. Ms. C. is introduced to a past client who now has a different name. She learns that he is highly respected in the community for his outstanding service to others. He trains and hires the unemployed and actively supports community and church projects. She recalls that she worked with his wife and child and visited him in prison where he was serving a seven-year sentence for armed robbery. His escape was apparently coordinated with the disappearance of his wife and child.

CASE EXAMPLE 1

Mr. and Mrs. A. and their 11-year-old son were allowed into Norway for humanitarian reasons. After spending an initial period in a camp, they were moved to a small community outside of Stavanger. They were Moslems and raised in a culture in which the father was expected to be the main provider for the family, Mr. A. could not find employment. Mrs. A. took a job as an assistant in a home for the elderly. After one year, she was laid off. They came to the social welfare office for assistance. The worker needed an interpreter since both parents spoke little Norwegian. After six months of welfare services, Mr. A. applied for return passage to Iran for himself and his son. Mrs. A. filed for a divorce and custody of her son. They asked their worker to help them resolve their conflict. After much discussion, it became clear that even if Mr. A. found work in Norway, he wanted to return home to Iran, and that Mrs. A. did not want to go with him. The question remained, what ought to be done about their son? When the worker asked 11-year-old Omar, he said that he knew he would have to go back with his father, but he liked living in Norway. It was an ethical dilemma involving conflicting values, principles, and laws.

Ethical Decision-making Process

*Engagement.* During engagement for ethical decision making, the worker listened to what Mr. and Mrs. A. were saying and feeling about what ought to happen with their son. The worker helped them recognize their ethical dilemma and encouraged both parents to express themselves.

Mr. A. found his unemployed state to be socially degrading. Because of an increase in unemployment in Norway, local employers were under pressure to hire only native Norwegians and not immigrants. Mr. A. wanted to be the provider for his wife and child. He also wanted to be able to have more than one wife, and he wanted his son to be with him wherever he went. He believed he had a right to the fulfillment of these expectations because they were accepted in his homeland. He believed things were better politically in Iran, and he wanted to return home, where he could work with his father and uncle. He had learned that there was an earthquake in his village and he felt he needed to go back to be of help to his extended family. He knew that the laws of Norway would not support his plans for marrying a second wife and taking his son from his mother.

Mrs. A. was becoming acculturated to the Norwegian way of life. She did not have a problem with working for herself and her family. She wanted to keep her son with her, and she hoped the worker would help her move closer to a sister who was living in Norway. Mrs. A. did not want to share her husband with other wives. She wanted to study Norwegian and get another job.

*Data Collection.* In studying the ethical dilemma, the worker recognized different ethical principles manifested in the laws and cultures of the two countries of Norway and Iran. Both Mr. and Mrs. A. were reflecting these differences as they expressed their values, goals, and expectations.

In Norway, the rights of women as well as men are recognized based on a principle of equality. The law upholds monogyny and does not usually give children to fathers when there is a marital breakdown. Norway has been known as a humanitarian country with strong social services for all. Recent financial constraints and increasing unemployment in the country, however, have led to the practice of hiring native Norwegians over immigrants.

In Iran, husbands are seen as superior to their wives. Men are able to marry more than one wife and have ownership of their children and household. Men have a right to self- and family-determination; women are expected to be subject to their husbands.

Mrs. A. valued independence and self-determination. She loved her son and husband and wanted to keep her son and have her husband to herself. She liked the freedom for women she found in Norway and did not value her homeland to the extent that she wished to maintain its laws and cultural norms.

Mr. A. loved his homeland and wanted to live out the values and norms of his culture. He wanted to be in control of his wife and child, and saw himself as a failure if he could not provide for them. He valued the custom of having more than one wife. He felt a strong loyalty and responsibility for his father and extended family. Mr. A. wanted to return home with his son where they could be with their relatives. He believed his son would have more respect and opportunity in Iran, where he would not be seen as an immigrant.

*Assessment.* In the assessment stage, the worker and Mr. and Mrs. A. began to look at the options for deciding what ought to be done about their son. The Ethical Prioritization Instrument was used to clarify the various dimensions of the dilemma and to arrive at a decision. First, the worker identified the decision, probable outcome, and central principles for each option (see Diagram 3–5).

As each option was considered, the worker began to judge and assign numbers for the extent of congruence between values and the extent of life quality for person(s) and environment. In both options, the "persons" involved in the ethical dilemma were Mr. and Mrs. A. and their son Omar. In option 1, Norway was the "environment" of focus because it was where Omar would reside according to the decision to have Mrs. A. and her son remain in the country. In option 2, the "environment" of focus was Iran because the option was for Mr. A. and his son to return there (Diagram 3–6).

*Option 1.* In the first value column of option 1, the worker placed a 3 because the decision to have Omar remain with his mother was in conflict with their cultural norms.

**DIAGRAM 3–5**   Case 1: Ethical Dilemma Prioritization

| OPTIONS | | |
| DECISION | OUTCOME | PRINCIPLES |
|---|---|---|
| 1. Son remains with Mother in Norway | 1. Son away from native culture, father, and relatives. Mother (1) provides for son's welfare (2) Seeks job (limited resources) (3) Searches for sister (4) Studies Norwegian | 1. Autonomy, Self-determination Freedom Quality of life Individuality Gender Equality Nonequality in hiring immigrants |
| 2. Son returns with Father to Iran | 2. Son relocated in native culture and living with his father and relatives Father expects to work and live at home with parents Father expects to remarry | 2. Paternal self- & family determination Polygamy Quality of life Upholding cultural norms Nonequality for women |

The fact that Mrs. A. was beginning to identify with other values and norms was recognized by scaling the value assessment with a +3 (Diagram 3–7). The quality of life was also assessed somewhat low (3) because single female-headed families were becoming increasingly poor in Norway as the economy was on the decline and welfare

**DIAGRAM 3–6**   Ecological Perspective: Case 1

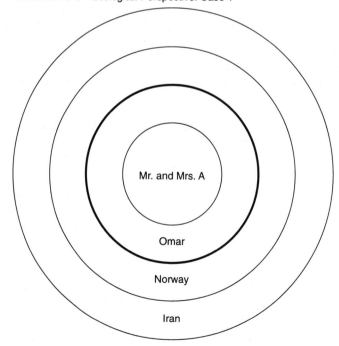

**DIAGRAM 3–7**   Ethical Dilemma Prioritization Instrument

QUESTION: What ought to be done by Mr. and Mrs. A. about Omar?

| | OPTIONS | | PERSON(S) | | ENVIRONMENT | | PRIORITY* | |
|---|---|---|---|---|---|---|---|---|
| DECISION | OUTCOME | PRINCIPLES | VALUES | LIFE | VALUES | LIFE | TOTALS | RANK |
| 1. Son with mother | Son removed from culture, father, relatives . . . | Autonomy Self-determination Freedom . . . | 3 | 3 | 8 | 3 | 17 | 2 |
| 2. Son with father | Son returned to native culture father, relatives . . . | Paternal self-determination Quality of life . . . | 7 | 7 | 9 | 8 | 31 | 1* |

*Option in conflict with ethics of worker.

services were being cut back. The fact that Mrs. A. was an immigrant who spoke little Norwegian was going to make it difficult for her to find a job. Being an immigrant with little family support would be a drawback for Omar also. Being away from his father and adjusting to his mother's new lifestyle might also impact Omar's development. Mrs. A. said that even if she moved closer to her sister, she was not sure that she would be accepted because she broke away from their native tradition. Mr. A. would experience great pain and embarrassment if he returned home without Omar and tried to explain why he did not take his son with him.

The environment value for option 1 in relation to the values of Norway was assessed as an 8. Having a son remain with his mother when there was a divorce and giving Mrs. A. the opportunity to choose her independence for herself and her son reflect principles in concert with the values and laws of Norway. The only drawback to the outcome of the option appeared to be the emerging devaluing of employment of immigrants.

The life or well-being of Norway in the light of option 1 was assessed as a 3. The use of the country's resources for an increasing number of dependent immigrants was identified by the country's officials as a drain on the economy. The increase in unemployment was being seen as directly relating to the increase in the number of immigrants into the country and their taking jobs from native people. The +3 reflected the country's history of being humanitarian and open to people of other nations. There was a recognition that the country was enriched socially and spiritually through its cultural diversity.

*Option 2.* In assessing the values of person(s) with the values reflected in option 2, the worker selected a rating of 7 because having a son go with his father is strong in the norms and culture of all three persons involved in the ethical dilemma. Mrs. A. is disregarding the norms and values of her original culture in wanting to identify with Norwegian values of gender equality and independence for women.

The life assessment score for person(s) is judged to be a 7 because Omar will be in his original culture and country with his father and relatives. His father would not be experiencing the stresses relating to his adjustment to Norway, and his mother would have the freedom to pursue learning the Norwegian language, finding a job, and locating near her sister without having to provide care for Omar at the same time. The decision would result in some psychological and emotional pain for mother and son due to their separation.

The environmental value score for option 2 is judged to be a 9 because the values and norms in Iran would strongly support the decision to have Omar remain with his father. If Mrs. A. were to return with them it would be a clear 10. The life score under environment is assessed as an 8. Living in Iran with his father and family would provide Omar with opportunities for developing according to his culture in all areas (physically, intellectually, spiritually, socially, etc.). Because his natural mother would not be in his immediate environment, he would be emotionally delayed. Mr. A. expects to help with the cleanup after the earthquake and to assist his father and uncle with their business. This was assessed also as a positive for the environment.

After a number is placed in each column for person(s) and environment assessment, the numbers along each item line are totaled and placed under the priority total column. They are then ranked according to numbers and prioritized in the rank column. Weighing the circumstances in the context of the ethical dilemma, it became apparent to the worker and the clients that having Omar go with his father would probably be the best decision at this time.

Although some of the value principles reflected in option 2 were contrary to the worker's personal and professional ethics (see * in Diagram 3–7), a transfer or referral was not needed. Mrs. A. agreed with option 2 after she considered all the dimensions of the dilemma. Under the circumstances, and through the assessment process, and worker could support the decision for Omar to return to Iran with his father. Mrs. A. said that she hoped that once she got a job and her son got older he would be able to come to stay with her. As work with the family continued, plans were made that included agreed-upon activities for Omar and his mother before his departure. Mr. A. agreed to allow Omar to keep in contact with his mother.

*Intervention.* The intervention stage is when the strategy for implementing the selected option is enacted. In this case, the mother withdrew her request for custody and the worker supported the plan for Omar to return with his father in her recommendation to the Magistrate. Mr. A. and Omar departed and the worker continued to work with Mrs. A.

*Evaluation.* The worker reviewed with Mrs. A. the plan that was carried out regarding Omar and helped Mrs. A. express her strong feelings of loss and loneliness. Mrs. A. wrote to her son and she received a letter from him. Mrs. A. said that from what he said in his letter, he seemed to be adjusting well.

*Termination.* The ethical dilemma seemed to be settled and the worker focused on helping Mrs. A. enroll in language classes. Mrs. A. wasn't sure that she wanted to move closer to her sister. She decided that she would wait until she finished taking language classes. She also was referred to a training program for medical assistants.

Occasionally, Mrs. A. would bring up the subject of wishing that she could have her son back, and the worker would review with Mrs. A. the circumstances leading to his departure.

## CASE EXAMPLE 2

Over the last two years, Church Social Services (CSS), a diocesan social service agency, has grown in number of programs and staff under the administration of Ms. B. In addition to funds acquired from grants and fees each year, 50% of the agency's budget comes directly from the diocese. Ms. B. was informed that the allocation from the diocese for the coming year was going to be reduced by 10%. It was expected that it would be a permanent cut. The diocese determined a flat salary increase for all employees in any church-related job. A reduction in staff salaries was not a budget line that could be considered to make up for the deficit. Ms. B. was faced with the dilemma of having to decide which programs would have to be reduced or terminated.

The programs of the agency were categorized under the following headings: Family Life, Migrant Services, Peace and Justice, Refugee Resettlement, Senior Adult Program, and Bethany House for adolescent girls. Each category included a number of programs. Family Life, for example, included adoption, domestic and international; direct assistance (financial); and pregnancy, individual, premarital, marital, and family counseling. Services were delivered through a central office coordinator and decentralized regional offices in the five regions of the diocese. Each regional office had one or two full-time professional staff, one or two part-time professionals, and a number of volunteers. Ongoing evaluations showed that existing programs were successfully meeting needs for diverse populations. Ms. B. faced the question: What programs ought to be maintained, reduced, or cut? She was experiencing an ethical dilemma in having to choose from a number of valuable programs.

### Ethical Decision-making Process

*Engagement.* During engagement, the administrator and members of the Board of Directors met with the finance council of the diocese to hear about the problem from the perspective of the diocese. The needs of the Church were seen as extensive, with no flexibility in being able to offer the agency more than 90% of the amount given in the previous year. Ms. B. met with the program coordinators and regional managers of the agency and told them about the expected cut in the agency's budget. Anxiety, defensiveness, anger, and denial were expressed by many. Ms. B. listened to their thoughts, feelings, and suggestions. They were assured and in agreement that every effort would be made to reduce costs with the least possible reduction of needed services for clients. The employees for each program were asked to take time to consider how costs might be reduced in their programs.

*Data Collection.* Using the problem, person and environment focal points of the data collection stage of the process, Ms. B. began by studying the problem. She had meetings with the Bishop and his financial officers to explore further the extent and severity of the problem. Although it was clear that there was no way in which they would give more than 90% of the allocation, they assured Ms. B. that they did not expect that they would have to reduce the allocation further in the next three years.

They did not, however, give her any hope that the allocation would be increased in the future. At meetings with program coordinators and regional managers, helpful ideas were presented for possible reductions. The suggestions for reduction or deletion of staff positions or client services often related to the expected departures of staff or client systems from their programs or regions. Questions were raised about the possible availability of other resources in the region or diocese to handle some of the needs currently serviced by the regional offices of the agency.

As Ms. B. explored possible external resources for providing some of the services of CSS, she discussed with local parishes the possibility of their providing direct financial assistance to the poor in their parishes. She also explored greater use of parishes' Social Action Committees to assist with the Advocacy for the Poor service of the Peace and Justice Office of the agency. New grant sources were located and information regarding application procedures was requested.

As part of data collection, Ms. B. identified those ethical principles and values that related to the dilemma she was facing in having to decide which programs had to be cut. She listed the following: the utilitarian principle of "greatest good for the greatest number"; the egalitarian principle of justice which stresses the needs of the most disadvantaged; the principle of nonmaleficence (no harm); and principles of beneficence (do good), truth, equality, equal opportunity, and justice. She also recalled the ethical responsibility of the agency and of the profession of social work to clients, employees, and the general public, as found in the NASW Code of Ethics and the agency's "Mission Statement." These include the commitment "to serve all people in need—the poor, the hurt, the estranged, and all those subject to discrimination; with equal emphasis being given to: advocacy for social and economic justice as well as addressing immediate needs with emergency resources."[23] She recalled the "primacy of clients' interest," and the ethical principles stating that social workers should act "with special regard for disadvantaged or oppressed groups of persons," and "to prevent and eliminate discrimination."[24]

*Assessment.* Ms. B. pondered the current budget and considered the possible options for reducing it to comply with the projected decrease for next year. She began by eliminating those programs that were self-supporting or grant funded (with expectation of renewal). The home for adolescent girls was not seen as an option because the Board had already committed itself to maintain the program for at least another year while an extensive study was being conducted by the evaluation committee to see if the program continued to be needed in the diocese. All other programs were seen as possible choices for reduction. She used the Ethical Dilemma Prioritization Instrument to assist her in the process. Each option was first listed according to decision, outcome, and principles (see Diagram 3–8).

The decision, projected outcome, and principles for each option were then assessed in relation to their impact on the persons and environment involved in the dilemma. The "persons" in this case were those constituting the agency having to make the cuts and the populations serviced by the programs identified in the options. The "environment" included the Church, region, and society of the "persons" (Diagram 3–9).

*Option 1.* The premarital counseling service was being conducted by a couple who worked part-time for the central office agency. They would travel to local regions

**DIAGRAM 3-8**   Case 2: Ethical Dilemma Prioritization

OPTIONS

| DECISION | OUTCOME | PRINCIPLES |
|---|---|---|
| 1. Cut pre-marital counseling | Local pastors provide service | Greatest good . . . Equal opportunity |
| 2. Cut direct assistance | Local parishes and public services would have to provide | Most disadvantaged Commitment to poor Greatest good . . . Equal opportunity Nonmaleficence Beneficence |
| 3. Cut services for migrants | Central coordinator's position cut, Services at regional offices continue | Most disadvantaged Commitment to poor Equal opportunity Greatest good . . . |
| 4. Cut elderly services | No coordinator for volunteer groups No substitute available | Greatest good . . . Equal opportunity |
| 5. Cut Peace and Justice Office | Give responsibility to parish social action committees and Board Legislative Committee | Needs of disadvantaged Social and economic justice Greatest good . . . |
| 6. Cut a regional office | No local professional services—Clients would go to closest region | Equal opportunity (access) Nonmaleficence Beneficence |

to meet with groups of couples about to be married. Over 100 couples received counseling each year. The administrator thought that it was a service that could be assumed at the local parish level by the pastor. Although the agency would no longer give people the opportunity to receive this service from CSS, and it was a "good" for a good number, the opportunity for premarital counseling would continue to be available, with easier access, if offered by the parish. Weighing all these factors, she assessed the value dimension as a 6 because the decision to cut from CSS, with the service continuing locally in the parish, was still supporting the value of providing the service. The quality of the new service remained to be seen. The administrator assumed that it would be positive in assisting the couples at least to the "life" dimension of a 6. In terms of the environment, the decision to cut the program at CSS and pass it on to the parishes might be a drain on the parish, but it certainly was in line with the values of the Church, the community, and society to offer such a service to local couples about to get married. Marriage and family were seen as primary values and of serious concern in the environment of church and society. The score of a 7 was given for environment value, and a 6 for "life" in the environment.

*Option 2.* Cutting direct assistance to the poor and giving this responsibility to the parishes was seen as having advantages and disadvantages. The agency had

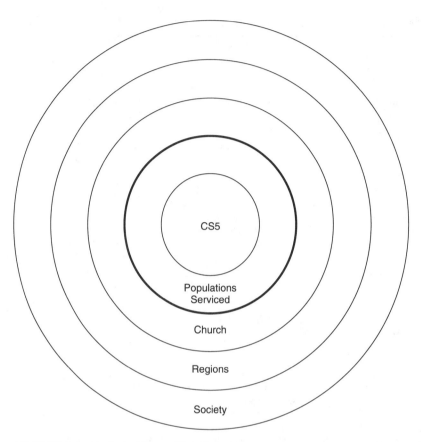

**DIAGRAM 3–9**    Ecological Perspective: Case 2

only a flat amount that could be used each year in the budget for this service. Parishes could have ongoing activities to provide emergency resources for those in need. There would, however, probably be an unequal amount of funds available in different parishes. The process of selection and distribution might also be a problem. Public welfare services were already drained as an increasing number of people were applying for assistance in the diocese. In assessing this option in relation to the values of the agency and people involved, Ms. B. gave it a 3. The egalitarian principle of justice, which stressed the needs of the most disadvantaged, was strongly apparent in the Mission of the agency. Letting go of this service was strongly opposed by members of the agency and Board. Even though the Bishop spoke to the pastors and asked them to assume this responsibility, there was fear that the poor in poor parishes would receive little help with emergency needs. The "life" dimension of person, meaning the impact of this option on the agency and those who received the service, was also assessed by a 3.

The environmental assessment of a 4 for values and a 4 for life quality reflected the recognition that there would be an extended drain on the parishes and public services as a result of this decision. The fact that at least some assistance would be available through the parishes was seen as a positive contribution to the environment. The environmental values of beneficence (doing good) and nonmaleficence (no harm) were supported somewhat by having parishes provide this service in the community.

*Option 3.* The coordinator of migrant services planned to leave the agency and take a job in one of the regional offices. Cutting this position would somewhat decrease the quality and extent of service to migrants but not eliminate the direct services offered regionally. Having a centralized coordinator added a resource who served as a consultant, supervisor, information giver and coordinator for the migrant services at regional offices. He also was an advocate and spokesman for migrants in the extended environment. The values and principles of the agency to serve the most disadvantaged would continue to be activated through the regional services. It was possible that fewer people might be served because regional staff would have to assume the tasks of the coordinator. The administrator, therefore, assessed the value dimension of person as a 4. The life dimension was given a 5 also because the effects of the decision were not expected to be a major detriment to the direct services.

Assisting migrants was not supported by some of the people and policies in the region or society. The values of equality and equal opportunity of society-at-large were in concert with the decision to maintain services for migrants. The decision to cut and yet maintain the service, therefore, received a 5, reflecting the conflict in values and policies of the environment in relation to the option. The slight possible increase of migrants not receiving CSS service might be seen as a negative for the environment. Keeping the regional services operating, however, led to an assessment of a 5 for the life dimension of the environment.

*Option 4.* The elderly of each region formed organizations that voluntarily reached out to seniors in their local areas by offering a variety of programs and services. The agency demonstrated support of their efforts by providing a part-time professional, who served as a coordinator of senior adult programs. This person assisted with training volunteers, advocating for the elderly, giving information, and coordinating programs and activities. The option to cut the coordinator's position would leave the volunteers with no formal leadership or voice in the structure of the diocese. Regional offices could not assume the tasks of the coordinator. In hearing about the possibility of their coordinator's position being cut, the elderly strongly expressed concern that they were not being treated justly, with equal opportunity for service, by the agency.

In assessing the value relationship of the option with the persons involved, Ms. B. gave it a 4. The agency was providing a "good" for a great number (200 elderly), but the population was not actually seen as among the "most disadvantaged" in the Church or society. The elderly serviced, however, did include some poor and handicapped (approximately 5%). Closing the office would have a major impact on the services being offered to seniors. They felt that they would be losing their "leader." Ms. B., therefore, assessed the life dimension as a 3. Even though the service loss would not directly affect them physically, it was going to be a major loss for them socially, emotionally, and, possibly, intellectually and spiritually.

In considering the environmental impact, Ms. B. was aware of the expressed values in society for human life and for the elderly, but she also knew that in the diocese and the region there were few resources for them. Closing the office for the elderly might lead to the breakdown of the local volunteer organizations and result in a felt service gap in the environment. The option, therefore, was seen as negatively impacting the environment in terms of value and life fulfillment. The scores of 2 and 2 were given.

*Option 5.* The Peace and Justice Office consisted of one full-time coordinator. At times, he contacted regional offices and local parishes for support in advocating for the oppressed. He was leaving to go to school for advanced study. The option proposed that the role enacted by his position would be passed on to regional offices, parish social action committees, and the Board's Legislative Committee. These groups were to some extent already active in social justice issues. Although closing the office would be in strong conflict with the values of the agency, the continued activity and involvement by the other identified groups would help the agency uphold this value commitment. Ms. B., therefore, assessed the value dimension of person as a 5. The life dimension for those serviced might be reduced through a decrease in the quality or extent of service. This dimension was, therefore, given a 5. Environmentally, maintaining the service, even though possibly somewhat reduced, would be in concert with the environmental values of equality and social justice and would, hopefully, continue to enhance the welfare for the most disadvantaged in society. Each of the environmental dimensions, therefore, received a 5.

*Option 6.* To close a regional office would strongly be in conflict with the values of the agency and have negative impact on the environment. The values of equal opportunity (access) and nondiscrimination would be called into question since the option would make it necessary for the people in that particular region to go to another region for service. Ms. B. assessed this option as the lowest, placing a 2 in each column. Two was given instead of 0 because services would be open to them in other regions.

The scores given for each option were totaled and prioritized (Diagram 3–10). The first three options were put into a plan for budget cutting. Parishes would be expected to provide premarital counseling services, and the Peace and Justice Coordinator position and the Migrant Ministry Coordinator position would be frozen. More cuts were needed. There was not enough money to maintain the direct assistance program. Regional managers said that they would help local parishes set up a process for providing direct emergency assistance. The Bishop said that he would help pastors find ways to raise funds for this service. There was still not enough money to sustain the Coordinator for the Elderly. With advice from the Board's finance committee, the budget was tightened enough to allow for some money to be used for the elderly. Instead of maintaining the existing position, the agency would purchase individual services from the person in the position. Local elderly organizations participated in prioritizing the tasks and duties of the coordinator and identified which services were most in need of being retained. No regional office had to be closed in the plan Ms. B. finally presented to the Board. The proposed budget was approved by the Board.

*Intervention.* During the intervention stage of the process, the decision to cut programs and operate within the reduced budget was implemented. Ms. B. shared the approved budget with agency coordinators and regional managers. She had private meetings with those employees directly affected by the cuts. All parties identified in

**DIAGRAM 3–10**    Ethical Dilemma Prioritization Instrument

QUESTION: Which programs ought to be cut?

| | OPTIONS | | PERSON(S) | | ENVIRONMENT | | PRIORITY* | |
|---|---|---|---|---|---|---|---|---|
| DECISION | OUTCOME | PRINCIPLES | VALUES | LIFE | VALUES | LIFE | TOTALS | RANK |
| 1. Cut pre-marital counseling | Pastors provide | Greatest good . . . | 6 | 6 | 7 | 6 | 25 | 1 |
| 2. Direct assistance | Parishes/public provide | Most disadvantaged | 3 | 3 | 4 | 4 | 14 | 4 |
| 3. Migrants | Cut co-ordinator, regional offices provide | Most disadvantaged . . . | 4 | 5 | 5 | 5 | 19 | 3 |
| 4. Elderly | No coordinator or substitute | Greatest good . . . | 4 | 3 | 2 | 2 | 11 | 5 |
| 5. Peace & Justice | SAC of parishes/ Board Leg. Com. provide | Most disadvantaged . . . | 5 | 5 | 5 | 5 | 20 | 2 |
| 6. Regional office | No local services | Equal opportunity . . . | 2 | 2 | 2 | 2 | 8 | 6 |

*Option in conflict with ethics of worker.

the plan as resources for continuing services were contacted. At a meeting of pastors, they voted to recommend that the premarital counseling program continue under the direction of the CSS agency. To make the program self-sufficient, it was proposed that couples would be charged a fee. If any couple could not afford to pay the fee, the parish would cover the cost of the service. This recommendation was approved by CSS, and the service was continued.

A few small grants were obtained, but they did not affect the budget significantly. They were for short-term projects in some regional offices. Two of them were to enhance services for migrants. Ms. B. and the regional managers increased their contacts with pastors and parishes. They offered advice and training for greater parish involvement in direct assistance for the poor and advocacy for social justice.

*Evaluation.* In evaluating the outcomes that resulted from the budget decisions that were made, Ms. B. saw resulting gaps and strain, particularly in leadership for peace and justice issues. She continued to monitor the direct assistance being offered at the parish level. Agency personnel and resources were being stretched to their limit. The need for additional resources was very evident. In sharing her evaluation with the Board, the decision was made to form a Development Committee of the Board with the specific purpose of fund raising for the agency. In addition, the Board approved of an action to take money from the principal of an agency foundation (interest was being used to support some programs) to pay the salary of an assistant to the Administrator.

A primary task for this person would be to work with the Board Committee on grant writing.

*Termination.* The question about the budget was ongoing as programs continued to be evaluated. There was strong hope that additional funding would be found to supplement the reduced budget and provide the additional staff and resources needed to advance the agency's mission and quality of service.

## CASE EXAMPLE 3

Ms. C. used to work in Public Welfare as an advanced generalist before she began teaching social work at the University. While attending a conference in another state, she looked up an old friend in the area who invited her to a neighborhood party. At the party, Ms. C. was introduced to Mr. Z., whom she recognized as a past client. He was using a different last name and acted as if he did not know her. Later, Ms. C. learned from her friend that Mr. Z. had moved into the area about six years ago. He was a highly respected member of the local community. He trained and hired the unemployed and was a church leader in projects for the poor. As her friend described Mr. Z.'s wife and two children (ages 5 and 12), Ms. C. realized that they could fit the description of the family she worked with about ten years ago. The mother and son had the same first names. At that time, there was no female child in the family. Ms. C. recalled that while working with Mrs. Z. and her son, she had visited Mr. Z. in prison where he was serving a seven-year sentence for armed robbery. Mrs. Z. always said that her husband was innocent and framed by his brother and nephew. At the time of Mr. Z.'s escape from prison, his wife and child were also missing. Ms. C. believed that he was still wanted by the police.

As Ms. C. started to leave the party, she was approached by Mrs. Z., who asked if she could speak with her. She said that her husband had told her that he knew Ms. C. had recognized him. She pleaded with Ms. C. not to report him. They were trying to forget the past and lead good, normal lives. She said her children did not know about her husband's imprisonment and that it would be devastating to all of them if it came out. Ms. C. asked Mrs. Z. if she wanted to spend all of their lives hiding the truth and running from the law. She encouraged Mrs. Z. to try to get her husband to turn himself in and place his case at the mercy of the authorities. Mrs. Z. said she knew that her husband would not do that.

In returning to her room, Ms. C. struggled over the situation. She believed that she had a responsibility as both a citizen and a professional to report Mr. Z., even though Mrs. Z. had confided in her and asked her to keep her husband's identity confidential. She used the ethical decision-making process and the dilemma prioritization instrument to help her sort out her values, thoughts, and feelings about the situation. She started by stating the question; What ought to be done by *me* about *my recognition of Mr. Z., an escaped prisoner?*

### Ethical Decision-making Process

*Engagement.* Ms. C. began by facing her own feelings about the situation. She pondered why she wished she had never attended the neighborhood party. It was apparent that the Z. family were doing well and making a valuable contribution to their community. She resisted because she did not like to think of the possible outcome that would result for the family and the community if Mr. Z. was returned to prison. Yet, she believed that she was expected to cooperate with the authorities and report the location of a convicted criminal. She wanted to be ethical and responsible.

*Data Collection.* Ms. C. called her home state to see if Mr. Z. was in fact still wanted by the authorities. She inquired also about the specific law that would require her to report his location. She found out that there was a federal warrant out for him for interstate flight to avoid confinement. If she knew of his whereabouts and did not report it, there was the possibility that she might be charged as an accessory to the fact.

*Assessment.* Using the ethical dilemma prioritization instrument, Ms. C. first listed her options, probable outcomes, and related ethical principles (Diagram 3–11).

To assess the impact of each option on the person and environment factors, Ms. C. considered the situation from the ecological systems perspective as depicted in Diagram 3–12. The "persons" identified in this case as directly involved in the situation were the worker and Mr. Z. and family. The "environment" was the community and society-at-large.

*Option 1.* Using the 0–10 scale of the prioritization instrument, Ms. C. assessed the person value for option 1 as a 7. The values and principles of truth, justice, equality and respect for law and order in society were strong for Ms. C. and, for the most part, in the value system of the Z. family. To report Mr. Z. was in keeping with these values and therefore highly in agreement with the values of the persons involved in the situation. It received a 7 instead of a 10 because for Mr. and Mrs Z. they wanted Mr. Z.'s case to be an exception to the law, which would be in conflict with the principle of

**DIAGRAM 3–11**   Case 3: Ethical Dilemma Prioritization

| OPTIONS | | |
|---|---|---|
| DECISION | OUTCOME | PRINCIPLES |
| 1. Report Mr. Z. to FBI | Mr. Z. confined<br>Family separation<br>Family in need of help<br>Community loss<br>Warrant supported | Truth, Full disclosure, Justice<br>Equality of treatment<br>Law and order |
| 2. Do not report Mr. Z. to FBI | Warrant ignored<br>Family intact<br>Community served<br>Mr. and Mrs. Z. continue to hide identity<br>Worker subject to possible arrest | Confidentiality<br>Family preservation<br>Self-Determination<br>Beneficence |

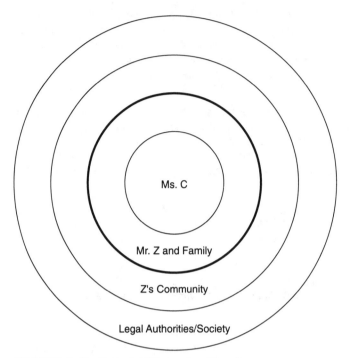

**DIAGRAM 3–12**    Ecological Perspective: Case 3

equality, which in this case was in terms of equal treatment for all who are found guilty under the law.

The life assessment of person was given only a 3 because the probable result of option 1 was the disruption of the family. The item was given three plus points because, at the same time, it would free the family from having to avoid or deny the truth of their father's background. The worker would also be freed from fear or guilt for not cooperating with the authorities.

The value assessment of the environment for option 1 received a 7 because the laws of society and of the community of the Z.'s were in concert with the values reflected in the option. It received a 7 instead of a 10 because the option, in the case of the Z. family, seemed to undercut the values of family and community service, which were also strongly supported in the environment. The life assessment of the environment was given a 5 because the community would suffer the loss of the contribution of Mr. Z. and the shock of learning about his background. At the same time, however, society would be strengthened with the assistance of its citizens in efforts to carry out justice and order for all.

*Option 2.* For option 2, Ms. C. gave the person value a 3. Although option 2 would assist in maintaining the Z. family, and reflect the values of family and community service, it would be contrary to the values of upholding law and order for all. The person life column received a 7 because failure to report would enable the family to

**DIAGRAM 3–13**   Ethical Dilemma Prioritization Instrument

QUESTION: What ought to be done by Ms. C. about her recognizing Mr. Z., an escaped prisoner?

| | OPTIONS | | PERSON(S) | | ENVIRONMENT | | PRIORITY | |
|---|---|---|---|---|---|---|---|---|
| DECI-SION | OUTCOME | PRINCIPLES | VALUES | LIFE | VALUES | LIFE | TOTALS | LIFE |
| 1. Report Mr. Z | Confinement of Mr. Z. Family separa-ration . . . | Truth Justice Equality Law & order | 7 | 3 | 7 | 5 | 22 | 1 |
| 2. Not to report | Warrant ig-nored Family intact . . . | Confidentiality Family Self-determi-nation Beneficence | 3 | 7 | 3 | 5 | 18 | 2 |

continue its current, productive life. It would cause some difficulty for Ms. C. in knowing that she failed to cooperate with legal authorities.

The environment value dimension was assessed as a 3 because failing to report was not supportive of the needs and expectations of society for upholding law and order and for applying equal treatment. It was also contrary to the values of the community of fair treatment and preserving the law. The life value of the environment for option 2 received a 5. If this option were selected, society would continue to have a wanted, convicted criminal at large and a citizen who knew where he was and failed to assist the authorities in locating him. On the other hand, the community and society would profit from the beneficent lifestyle of the Z. family. The fact that the community was under a false assumption of the identify of Mr. Z. was also considered.

As Ms. C. totaled the scores for each item, she could see why she had mixed feelings about what needed to be done in this situation. As shown in Diagram 3–13, option 1, to report Mr. Z., received priority (total of 22). Option 2, not to report, received a score of 18, which indicated that there were reasons for questioning what ought to be done. Ms. C. saw more clearly, however, what she needed to do.

*Intervention.* The worker carried out the decision to report Mr. Z. to the authorities by first finding out the address of the family. She then contacted the local police, who put her in touch with the FBI.

*Evaluation.* After returning home, Ms. C. called her friend and asked how the Z. family was doing. She was told that Mr. Z. had been arrested. Ms. C. inquired how Mrs. Z. and the children were managing. Her friend said that she did not know, but she heard that they might be moving.

*Termination.* Although the worker had a clear conscience in this case, she regretted that she could not do more with the family. She wondered if she would see or hear from them again.

## SUMMARY

An expansion of the value dimension of practice for advanced generalists has been offered in this chapter. Knowledge of, and commitment to, the basic social work values and principles for practice are insufficient for meeting the needs of advanced generalists challenged by complex ethical dilemmas calling for justifiable decisions and effective resolutions. As demonstrated in this chapter, the value base of generalists can be augmented with an ability to apply their ecological systems perspective, general method, and prioritization skills to ethical situations. The ethical decision-making model that has been presented in this chapter equips the worker with a framework for making ethical choices based on a holistic consideration of both the principles and values underlying each possible decision as well as the unique combination of circumstances and context for each option considered. The Ethical Dilemma Prioritization Instrument, as demonstrated in case examples, serves as a tool to organize information and guide the thought processes of the worker.

Additional research, models, tools, and techniques are needed to assist advanced generalists as they face daily ethical challenges that use enormous amounts of their time and effort. An openness to, and recognition of, the similarity in dilemmas facing human service professionals in other disciplines and other countries may expand the realm of possible resources for research and practice by advanced generalists.

## NOTES

1. Thomas P. Holland and Allie C. Kilpatrick, "Ethical Issues in Social Work: Toward a Grounded Theory of Professional Ethics," *Social Work* 36, no. 2 (March 1991): 138.

2. M. Abramson, "Ethical Issues in Social Work Practice with Dying Persons," in L. H. Suszychi and M. Abramson, eds., *Social Work and Terminal Care* (New York: Praeger, 1984), p. 129.

3. M. Vincentia Joseph, *Developing and Teaching Models of Ethical Decision Making* (Chicago, Ill.: Loyola University of Chicago, 1988), pp. 1–2.

4. *Code of Ethics of the National Association of Social Workers.* NASW Policy Statements 1 (Washington, D.C.: NASW, 1980).

5. David Wagner, "Fate of Idealism in Social Work: Alternative Experiences of Professional Careers," *Social Work* 34, no. 5 (September 1989): 389.

6. *Curriculum Policy for the Master's and Baccalaureate Degree Programs in Social Work Education* (New York: Council on Social Work Education, 1983), p. 5.

7. Ibid.

8. Felix P. Biestek, S.J., *The Carework Relationship* (Chicago: Loyola University Press, 1957).

9. J. F. X. Paiva, "A Conception of Social Development," *Social Services Review* 51, no. 2 (June 1977): 329–336.

10. Kenneth J. Hermann, Jr. "Social Workers and the United Nations Convention on the Rights of the Child," *Social Work* 36, no. 2 (March 1991): 102.

11. Joseph, *Developing and Teaching Models,* p. 13.

12. Andrew Jameton, *Nursing Practice: The Ethical Issues* (Englewood Cliffs, N.J.: Prentice-Hall, 1984), pp. 67–69. Adapted by permission.

13. Elsie L. Bandman and Bertram Bandman, *Nursing Ethics in the Life Span* (Norwalk, Conn.: Appleton-Century Crofts, 1985), p. 79.

14. Mark Siegler, "Decision-Making Strategy for Clinical-Ethical Problems in Medicine," *Archives of Internal Medicine* 142 (November 1982): 2178–2179. © 1982, American Medical Association.

15. David C. Thomasma, "Training in Medical Ethics: An Ethical Workup," *Forum on Medicine* (December 1978): 34–36.

16. Joseph, *Developing and Teaching Models,* pp. 11–14.

17. Reproduced by permission of the publisher, F. E. Peacock Publishers, Inc., Itasca, Illinois. From Frank Lowenberg and Ralph Dolgoff, *Ethical Decisions for Social Work Practice,* 4th ed., © 1992, p. 54.

18. Ibid., p. 60.

19. Holland and Kilpatrick, "Ethical Issues," p. 140.

20. Maria O'Neil McMahon, *The General Method of Social Work Practice,* 2nd ed. (Englewood Cliffs, N.J.: Prentice Hall, 1990), p. 339.

21. Ibid., pp. 157–160.

22. Lowenberg and Dolgoff, *Ethical Decisions for Social Work Practice,* p. 60.

23. Catholic Social Ministries, Diocese of Raleigh, "Mission Statement," March 1990, p. 1.

24. *Code of Ethics,* NASW, pp. 4, 9.

# 4
# Knowledge
# for Advanced
# Generalist Practice

*INTRODUCTION*

Human beings innately want to know. They seek to understand reality. The goal of this quest may be seen as the completion of a puzzle called "truth." Theories are pieces of a puzzle that may offer a component picture of reality and, when juxtaposed with other pieces, may promote a growing understanding of the truth.

Various epistemologies explain the nature, scope, origin, and methods for acquiring knowledge. For example, according to logical empiricism, knowledge can be obtained and objectively verified through sensory data and scientific technique. The values or biases of the person conducting the inquiry can be controlled through mathematical techniques. Existentialism offers a contrasting view of knowledge, stressing the need to focus on subjective experience, living, and interactions in current reality rather than objective reasoning based on fact. Emphasis is given to the need for human beings to understand self and others in their current reality and to strive for "authentic existence."[1]

Jurgen Habermas[2] brings the objective and the subjective together, combining facts with ideas. He states, "The only knowledge that can truly orient action is knowledge that frees itself from mere human interests and is based on Ideas—in other words, knowledge that has taken a theoretical attitude." He points out that facts alone do not provide knowledge. It is only through understanding of the meaning of the facts that one can begin to arrive at knowledge. In an effort to understand, researchers develop theories to compare facts and study relationships. As described by Fred Kerlinger,

> A theory is a set of interrelated constructs (concepts), definitions, and proposition that present a systematic view of phenomena by specifying relations among variables, with the purpose of explaining and predicting the phenomena.[3]

Theory building is a process for developing knowledge. According to Francis Turner, theory building "is a complex and intricate human activity involving the whole spectrum of our intellectual and emotional potential."[4] The process begins with the experiencing of a particular phenomena. The experience is then generalized and conceptualized. Relationships of concepts are considered and efforts are made to test out a "theory" about the phenomena. Results are then analyzed and operationalized.

Not all theory is verified through scientific testing of facts. Herbert Strean describes theory as "a more or less verified explanation of observed facts or phenomena."[5] In a broad sense, "theory" may be used to refer to knowledge derived through accumulated practice wisdom or the systematic formulation of ideas.

Theories used in helping professions may be divided into the categories of (1) theory for understanding and (2) theory for practice. Theories may also be classified as personality, political, or practice theory. The knowledge needed for effective professional social work practice encompasses a broad range of theories and extensive information about persons, problems, places, programs, and policies.

In this chapter, attention will be given to knowledge needed for advanced generalist practice. A study of the multifaceted history of theory in social work is presented as a predecessor to the comprehensive approach to theory development found in advanced generalist practice. An international perspective of advanced ecological systems theory was depicted in Chapter 2. An entire chapter was given to this dimension of knowledge because it is an essential, pervasive, theoretical perspective in advanced generalist practice. The knowledge component of social policy, national and international, for advanced generalist practice will be addressed in Chapter 8. Throughout this chapter, the meaning of knowledge in social work, advanced knowledge about person in environment, and holistic paradigms for advanced generalist practice will be explored.

### Knowledge in Social Work

In 1957, Ernest Greenwood, in his "Attributes of a Profession," stressed the need for a profession to have an identifiable body of theory that is communicable and constantly tested for relevance.[6] He differentiated scientific theory from practice theory, saying that "scientific theory is descriptive, practice theory is prescriptive."[7] Social work's body of knowledge is both descriptive and prescriptive. Max Siporin distinguishes between social work's descriptive knowledge, which is acquired from the social and behavioral sciences, and practice theory, which "prescribes action for change" and exists primarily "in the form of *practice wisdom* rather than in a codified, scientifically tested form."[8] Although most practice theory was based on practice wisdom in the past, there is a strong movement within the profession toward the development of scientifically tested practice theory to prescribe the actions of the "scientific practitioner."[9]

Several authors have addressed the need for an empirical base for practice theory in professional social work. For example, Scott Briar writes, "Intervention theories that do not lend themselves to empirical specification are of questionable value for a scientific profession."[10] Lawrence Shulman argues that "we are still in the early stages of building an empirically based, holistic social work practice theory." Although we often borrow empirically based theories from other disciplines that "are closely tied to prescriptions for worker interventions," Shulman points out that they may not appropriately fit social work practice because "they sometimes seem to ignore our profession's traditional concern for social policy and social justice issues that affect our clients and that underpin our professional value system."[11] Francis Turner describes theory building based on empirical research as "a stance still greatly neglected by our field." He writes:

> In this mode, various concepts related to our field are operationally defined and tested through the formulation of hypotheses and the examination of resultant data. . . . Many more projects of this type are needed and can be expected in the next few years.[12]

Turner identifies a variety of different approaches that have been used to build theory in the profession. These include a study of components and concepts of processes, formulation of models and theoretical frameworks, comparative studies of theories, conceptualizations of the nature of theory and theory building, descriptions of practice approaches drawn from practice experience and reflection, efforts to develop an integrated or eclectic model of theory, and empirical research.[13]

Social work has been described as both an art and a science since its inception as a profession. This duality within the profession continues to be reflected in the debated approaches used to pursue knowledge and secure professional identity. A review of the history of social work reveals an interesting cyclical progression in the development of knowledge, moving from a morality base to practice wisdom, to empirical research, to an encompassing integrated effort that accepts diversity in approaches, to a questioning of the need for any theory, to a return to and recalling of the morality of social work. Limiting the acquisition of knowledge, both descriptive and prescriptive, for the multifaceted profession of social work to any one approach may certainly be questioned. To find a holistic perspective that comprehensively reflects the duality and diversities within the profession is an ongoing challenge.

### History of Theory in Social Work

The idealism of the founders of the profession influenced the early development of thought and action in social work. Originally, the theory used in social work was based on morality. The writings of the leading spokespersons for organized charity before 1900, such as Josephine Shaw Lowell or Alexis de Tocqueville, were centered on a series of moral arguments.[14] In the early 1900s, social work leaders, such as Mary Richmond and Edward Devine, emphasized the value of practice wisdom as the professional knowledge base instead of the prevailing application of individual moral judgments.[15]

Schools or social work in the early 1900s grew out of in-service training programs of charity agencies. An early debate in the formation of the curriculum of the schools was in regard to its focus on either (1) fundamental social policy issues based on social theory with a reform orientation or (2) individual and family issues based on practice wisdom with a casework orientation. In the beginning of the New York School of Philanthropy, prior to 1912, emphasis was placed on social theory, with courses in direct practice offered only as electives. Social work, along with sociology and economics, identified with a concern for social problems and a commitment to social reform. After 1912, the influence of Mary Richmond predominated and the school developed a two-year curriculum emphasizing preparation for direct practice. In addition to knowledge about social institutions and legislation, Richmond stressed the need to know about the spiritual and physical well-being of persons as endemic to social work.[16]

Abraham Flexner in 1915 spoke at the National Conference of Charities and Correction in Baltimore. He disparaged the use of practice wisdom for a profession's body of knowledge, stressing the need for theoretically coherent scientific knowledge, as found in medicine.[17] Turning to the field of psychoanalysis in the 1920s, social workers attempted to become more scientific in their thinking as they developed the diagnostic schools of learning. Further searching for understanding and direction in practice led them to study classical behaviorism and Rankian theory. Functional schools of social work emerged in the 1930s and 1940s. Whereas Freudian theory stressed the unconscious and ego and behavioral theory focused on the conditioning of behavior, Rankian theory emphasized such concepts as the human will, relationship, and process.[18]

In the 1950s, social workers relied heavily on the social and behavioral sciences to develop their theory base.[19] At the same time, the profession encouraged the use of a variety of theoretical approaches and conceptual frameworks. Attempts were made to reconcile the diagnostic and functional schools and to move toward a more unified practice that encompassed diversity in thought and action.

In the 1960s, questions of the profession's legitimacy, status, and survival emerged. Social work educators and practitioners began to stress the need for more empirical research to validate the theoretical base of social work. Knowledge acquired through quantitative design and analysis began to be seen as superior to knowledge from practice wisdom or qualitative study. Although social work education was intrinsically tied to professional practice, pressures from outside led educators to give priority to scholarly research over teaching and service. As described in a monograph of the National Association of Deans and Directors of Schools of Social Work:

> The sense of urgency regarding an augmented scholarly enterprise in social work education derives from the 1960's and 1970's, when it became clear that the profession's normal and accustomed approaches to problem solving were often not effective; that social welfare programs were at risk of losing out in the struggle for scarce societal resources unless a better case could be made for their efficacy; that the profession itself would lose its place in policymaking councils unless it had new ideas for addressing problems; and, that the mechanisms for developing, testing and disseminating practice knowledge were weak.[20]

In the 1980s, a major development was the integration of practice and empirical research through the use of single-system design. This research methodology is a systematic study of a single case, utilizing operationalized goals and techniques for measuring progress and outcomes. Clinical relationships are reduced to component parts for standardization and objective measurement.[21]

In recent years, questions have been raised about the appropriateness of relying on objective instruments and mathematical techniques to assess clinical relationships and human progress.[22] Followers of the critical theory of Habermas argue that empirical methods should be joined with a hermeneutic approach that reflects on the impact of motives and self interests in framing a problem and calls for a consideration of alternatives and possible reformulation of research questions.[23] In addition, as pointed out by Ruth Dean and Barbara Fenby, critical theory "considers humanity's ability to reflect on history to be an agent of societal change." Dean and Fenby also suggest the use of "deconstruction fiction," which questions the validity of existing structures, as a valuable theoretical position for knowledge development.[24] Social workers have begun to use qualitative and quantitative research techniques during practice assessment, intervention, and evaluation. This type of "multiple triangulation" is seen as providing "the tools required to get at the interactions and transactions constituting the reality of the phenomena" that is "the heart of social work practice, a reality that is filled with concrete acts and symbolic meanings."[25]

Howard Goldstein questions the "underlying assumption . . . that effective or "good" practice must be rooted in an established theoretical foundation."[26] He proposes a "humanistic approach" to professional knowledge that emphasizes 'the real-life nature of the helping experience."[27] In her article entitled "Social Work: A Profession Chasing Its Tail," Marion K. Sanders suggests that social work "may have gained a profession by forfeiting a mission."[28] Alan Keith-Lucas points out the limitations of empirical research for contributing "useful new knowledge" to practice and stresses his concern that "Social work today has virtually deserted the poor."[29] Several contemporary writers are encouraging the profession to recall and return to "The Moral Purposes of Social Work," which was the original basis for theory in the profession.[30]

It appears, therefore, that social workers have gone full circle in a cyclical progression as they consistently strive for enriched and expanded professional knowledge for understanding and direction. A variety of methods continue to be used in the pursuit of an identifiable body of theory. Practice wisdom, empirical study, existential learning, moral direction, and other approaches have all served as valuable sources for acquiring knowledge. The use of diverse methods and approaches has helped to advance knowledge and to renew the interest and commitment of professionals. As Robert Perlman and Arnold Gurin write:

> While definitions and boundaries are necessary in the clarification of a professional field, they can, if used excessively, or prematurely, prevent that field from discovering its own potentialities. The diversity that now exists is an asset in enabling this field of practice to engage in experimentation and innovation.[31]

### The Search for Theoretical Holism

"Holism" is defined as "a totality in perspective, with sensitivity to all of the parts or levels that constitute the whole and to their interdependence and relatedness."[32] Throughout the history of social work, there has been frequent reference to the desire for a unifying theory, sometimes refered to as a macro, integrated, grand, or holistic theory. In the past, theories that have been offered as hopeful possibilities have included Lewin's Field Theory, Von Bertalanffy's General Systems Theory, Blumer's Symbolic Interactionism, or the Planned Change Theory as developed by Lippitt, Watson and Westley.[33] The desire for a single theoretical base for social work is understandable in the light of the vast array of theories and research studies currently used by practitioners. Students often find the extensive realm of possibilities in theory selection confusing and overwhelming.

The creation of a holistic theory that would enable a social worker to comprehend the distinctive elements of practice as they interact within the context of the whole may be a continuing quest throughout the life of the profession. Whereas some leaders in the profession have supported this quest with urgency, others have strongly opposed it, seeing the endeavor as narrowing and futile. Shulman, for example, stresses the need for "an integrated, method-focused, empirically based theory of practice" and describes his "sense of urgency that a beginning is needed."[34] Harry Specht, on the other hand, writes, "Whether it is systems theory, social exchange theory, organizational theory, or some other theory, professionals who are educated primarily in the use of one theory to explain and guide their practice will necessarily have an exceedingly narrow vision of the people with whom they deal and the contexts in which they practice."[35]

Instead of creating a single, all encompassing theory for practice, some writers have attempted to discover a holistic framework to serve as a guide for organizing or clustering theories into a systematic pattern to show commonalities and relatedness. Pearman, for example, categorized theories in the behavioral and social sciences for social work under the headings: Psychological Sciences, Anthropology, Sociology/Social Psych, Economics, and Political Sciences (Diagram 4–1).[36] Francis Turner organized 21 social work practice

**DIAGRAM 4–1**   Behavioral and Social Sciences

| PSYCHOLOGICAL SCIENCES | ANTHROPOLOGY | SOCIOLOGY AND SOCIAL PSYCHOLOGY | ECONOMICS | POLITICAL SCIENCE |
|---|---|---|---|---|
| Psychoanalytic theory | Value concepts | Social organization and basic | Systems orientation | Systems orientation |
| Other theory from psychiatry, e.g., reality theory | Dominant culture Subcultures Relationships to individual be- | systems Power structure Community | Macro-economics and employ- ment | Political science theory Compensatory |
| Other psychological theory, e.g., learning theory, operant psychol- ogy | havior collective behavior Culture conflict | concepts Social change concepts includ- ing conflict | Public finance Monetary theory Welfare theory Distribution theory | policies for disadvantage in the eco- nomic system |
| Research technol- ogy | Research tech- nology Relationship | theory Demography Small group | Cost-benefit analysis Human resources | Political realities Relation of pub- lic and private |
| Personality theories | between values and social | theory Research tech- | investment concepts | agencies Check-and- |
| Human growth Psychological theory related to impact of client participation | systems | nology Role theory Social stratifi- cation | Equilibrium concept Research technology | balance con- cept Techniques for political inter- vention Research tech- nology |

theories according to six categories with 33 selected attributes. The six categories are (1) general attributes, (2) perception of person, (3) perception of functioning, (4) therapeutic qualities, (5) the therapist, and (6) therapeutic application.[37] Max Siporin identified seven major theoretical helping frameworks which, although "relatively underdeveloped," are being utilized in social work practice. They are "social provision, interactional, psychoanalytic, sociobehavioral, existentialist, problem-solving, and ecological-systems theory." He described ecological systems theory as a "general theoretical model," and "a generic framework for social work practice." Problem solving is seen as ideally requiring "rational planning and decision procedures with individuals and groups, involving a phased sequence of tasks."[38]

The search for holistic framework for identifying relevant theories has been an endeavor common also to the field of generalist practice and advanced generalist practice. The field clearly embraces and integrates two of the approaches described by Siporin, namely, the problem-solving approach and ecological systems theory. Both approaches serve as guiding frameworks for the identification and selection of theories for generalist and advanced generalist practice as developed in this chapter.

### Knowledge in Generalist Practice

A key element of generalist practice has been identified as "an open selection of theories and interventions" (see Chapter 1, Diagram 1–7). Depending on the problem in focus, the generalist may be eclectic in chosing theories and approaches as needed for effective intervention. At the same time, the worker keeps in mind basic parameters of eclecticism. As brought out by Siporin,

> Being eclectic means to select what is best from various doctrines. Eclecticism does have a basic requirement, that whatever is borrowed or developed needs to be consistent with other elements of social work's body of values and knowledge.[39]

The theories selected by generalists need to be appropriately matched with their values, roles, and skills. Whereas social work generalists rely heavily on practice theories of a cognitive nature (e.g., problem solving, task centered, reality, cognitive theory), they would not by their nature and education select highly specialized practice theories and interventions (e.g., Gestalt, psychoanalysis, hypnosis). When needed, the generalist would make a referral to an advanced worker or specialist with the necessary expertise.

There are two central paradigms that guide social work generalists in their knowledge development and theory selection. A "paradigm" is a basic assumption or illustration that guides a discipline in its application of knowledge in a particular area. It is a "disciplinary matrix" that shares symbolic generalizations, models, values and examples.[40] A paradigm is not as inclusive as a theory, but may serve to explain a central idea of a theory. An example is the medical model of "study, diagnoses, and treatment," which was used extensively as a guiding framework for practice in the early history of social work. Two paradigms used in generalist practice are: (1) the ecological systems theory perspective and (2) the problem-solving process of the general method.

The ecological systems perspective of "person in environment" has served as an organizing paradigm for clustering the foundation theories commonly used in practice. In the ecological systems paradigm, depicted in Diagram 4–2, the three headings used are "Person," "In," and "Environment." The theories placed under the three headings are primarily theories for understanding. They inform the practitioner rather than guide the actions of the practitioner, as found in practice theories.

The General Method, a six-stage problem-solving process, serves as a paradigm for guiding a worker in the selection and use of practice theories and techniques for generalist practice. Within each stage of the process, a worker's actions may be directed through input from diverse theories. For example, in engagement, generalists may use the practice theory and communication skills developed by Robert Carkhuff and William Anthony.[41] If working with a family, theory about dysfunctional communications patterns as proposed by Virginia Satir may assist with data collection.[42] When selecting a planned intervention for work with a community, the worker may consider Jack Rothman's practice models of locality development or social action.[43] During assessment, the worker may find support from task-centered practice, described by William Reid and Laura Epstein, as contracts are developed listing tasks to be accomplished for problem resolution.[44] Throughout the process, the problem-solving theory of Helen Harris Pearlman may provide the worker with guidance and understanding in the process of helping.[45]

It is apparent that generalists use a variety of sources for acquiring and using knowledge in the profession. In addition to theories that have been sci-

**DIAGRAM 4–2**  An Ecological Perspective of Foundation Theory for Social Work

| ECOLOGY | | |
|---|---|---|
| PERSON | IN | ENVIRONMENT |
| Ego psychology | Role | Organizational theory |
| Developmental theories | Socialization | Political science |
|   Biological | Behavioral theory | Economic theory |
|   Sexual | Communication | Cultural anthropology |
|   Psychosocial | | |
|   Cognitive | Stress theory | Systems theory |
|   Moral | Ecological-systems theory | |
|   Spiritual | | |
| Self-actualization | | |

entifically verified, such as those from the behavioral sciences, several theories used, such as those taken from the field of family treatment, may be based more on practice wisdom and experience. The problem-solving and task-centered practice theories used in the six-stage process paradigm have been supported by empirical research. Ecological systems theory, which is the fundamental theory in the advanced ecological systems paradigm, has minimal scientific data to support it.[46] As a subsystem of general systems theory, it has been adopted by several disciplines because of its effectiveness in explaining complex phenomena.

## KNOWLEDGE IN ADVANCED GENERALIST PRACTICE

At the advanced generalist level, the practitioner acquires knowledge of advanced theories for application to complex problems. Advanced generalists build on the paradigms and related theories used in generalist practice. Through further study, they extend their knowledge for greater understanding and skill. A variety of theories are applied to multilevel situations in both their direct and indirect practice roles of front line service provider, middle manager, supervisor, administrator, and policy maker.

### The Advanced Ecological Systems Paradigm

For the advanced generalist, the advanced ecological systems perspective pictured in Diagram 4–3 serves as a paradigm to guide practitioners in their identification and selection of theories. All the systems in the paradigm are perceived of together as an interdependent and integrated whole. At the same time, each system is seen as separate with its own subsystems. There is a broad range of theories available for each system and subsystem in the paradigm. A worker may select for advanced study theories about "person" (with the six subsystems of educational, economic, political, psychological, physical, sexual, social, and spiritual) and theories about the triplex environment: the nurturing environment (family, friends, culture, community, and significant others); the sustaining environments (society's institutions, programs, and services); and the global environment (people, problems, policies, and programs of different countries).

The study and selection of theories for knowledge development in advanced generalist practice are individualized according to the needs of each person preparing to become an advanced generalist. An individualized learning assessment is made to ascertain which systems or subsystems are most in need of further development by the individual for effective advanced generalist practice. Depending on the individual's life and work experience and acquired knowledge, there may be gaps or weaknesses in particular areas of knowledge to be addressed through advanced study. An example of how each

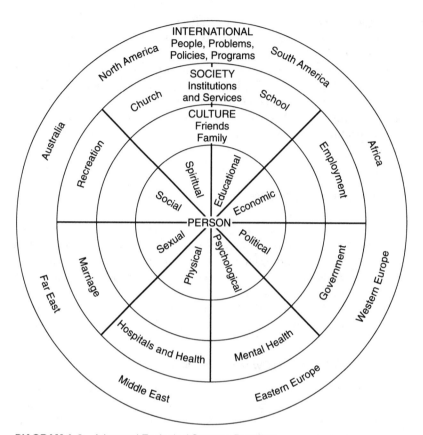

**DIAGRAM 4–3**   Advanced Ecological Systems Paradigm

system is considered for identification of knowledge gaps or needs is found in Diagram 4–4. As each system within a circular boundary is highlighted, the basic questions are: (1) What does this worker know about this system and its subsystems and (2) What does this worker need to know about this system and its subsystems for effective practice as an advanced generalist? Following a learning assessment for each of the systems in Diagram 4–4, the worker returns to the holistic advanced ecological systems perspective of Diagram 4–3 and asks: What knowledge do I have and what do I need to develop to understand the interrelationships among these systems.

*Knowledge about "Person"*   Advanced generalists build on generalist knowledge of "Person" and acquire broader and deeper knowledge for greater understanding. In order to identify which theories about "Person" should be selected for study in advanced generalist practice, the concept of "Person(s)" and the various subsystems of "Person," as identified in Diagram 4–4 A, are considered separately. Again, the question asked for each is: "In this area, what

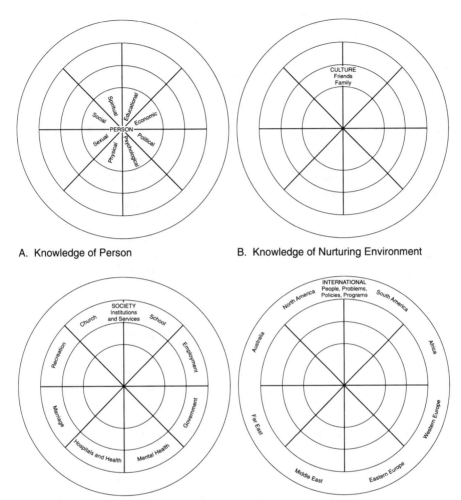

A. Knowledge of Person

B. Knowledge of Nurturing Environment

C. Knowledge of Sustaining Environment

D. Knowledge of International Environment

**DIAGRAM 4–4**   Individualized Knowledge Assessment

further knowledge do I need to develop for effective practice as an advanced generalist?" Turner[47] aides in the selection of theories ("Thought Systems") in several distinguishing areas of "person" as found in Diagram 4–5. The thought systems listed in the diagram include theories that both inform and guide social workers. The identified areas have commonalities with those dimensions of person as found in Diagram 4–4 A. The worker may select some of the theories identified in Turner's framework or seek out other theories or sources of knowledge relating to specific areas of person. For example, the worker may know little about AIDS and need to turn to the literature from medical disciplines for this information. An example of an individualized assessment of

**DIAGRAM 4–5**   Knowledge about Person

| DISTINGUISHING AREA OF FOCUS | RELEVANT THOUGHT SYSTEM |
| --- | --- |
| Person as a psychological being (psychological) | Psychoanalytic Functional Gestalt |
| Person as thinker (educational) | Cognitive |
| Person as learner (educational) | Behavior modification |
| Person as contemplator (spiritual) | Meditation Existentialism |
| Person as communicator (social) | Communications |
| Person as doer (economic) | Problem-solving Task-centered Crisis |
| Person as biological entity (biological) | Neurolinguistics |
| Person as individual (psychological) | Ego-psychology Client-centered |
| Person as family member (sexual, social) | Family Transactional analysis |
| Person as group member (social) | Group |
| Person in relation to society (political) | Psychosocial Systems Role Feminism Marxism |
| Person in relation to the universe | Ecological |

"Person" knowledge for an advanced generalist student is found in Diagram 4–6.

*Knowledge about Environment*   The triplex environment of the advanced ecological systems paradigm (Diagram 4–4, B, C, D) serves as a guide for identification and selection of knowledge about the environment needed for advanced generalists. Each environmental system (nurturing, societal, international) is considered separately with its component parts. Again, the individual workers asks: What do I know; What do I need to know in this area to be prepared for advanced generalist practice? In looking at the nurturing environments, there may be certain cultures or family types that a worker knows little about. Greater study of communities in rural or urban environments may need to be undertaken. In considering sustaining environments, there may be programs, policies, services, or processes that need to be understood. The worker may know little about federal laws, grants, or funding procedures. During an analysis at the international level, the worker may recognize a deficiency in knowledge about foreign policy or global needs. There may be the expectation that upon completion of a program to prepare for advanced generalist practice, the student will work with a number of people from a country about which

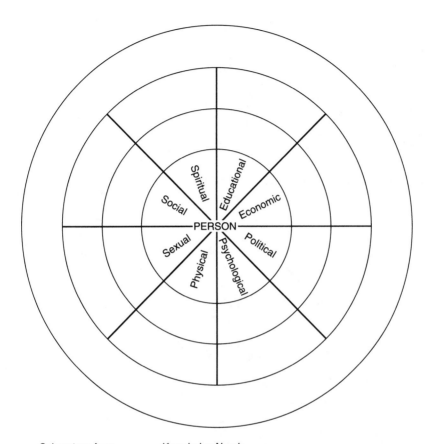

| Subsystem Area | Knowledge Needs |
| --- | --- |
| Education | Learning Styles, Motivation Theory |
| Economic | Money Management Theory |
| Political | Marxism, Feminism |
| Psychological | DSM III R, Ego Psychology, Psychopharmacology |
| Physical | Disease: AIDS, Cancer, Addictions |
| Sexual | Sexual Impotence |
| Social | Work/Leisure Theory |
| Spiritual | Spirituality, Meditation |
| Person | Humanistic Psychology, Self-Actualization |

**DIAGRAM 4–6**   "Person" Knowledge Needs Assessment

he or she knows very little. Diagram 4–7 offers an example of a triplex environmental knowledge assessment.

The knowledge identified as needing further development for an individual may be so extensive that the individual may need to prioritize theories and create an ongoing learning plan that could extend beyond the period of time for formal learning in a degree program. Advanced generalists along with other human service professionals know that professional learning is a lifelong process. An example of a prioritized, individualized learning plan for an

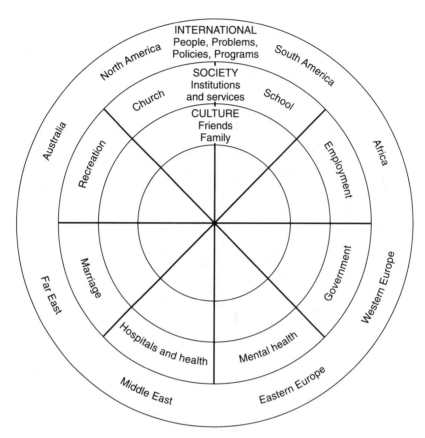

| Nurturing Environment | Social Environment | International Environment |
|---|---|---|
| Creative Learning Environments | Cybernetics | Political Ideologies |
| I.Q. Stimulation | Laws re. Schools | World Health Organization |
| Co-ops, Credit Unions | Macro Economics | World Bank Trade |
| Family/Town Law | Poverty in U.S.A. | International Law re: Child Custody, Illegal Aliens |
| Symbolic Interaction | Social Control Theory | Viet Nam–Status Systems |
| Community Health | National Institute of Mental Health | Yugoslavia |
| Divorce Law | Wellness Theory | Cross-Cultural Studies |
| Family Violence | Conflict Theory | |
| Spanish Language | Psychiatric Nursing | |
| Cults | Buddhism | |

**DIAGRAM 4–7**    Triplex "Environment" Knowledge Needs Assessment

advanced generalist student using the advanced ecological systems paradigm is found in Diagram 4–8. Although there were several areas identified as needing further study, the student selected those knowledge areas assessed as most in need of understanding upon completion of an advanced generalist social work program and prior to entry into an expected service delivery system. Other

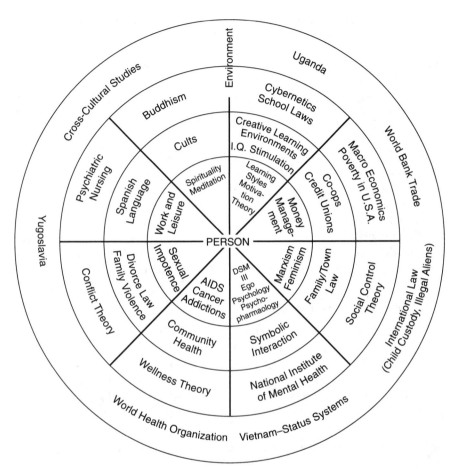

**DIAGRAM–4–8** Advanced Ecological Systems Paradigm: Individualized Selection (Needs Assessment) of Advanced Knowledge for Understanding

areas of knowledge seen as desirable would need to be pursued through post-graduate continuing education opportunities.

The use of the advanced ecological systems perspective as a paradigm for theory selection as proposed in this chapter is an expansion of ideas proposed by earlier writers in the field. For example, Carol Meyer described the ecosystems perspective in relation to theory selection as follows:

> At the theory level, the perspective can provide for various means of organizing and structuring the unit of attention and the environment. This structuring is necessary to understand the transaction taking place at the interface; it is left to the practitioner and client or client group to choose a frame of reference within which to work. In doing this, the perspective augments each practitioner's per-

ception of the world and respects the multidude of conceptualizations that are often necessary to account for the phenomena.[48]

Siporin describes the ecosystems perspective in this way:

> The ecological systems model is not a unitary theory but it is a basic framework, an umbrella-like structure we need for assessment and interventive purposes. It accepts behavior and personality theories.[49]

The paradigm as proposed in this chapter serves as "an umbrella-like structure" for "organizing and structuring the unit of attention" for the knowledge development of advanced generalists in relation to the various theories and bodies of information that are available about the units of person and environment. In addition to the use of the advanced ecological systems paradigm for the selection of theories primarily for *understanding*, advanced generalists use a second paradigm, with an advanced problem-solving process pespective, for the identification and selection of *practice* theories to guide their actions and interactions.

### The Advanced Problem-solving Paradigm

As stated earlier, essential elements of generalist practice include (1) a problem-solving process, (2) a multilevel approach, and (3) an open selection of theories and interventions (Chapter 1, Diagram 1–7). Framing the six-stage problem-solving process of the general method with the eight-system levels as shown in Diagram 4–9 provides a paradigm for selection and study of practice theories and techniques that guide the actions of the advanced generalist.

**DIAGRAM 4–9**  Advanced Problem-solving Paradigm: Individualized Selection of Theories, Models, and Techniques for Advanced Generalist Practice

| | | MULTILEVEL SYSTEMS (clients, employees, agencies, other) | | | | | | |
|---|---|---|---|---|---|---|---|---|
| | | Individual | Family | Group | Community | Institution | Society | World |
| **PROBLEM-SOLVING PROCESS** | Engagement | | | | | | | |
| | Data Collection | | | | | | | |
| | Assessment | | | | | | | |
| | Intervention | | | | | | | |
| | Evaluation | | | | | | | |
| | Termination | | | | | | | |

*Problem-solving Process*   Using the problem-solving process is generic to the nature of generalist and advanced generalist practice. The six-stage process of the general method is a thread or theme that may be used in multiple ways to support workers in their movement toward accomplishing goals. It serves as the iron beams to provide a basic structure for adding the walls and materials of theories and techniques to build an effective service delivery. The practitioner is not constricted by any one theory or intervention. The proposed problem-solving paradigm in Diagram 4–9 stimulates thought and discussion about the use and fit of various theories within advanced generalist practice.

*Multilevel Systems*   Advanced generalists use the problem-solving process while working with individuals, groups, or larger systems in their roles of direct service provider, supervisor, manager, administrator, or policy maker. In selecting a program of study to prepare for advanced generalist practice, the individual under academic advisement uses the paradigm to identify gaps and needs in practice knowledge for work with a variety of systems. The vast array of available practice theories, such as those listed in Diagram 4–10, are surveyed, and selection for further study is made in the light of spaces on the paradigm that are identified as voids in the student's practice knowledge. If students, for example, recognize a need to know how to help a community prioritize their problems, they may select to study the nominal group approach.[50] If there is a need to know how to help family members engage in sharing their perception of the family (problem) and

**DIAGRAM 4–10**   Direct and Indirect Practice Theories

| PRACTICE THEORIES AND APPROACHES | |
| --- | --- |
| DIRECT | INDIRECT |
| Behavior modification | Control/power theories |
| Bioenergetics/biofeedback | Cybernetics/information theory |
| Client-centered practice | Decision-making models |
| Cognitive therapy | Econometrics |
| Crisis intervention | Exchange theory |
| Existential psychotherapy | Expectancy theory |
| Gestalt therapy | Incremental planning |
| Life skills counseling | Inequality theory |
| Mediation | Interactional management |
| Meditation | Management by objectives |
| Neurolinguistic programming | Organizational management |
| Play therapy | Policy science |
| Psychoanalytic theory | Political economy theory |
| Psychodrama | Redistribution theory |
| Psychosocial therapy | Scientific management |
| Primal theory | Situational leadership |
| Reality therapy | Social change theory |
| Task-centered practice | Theory X and Y |
| Transactional analysis | Theory Z |

of what they would like to see the family become (goal) they may select to study such techniques as sculpturing or cluster analysis, found in theories of family therapy.[51] If the individual knows little about management and how to work differentially with employees, situational leadership theory may be of assistance.[52]

*Vertical and Horizontal Selection*    As the use of a theory or technique is explored, the individual is encouraged to consider the theory both vertically and horizontally. One theory may be selected for use in guiding the actions of the worker throughout the six-stage process (vertical). Another theory may offer techniques or an approach to practice that can be carried across system levels (horizontal). For example, behavioral theory may be found valuable for guiding the actions of the worker throughout the entire six-stage process while working with an individual (vertical). The technique of eco-mapping, on the other hand, may be used during data collection while working with an individual, a group, a family, a community, and an organization or larger system (horizontal). In some situations, an advanced generalist may use several theories (vertical and horizontal) to carry out the six-stage process. Diagram 4–11 depicts the use of the advanced problem-solving paradigm for an individualized assessment and selection of practice theories and techniques for advanced generalist practice.

## THE STUDY OF A THEORY

In using the suggested paradigm, once a theory or technique has been identified as desirable knowledge for an individual preparing for advanced generalist practice, a range of frameworks is available to guide in the study process. For

**DIAGRAM 4–11**    Advanced Problem-solving Paradigm: Individualized Selection of Theories, Models, and Techniques for Advanced Generalist Practice

| | | MULTILEVEL SYSTEMS (clients, employees, agencies, other) | | | | | | |
|---|---|---|---|---|---|---|---|---|
| | | Individual | Family | Group | Community | Institution | Society | World |
| **PROBLEM-SOLVING PROCESS** | Engagement | Neuro-Linguistics Programing (NLP) | Cluster Analysis | Nominal Group Approach | | Interactional Management | | |
| | Data Collection | | Sculpturing Ecomapping | | | | | Information Search Skills |
| | Assessment | | | | Social Change Theory | | | |
| | Intervention | Stress Management Behavior Modification | | Caseload Management | | Situational Management PPBS | Policy Development | |
| | Evaluation | | | | | MBO | | |
| | Termination | | | | | | | |

a cursory view of the theory, a basic framework may be followed consisting of five subheadings:

1. Definition (define the name given to the theory)
2. Sources (primary references)
3. Statements ( central ideas, descriptions, and relationships of concepts in the theory)
4. Concepts (main concepts found in the theory)
5. Practice example (use of theoretical statement or concept in practice)

Diagram 4–12 illustrates the use of this approach in an initial study of role theory.

For a more in-depth study of a practice theory, the Framework for Analysis of Practice Models provided by Carol Meyer may be followed. It consists of the following set of questions to be asked about a theory:

1. Ideological biases. What nonempirical commitments are held by the model?

2. Values. What beliefs relevant to social work are expressed in the model?
3. Knowledge base. What theories and ideas does the model draw upon?
4. Unit of attention. Is the model to be used with individuals, families, groups, communities, organizations?
5. Problem definition. How does the model determine what is a problem for its attention?
6. Congruent and explicit interventions. Is the interventive methodology consistent with the other parts of the framework, such as those mentioned in numbers 1 to 5? And are the model's techniques of a specific or a general design?
7. Uses of the professional relationship. To what degree is the professional relationship used as context and/or process in the model? Is it used as means or ends in interventions?
8. Desired outcomes. What does the model define as its goals of intervention?
9. Uses of time. Does the model suggest or require short- or long-term interventions? Is time used as a dynamic in assessment and intervention?
10. Differential use of staff. Does the model require that only graduate social workers can practice it, or can it be used by a variety of staff levels and types?
11. Work with self-help groups. Can the model be made applicable to nonclient groups?
12. Availability to effectiveness research. Is the model explicitly defined, so that its use in practice can be evaluated empirically?[53]

Examples of the use of this framework as applied to psychosocial theory, problem-solving theory, behavioral theory, and crisis intervention may be found in Meyer's book entitled *Clinical Social Work in the Eco-systems Perspective.*[54]

**DIAGRAM 4–12**    Framework 1: Role Theory

I. Definition:
Role refers to an expected pattern of behavior performed by a person in an interaction situation (Sarbin & Allen).

II. Selected Sources:
Bruce J. Biddle, *Role Theory: Expectations, Identities, and Behaviors* (New York: Academic Press, 1979).

Liane Vida Davis, "Role Theory," in Francis J. Turner (ed.), *Social Work Treatment: Interlocking Theoretical Approaches,* 3rd ed. (New York: The Free Press, 1986).

Helen Harris Perlman, *Persona: Social Role and Personality* (Chicago: University of Chicago Press, 1968).

Theodore Sarbin and V. L. Allem, "Role Theory," in Gardner Lindsey and E. Aronson (eds.), *Handbook of Social Psychology* (Cambridge, MA: Addison-Wesley, 1968).

III. Basic Statements:
1. The focus of role theory is on behavior.
2. Role is interactional. It occurs in the social context of complementary roles.
3. Role enactment is dependent on role expectations.
4. Role relates to and derives from status. Through occupying status, one can assume a role.
5. Individuals occupy more than one role at a time. The collection of roles a person occupies is called a role set.
6. Persons are taught roles through the process of socialization.
7. When an actor is confronted with incompatible expectations within one role or between roles, role conflict may be experienced.

IV. Basic Concepts:

| | | |
|---|---|---|
| Role enactment | Gender roles | Status |
| Role complementarity | Role expectations | Role set |
| Role skills | Role location | Socialization |
| Self-role congruence | Role conflict | Norms |

V. Case Example:
Mrs. K. came to the Employee Assistance Office to talk about the pressures she was experiencing as a single mother and a business executive. Her current position required extensive travel to meetings out of town. Her two children were active in school and sports. She frequently missed parent-school meetings and events of significance to her children. She was experiencing headaches and occasional chest pains. Her doctor recommended counseling. The EPA counselor, an advanced generalist, recognized Mrs. K.'s role conflict and resulting stress.

If an extensive examination of a theory is seen as desirable, the student could follow Turner's framework for comparing social work practice theories calling for an exploration of thirty-three attributes. Framework 2 is an example of this approach as applied to Existentialism[55] (Diagram 4–13).

## THE HOLISTIC APPROACH IN ADVANCED GENERALIST PRACTICE

A worker may use the two paradigms (advanced ecological systems and advanced problem solving) as tools for identifying the theories or techniques that would be helpful to providing service for a particular case or work assignment. Often, a number of theories or techniques may be used. In the case described in framework 1, for example, the worker saw the need to use role theory and stress theory during assessment and intervention with the client system. A key point to describe advanced generalist practice is the fact that the practitioner is not limited to the use of only one of a few theoretical approaches. Depending on the situation of service, creative combinations and innovations are applied as each step of the process is planned and executed.

Advanced generalists think and act holistically. They see the whole and the interrelationship of past with present and future. Some theories emphasize the past, focusing on memories, repressed experiences, or earlier traumas. Examples of past-oriented theories include psychoanalytic and primal theories. Uncovering the past is seen as a source of cure and release of energy. Some theories are present oriented, with concentration on one's current life-space and choices, such as reality therapy and existentialism. Other theories stress the future, using imagination and imagery, or emphasizing articulated goals as a source of motivation and reality change. Cognitive and psychosocial theories, for example, emphasize the future.

Sometimes theories contrast with each other due to a difference in ideological or philosophical views of human nature. In client- centered and functional theories, for example, a basic proposition is that human beings are innately good with motivation and potential for change. In psychosocial theory, although persons are seen as fundamentally good, they are believed to be easily influenced negatively. In other theories, such as general systems, communication, and Gestalt, human beings are seen as neutral—neither good nor bad. Advanced generalists strongly adhere to the value system at the origin of the social work profession namely, Judeo-Christian, which views human nature as neither good nor evil, but with the potential for both.[56] Depending on the problem and the timing in the process, theories and techniques are carefully selected by the advanced generalist and juxtaposed for comprehensive understanding and intervention. When it is apparent that theories do not "fit" with each other, the worker is eclectic and selects the most appropriate theory based on an individualized assessment of the context for each particular problem-person-environment situation.

## SUMMARY

Although some social work students in graduate programs may select a concentration in one pie slice area of Diagram 4–7 or in one type of intervention (e.g. casework, group work, community organization; direct or indirect; micro or macro) and focus on theories related to that area of practice, students selecting an advanced generalist concentration use fundamental paradigms that encourage the use of multiple approaches and techniques for holistic practice

**DIAGRAM 4–13**  Framework 2: Existentialism

| SYSTEM ATTRIBUTES | EXISTENTIALISM |
|---|---|

**I. General Attributes**

A. Historical roots and connections
  - i. Originated from philosophy: Kierkegaard, Buber, Sartre, Marcel, May, Frankl
  - ii. Principal social work authors: D. Krill, D. Weiss, R. Sunsheimer

B. Level of development
  - i. Philosophical base well developed, rich literature
  - ii. Interventive base moderately well formulated

C. General theory or Single domain theory
  - General: Applicable to all life situations; specific emphasis on place of anxiety, freedom, and choice

D. Focus on general laws or specific behavior
  - General

E. Basic assumptions
  - i. Equality of persons
  - ii. Persons are free agents
  - iii. We are responsible for our choices
  - iv. Our capacities are unlimited
  - v. Suffering and anxiety are part of reality

F. Empirical base
  - i. Strong commitment to research
  - ii. Growing body of phenomenological research

**II. Perception of Person**

A. View of basic human nature
  - i. Individuals are essentially good and noble
  - ii. We cannot escape our natural state, which is anxiety created by disillusion; and the reality of suffering and death

B. View of person's activity orientation
  - i. Operates in present
  - ii. Existence is being and being is becoming
  - iii. We accomplish through experiencing

C. View of relational orientation
  - i. Basic emphasis is the individual
  - ii. Dialogue and encounter with others and world are necessary
  - iii. Societal responsibility is to value others as equals

D. View of person's time orientation
  - i. Reality is here and now, but the future is important
  - ii. The immediate moment is the most genuine way of discovering person's identity

E. Perception of person as rational or irrational
  - i. Strongly rational in as much as we are is free to make own choices
  - ii. We are not just rational, though we need to be in touch with experiential self

F. Perception of person as mechanistic or purposive
  - i. Purposive
  - ii. Responsible for own uniqueness
  - iii. Strongly anti-mechanistic

**III. Perception of Functioning**

A. Nature and importance of conscious-unconscious
  - Person is in control and free to make choices; unconscious is not relevant

B. Importance of heredity
  - Minimal: We are all equal in worth, dignity and uniqueness

C. Importance of person's history on current functioning
  - Downplay past: It is seen as an excuse for actions and denial of responsibility

D. Importance of a developmental view of human personality
  - Development is seen as movement toward becoming; little emphasis on formal developmental stages

E. Nature of mature functioning
  - i. Authenticity is the basis of maturity
  - ii. Discovery of personal uniqueness through relating to subjective experiences and in respecting authenticity process in others

DIAGRAM 4–13 (Continued)

| SYSTEM ATTRIBUTES | EXISTENTIALISM |
|---|---|

**III. Perception of Functioning (continued)**

F. Principal motivators of behavior
- i. Anxiety causes movement
- ii. Persons have freedom to choose
- iii. Integrating, creative force for growth, is core of personality

G. Nature of personality change
- i. Movement toward reaching potential
- ii. Never fully achieved
- iii. Always becoming
- iv. Person has capacity to radically shift
- v. Influencing of others is a strong agent of change

**IV. Therapeutic Qualities**

A. Targets — Individual, couple, family and group; emphasizes the individual

B. Range and importance of change agents
- i. Intrapersonal insight
- ii. Encounter with therapist and group

C. Place of relationship in planned change
- i. Essential heart of therapy
- ii. Feedback gives basis for subjective understanding
- iii. Encounter is a meeting between equals—a coming together in a meaningful way

D. Importance of setting — Unimportant as long as it does not hinder equality

E. Specific techniques
- i. Techniques designed for here-and-now heightening of awareness
- ii. Self-understanding through reflective thinking
- iii. Techniques borrowed from other disciplines
- iv. Encourages rich use of techniques from all sources

F. Problems and situations for which theory is useful — Best suited for clients whose problem involves loss of direction, value confusion, shaken identity, life changes, post-crisis

**V. The Therapist**

A. Knowledge required by therapist — Acceptance of own being and dignity and worth of other, plus knowledge of experiences of others

B. Skills required by therapist
- i. Relating; empathy; encouraging worth; finding meaning in suffering; openness
- ii. Strong emphasis on respect for uniqueness of other therapists

**VI. Therapeutic Application**

A. Precision of application
- i. Nonspecific
- ii. Each person unique and application is specific to individual
- iii. Eclectic in technique

B. Focus of therapy
- i. Stresses unique perception of each person's inner world
- ii. Looks at past and its effect on present
- iii. But essentially present oriented

C. Incorporation of existing knowledge — Philosophical base specific and can incorporate knowledge from similar theoretical bases, but tends to be isolated from other theories

D. Goal setting — Goals unique to each person; these are worked out mutually between client and therapist

E. Interdisciplinary utility — Used across disciplines and helps bring disciplines together

F. Therapeutic terminology
- i. Counsellor
- ii. Counselee
- iii. Encounter
- iv. Dialogue
- v. Authenticity

in any area of the field of human service. As members of a profession founded in diversity of thought and action, social workers continue to be challenged with the task of building a body of knowledge that contains the general and specific theories and techniques they need for effective practice.

In this chapter, the meaning of knowledge and the history of theory in social work have been presented. Particular attention has been given to the identification and selection of knowledge for advanced generalist practice. Two paradigms were presented as guiding frameworks for advanced generalists. The paradigms may be used, in general, to identify learning needs and, in particular, for application to a case or work assignment.

The advanced generalist selects from an extensive range of descriptive and prescriptive theories for both direct and indirect practice with multiple systems. The knowledge selected may come from a variety of disciplines and diverse approaches to knowledge development. The advanced generalist uses, applies, and contributes theory to the profession's body of knowledge. A holistic perspective and commitment to life-long learning are central to the professional socialization of advanced generalists.

The holistic practitioner needs to have a clear service mission and commitment, comprehensive knowledge, and flexibility in methodology for effective direct and indirect practice. Following the study of *values* and *knowledge* for advanced generalists, attention will be given in the next chapter to the third essential dimension of practice, namely, *methodology*.

## NOTES

1.  Henri F. Ellenberger, "A Clinical Introduction to Psychiatric Phenomenology and Existential Analysis," in Rollo May, Ernest Angel, and Henri Ellenberger, eds., *Existence* (New York: Simon and Schuster, 1967), p. 118.

2.  Jurgen Habermas, *Knowledge and Human Interests* (Boston: Beacon Press, 1971), p. 301.

3.  Fred N. Kerlinger, *Foundations of Behavior Research,* 2nd ed. (New York: Holt, Rinehart and Winston, 1973), p. 9.

4.  Francis J. Turner, ed., *Social Work Treatment: Interlocking Theoretical Approaches,* 3rd ed. (New York: The Free Press, 1986), p. 4.

5.  Herbert F. Strean, ed., *Social Casework: Theories in Action* (Metuchen, N.J.: Scarecrow Press, 1971), p. 5.

6.  Ernest Greenwood, "Attributes of a Profession," *Social Work* 2, no. 3 (July 1957): 44–55.

7.  Ernest Greenwood, "The Practice of Science and the Science of Practice," in Warren G. Bennis, Kenneth D. Benne, and Robert Chin, eds., *The Planning of Change* (New York: Holt, 1961), pp. 73–82.

8.  Max Siporin, *Introduction to Social Work Practice* (New York: Macmillan Publishing Co., 1975), p. 118.

9.  Joel Fischer, "The Social Work Revolution," *Social Work* 26, no. 3 (May 1981): 205.

10.  Scott Briar, in S. Jayaratne and R. Levy, *Empirical Clinical Practice* (New York: Columbia University Press, 1979), p. x.

11. Lawrence Shulman, *Interactional Social Work Practice* (Itasca, Ill.: F. E. Peacock Publishers, 1991), p. 10.

12. Francis J. Turner, *Social Work Treatment: Interlocking Theoretical Approaches,* 3rd ed. (New York: The Free Press, 1986), p. 9.

13. Ibid., pp. 6–10.

14. Josephine Shaw Lowell, *Public Relief and Private Charity* (New York: George P. Putnam's Sons, 1884); Alexis de Tocqueville, "Memoir on Pauperism," originally published in 1835 and reprinted in *The Public Interest,* no. 70 (Winter 1983): 102–120.

15. David M. Austin, "The Flexner Myth and the History of Social Work," *Social Service Review,* no. 55 (September 1983): 366.

16. Ibid, pp. 358–59.

17. Abraham Flexner, "Is Social Work a Profession?" *Proceedings of the National Conference of Charities and Correction,* (Chicago: Hildmann Printing Co., 1915), pp. 576–590.

18. Howard Goldstein, "Toward an Integration of Theory and Practice: A Humanistic Approach,": *Social Work* 31, no. 5 (September–October 1986): 353.

19. Jean R. Pearman, *Social Science and Social Work* (Metuchen, N.J.: The Scarecrow Press, 1973), p. 11.

20. Maria O'Neil McMahon, Michael Reisch, and Rino J. Patti, *Scholarship in Social Work: Integration of Research, Teaching and Service* (Columbia, S.C.: National Association of Deans and Directors of Schools of Social Work, 1991), p. 7.

21. Martin Bloom and Joel Fisher, *Evaluating Practice: Guidelines for the Accountable Professional* (Englewood Cliffs, N.J.: Prentice Hall, 1982).

22. For example, A. Ivanoff, E. A. R. Robenson, and B. J. Blythe, "Empirical Clinical Practice from a Feminist Perspective," *Social Work* 32, no. 5 (September–October 1987): 417–423; R. A. Ruckdeschel and B. E. Farris, "Assessing Practice: A Critical Look at the Single-Case Design," *Social Casework* 62 (September 1981): 413–419; and, M. Heinerman, "The Obsolete Scientific Imperative in Social Work Research," *Social Science Review* 55 (September 1981): 371–397.

23. Anthony Giddens, "Jurgen Habermas," in Quentin Skinner, ed., *The Return of Grand Theory in the Human Sciences* (Cambridge: Cambridge University Press, 1985), p. 127.

24. Ruth G. Dean and Barbara L. Fenby, "Exploring Epistemologies: Social Work Action as a Reflection of Philosophical Assumptions," *Journal of Social Work Education* 25, no. 1 (Winter 1989): 53.

25. Paula Allen-Meares and Bruce A. Lane, "Social Work Practice: Integrating Qualitative and Quantitative Data Collection Techniques," *Social Work* 23, no. 5 (September 1990): 452, 456.

26. Goldstein, "Toward an Integration," p. 352.

27. Ibid., p. 356.

28. Marion K. Sanders, "Social Work: A Profession Chasing Its Tail," *Harper's Magazine* (March 1957), as quoted by Alan Keith-Lucas, "A Socially Sanctioned Profession?" in P. Nelson Reid and Philip R. Popple, eds., *The Moral Purposes of Social Work* (Chicago: Nelson-Hall Publishers, 1992), p. 51.

29. Keith-Lucas, "A Socially Sanctioned Profession?" pp. 61 and 51.

30. Reid and Popple, *The Moral Purposes of Social Work.*

31. Robert Perlman and Arnold Gurin *Community Organization and Social Planning* (New York: Wiley, 1972), p. 55.

32. Maria O'Neil McMahon, *The General Method of Social Work Practice: A Problem-Solving Approach,* 2nd ed. (Englewood Cliffs, N.J.: Prentice Hall, 1990), p. 2.

33. Kurt Lewin, *Principles of Topological Psychology,* trans. Fritz and Grace Heider (New York: McGraw-Hill, 1936); C. V. Bartalanffy, "General Systems Theory," *General Systems Yearbook,* vol. 1, no. 4 (1956); Herbert Blumer, *Symbolic Interactionism; Perspective*

*and Method* (Englewood Cliffs, N.J.: Prentice Hall, 1969); Ronald Lippitt, Jeanne Watson, and Bruce Westley, *The Dynamics of Planned Change* (New York: Harcourt, Brace and World, 1958).

34. Shulman *Interactional Social Work Practice,* pp. 9, 10.

35. Harry Specht, *New Directions for Social Work Practice* (Englewood Cliffs, N.J.: Prentice Hall, 1988), p. 275.

36. Jean R. Pearman *Social Science and Social Work* (Metuchen, N.J.: The Scarecrow Press, 1973), p. 18.

37. Francis J. Turner, "Social Work Practice Theories: A Comparison of Selected Attributes," unpublished, May 1988.

38. Siporin, *Introduction to Social Work Practice,* pp. 137–153.

39. Ibid., p. 153.

40. Thomas Kuhn, *The Structure of Scientific Revolutions,* 2nd ed., International Encyclopedia of Unified Science, vol. 2, no. 2 (Chicago: Chicago University Press, 1962), pp. 43 and 182.

41. Robert R. Carkhuff and William A. Anthony, *The Skills of Helping: An Introduction to Counseling Skills* (Amherst, Mass.: Human Resource Development, 1979).

42. Virginia M. Satir, *Conjoint Family Therapy* (Cambridge, Mass.: Harvard University Press, 1967).

43. Jack Rothman, "Three Models of Community Organization Practice," in *Social Work Practice* (New York: Columbia University Press, 1968), pp. 16–47.

44. William J. Reid and Laura Epstein, *Task-Centered Practice* (New York: Columbia University Press, 1977).

45. Helen Harris Pearlman, *Social Casework: A Problem-Solving Process* (Chicago: University of Chicago Press, 1967).

46. Turner, "Social Work Practice Theories."

47. Turner, *Social Work Treatment,* p. 15.

48. *Clinical Social Work in the Eco-Systems Perspective,* Carol H. Meyer, ed., p. 57. © 1983, Columbia University Press, New York. Reprinted with the permission of the publisher.

49. Max Siporin, "Practice Theory for Clinical Social Work," *Clinical Social Work Journal* (Spring 1979): 83.

50. Andrew Van de Ven and Andre L. Delbecq, "Nominal versus Interacting Group Processes for Committee Decision-Making Effectiveness," *Academy of Management Journal* 14, no. 2 (June 1971): 203–212.

51. Donald A. Bloch, ed. *Techniques of Family Psychotherapy: A Primer* (New York: Grune and Stratton, 1973), p. 60.

52. Paul Hersey and Kenneth H. Blanchard, *Management of Organizational Behavior: Utilizing Human Resources,* 4th ed. (Englewood Cliff, N.J.: Prentice Hall, 1982).

53. Meyer, *Clinical Social Work,* pp. 79–80.

54. Meyer, *Clinical Social Work,* pp. 75–214.

55. Turner, "Social Work Practice Theories." Reprinted with permission.

56. Alan Keith-Lucas, *Giving and Taking Help* (Chapel Hill: University of North Carolina Press, 1972), pp. 138–143.

# 5
# The Methodology
# of Advanced Generalists

## *INTRODUCTION*

A *method* is "an orderly systematic mode of procedure."[1] The term method refers to the way or process one uses to accomplish certain goals. In this chapter, a methodology is identified that describes the general way advanced generalists proceed as they mobilize various theories, tools, and techniques for direct and indirect practice.

From the beginning of contact with any system, the advanced generalist uses a systematic way to proceed called the General Method (see Diagram 1–6). It begins with efforts to engage the system. Whether the system is a client or a target system, a supervisee or an administrator, a resource or a political institution, the advanced generalist uses select words and actions to cross the boundary and engage the system in a meaningful transaction. Proceeding through a process that involves data exchange, assessment, decision making and planning, evaluation, and termination, the practitioner assumes a variety of roles and uses appropriate theories for understanding and intervention to accomplish clearly defined goals. In this chapter, the general method as presented with encompass use in a holistic practice that includes the direct and indirect practice roles of advanced generalist practice.

As stated earlier, the entry-level generalist is prepared primarily for direct, face-to-face contact with client systems. The advanced generalist, on the other hand, is expected to assume responsibilities that may exceed direct client service and include such indirect practice roles as supervisor, manager, administrator, planner, and researcher. The full scope of services expected of advanced generalists calls for a practitioner who is capable of seeing the whole, pinpointing and prioritizing the problem(s), applying relevant theory or theories, and intervening at appropriate levels with an effective methodology.

All the essential elements of advanced generalist practice as identified in earlier chapters (e.g., advanced ecological systems perspective, advanced knowledge, international social work/welfare, ethical decision making, advanced research and technology, advanced general method) provide perimeters and incentives for the advanced generalist to deal with each situation with clarity of purpose and guidance for action. The systematic way in which advanced generalists use these elements as they proceed in their roles of direct service provider (e.g., counselor, problem solver, therapist) and in their indirect practice roles (e.g., supervisor, manager, administrator) will be explored and demonstrated in the following pages.

### Definition of Terms

Within the profession of social work, several terms are used to describe the actions of social workers. A variety of definitions may be found for direct practice, indirect practice, integrated practice, direct intervention, indirect intervention, psychotherapy, supervision, management, administration, and holistic practice. It is necessary, therefore, to clarify the meaning of these terms as they will be used in this chapter.

*Direct practice* refers to front-line work with client systems. The social worker may use a variety of actions, interventions, strategies, methodologies, and resources with or in behalf of the clients being served. Client systems may be individuals, families, groups, or larger systems, provided they fit the description of a *client system*. As stated by Allen Pincus and Anne Minahan, "client systems" are "people who sanction or ask for the change agent's (worker's) services, who are the expected beneficiaries of service, and who have a working agreement or contract with the change agent."[2] Generalist social workers at the entry level are prepared for direct practice with client systems.

*Indirect practice,* on the other hand, refers to the practice of social workers that does not involve their working directly with client systems. It includes such areas as administration, supervision, management, policy development, and planning. This type of practice is usually conducted by advanced professionals who have had years of experience in direct practice. Advanced generalists are prepared for direct and indirect practice.

*Integrated practice* is a term used when social workers are concurrently engaged in direct and indirect practice modalities. An example would be a practitioner who carries a case load and at the same time supervises other workers or manages a program.

*Direct intervention* is one type of action taken by social workers within the context of direct practice. It involves face-to-face contact with clients and can extend from a brief interview to ongoing contact in an intensive helping relationship. The worker works directly with the client system.

*Indirect intervention* refers to another category of actions taken by a worker while working in direct practice with client systems. This includes interactions between a worker and other systems that affect clients in order to bring about changes needed for clients to achieve their identified goals. These systems may be voluntary resources or resistant power systems that impact the problems or needs of client systems. The latter may be referred to as *target systems*.[3]

*Psychotherapy* is an advanced direct intervention used in direct practice and has been characterized according to the following four features:

1. Developing of a strong, empathic relationship with the client or patient
2. Providing emotional support
3. Aiding the client or patient to develop insight into the causes of behavior/feelings
4. Enabling the client to change behaviors/feelings/cognitions[4]

Advanced generalists may have the ability to provide psychotherapy when it is assessed as the appropriate way to proceed in the helping process with their clients.

*Supervision* is a process in which authorized individuals direct, coordinate, enhance, and evaluate the on-the-job performance of assigned supervisees. Supervisors perform administrative, educational, and supportive functions and are held accountable for the work of their supervisees.[5] As stated, supervision is one type of indirect practice. Alfred Kadushin, for instance, describes supervision as "indirect service":

> Supervisors do not directly offer service to the client, but they do indirectly affect the level of service offered through their impact on the direct service supervisees. Supervision is, thus, an indirect service.[6]

*Management* has been defined as "the process by which the elements of a group are integrated, coordinated, and/or utilized so as to effectively and efficiently achieve organizational objectives."[7] *Middle managers* in human services are often described as those who stand in the middle or who are caught between the higher administrators of an organization and those who are providing direct service under the management of the manager. More specifically, as described by Henry Havassy, middle managers meet the following three conditions:

1. They report to organizational superiors who have little or no direct contact with the actual service-delivery context.
2. They manage line supervisors or direct service providers who have contact with the client community but little or no direct contact with the higher levels of the vertical organization.
3. Their work site is located in the service-delivery community.[8]

*Administration* in human services is defined as having two functions: "the conscious direction of the internal relationships and activities of the enterprise toward the achievement of goals" and "the conscious intervention in the interacting forces operating between the agency and the larger community."[9] In the broadest sense, administration may be the term used to describe the activities of a range of personnel referred to as "administrative staff members." These may include chief executive officers (CEOs), directors of programs or units, managers, and supervisors. In this text, an attempt will be made to separate the practice of supervisors, managers, and top executives and administrators.

*Holistic practice* is a concept that will be used to describe the practice of an advanced generalist who is prepared to intervene with a broad range of interventions in the service of a variety of clients and to practice indirectly at different levels with and within different systems. This practitioner retains the "problem focus" and responds as needed to each problem or issue without constraint by any particular theory, intervention, or type of practice limitation (e.g., direct vs. indirect, micro vs. macro, clinical vs. nonclinical). At any given time, the advanced generalist may be providing, mobilizing, or managing multiple interventions. The "holistic" practitioner sees the whole, partializes as needed for study, decides and selects responses and resources, and completes service provision when it is time to end the process.

## THE ADVANCED GENERALIST IN DIRECT PRACTICE

The client system of advanced generalists may be individuals, families, groups, communities, organizations, or institutions. Client problems in need of professional attention may call for diverse interventions. The advanced generalist recognizes a broad scope of possible direct interventions (Diagram 5–1), extending from limited direct face-to-face contact for information or referral, to establishing an ongoing supportive relationship, to collaborative problem solving, to particular behavioral approaches, to insight-giving psychotherapy. Each intervention on the scale in Diagram 5–1 may be applied to any size client system. The "life skills counseling," for example, could be a life skills counsel-

**DIAGRAM 5–1**   Direct Service Interventions

| | | | | | |
|---|---|---|---|---|---|
| 0 | 1 | 2 | 3 | 4 | 5 |
| No face-to-face contact | Little/brief contact | Supportive contact/may be on-going | Collaborative problem solving | Advanced approaches, behavior focused | Intensive psychotherapy |

0= No face-to-face contact with client, worker may mobilize resources, client may use self-help groups

1= Little/brief contact, mainly information/referral (teacher/counselor)

2= Supportive relationship, may be for extended time period, could include life skills counseling, client centered approach (counselor)

3= Problem solving, collaborative, task-oriented (problem solver)

4= Advanced skills, usually focused on behavioral change, transactional analysis, rational therapy, behavior modification (advanced practitioner/therapist)

5= Psychotherapy, insight giving, may last for long time, working for change in thoughts, feelings, and behavior (advanced practitioner/psychotherapist)

6+ . . .= Those treatments, such as psychoanalysis, outside range of social work (unless social worker is also lay analyst or other specialist)

ing group. The insight-giving "psychotherapy" may apply to family or group therapy. "Collaborative problem solving" could be the approach used in community organization. This range attempts to reflect the worker's skill level and the intensity of contact with the client system. The duration of contact and the degree of intensity of worker/client relationship is dependent upon each individualized need and selected intervention.

Although each interval on the scale in Diagram 5–1 is not necessarily equal, and a number of various types of additional approaches could be identified, the diagram conveys the extensive range of options facing an advanced generalist when working directly with a client system. While using any one type of intervention on the scale, one or all to the left may be included in the worker's interventions with different problems for the same client system. For example, a worker may be providing psychotherapy for insight into a client's dependency, while at the same time working collaboratively with the client in problem solving regarding a need for employment.

The counseling and problem-solving approaches (0–3) used in direct practice by entry-level social work generalists have been presented in the author's earlier work.[10] At the advanced level, practitioners expand knowledge and skills for an extended range of possible interventions. Depending on one's interests, abilities, and opportunities for study and practice, advanced generalists may pursue their development in such treatment modalities as those listed in Diagram 5–2. Practitioners are not expected to be highly skilled in all types of intervention. Advanced generalists acquire additional competence in some of the advanced approaches. They grow in knowledge about the more sophisticated interventions and enhance their ability to better identify and match need with treatment, making appropriate referrals as necessary.

**DIAGRAM 5–2** Direct Practice Interventions

| | |
|---|---|
| Behavior modification | Play therapy |
| Crisis intervention | Psychoanalytic psychotherapy |
| Existential psychotherapy | Rational therapy |
| Gestalt therapy | Reality therapy |
| Neurolinguistic programming | Transactional analysis |

In addition to the interventive approaches identified in Diagram 5–2, there are a number of tools and techniques that may be selected to assist the worker in direct practice. These may include contracting, sculpting, genograms, nominal group approach, field-force analysis, psychodrama, mediation, imagery, and muscle relaxation techniques.

### Problem Solving: The Advanced General Method in Direct Practice

In generalist and advanced generalist practice, the selection of an intervention follows the engagement and data collection stages of the problem-solving general method. During assessment, the third stage of the method, the worker carefully selects the type of intervention believed most appropriate to the person-problem-situation. In direct practice at the advanced level, the selection may include the worker's assuming the role of psychotherapist, provided there has been advanced study, practice, and supervision in this type of intervention. Throughout the process of working with the client system as therapist, the worker maintains the guiding framework of the general method. Even though the therapy may be finished with a client, the worker will not conclude the service without taking time for evaluation and termination, the fifth and sixth stages of the general method. It may be that there are additional problems or needs that will call for other types of intervention by the worker and, thus, the need to return to the initial stages of problem solving. It may be that the practitioner was also providing counseling or problem solving (general direct interventions) or working with outside services or target systems (indirect interventions) relating to other problems while the client system was in therapy with the worker. The time to assess the progress being made with all interventions and to recognize the possible need to reformulate the contract would be during the evaluation stage of the process.

In Diagram 5–3, for example, the A line depicts the six-stage general method. Intervention in the general method refers to the carrying out of the tasks in the contracted plan that were identified with the client system during the assessment stage. Throughout this stage, the worker may be seen as providing general counseling and problem solving while maintaining the role of case manager, monitoring the implementation of the plan. The B line reflects the possible use of advanced interventions by the worker, such as psychotherapy, while, at the same time, the other tasks of the contract are being executed.

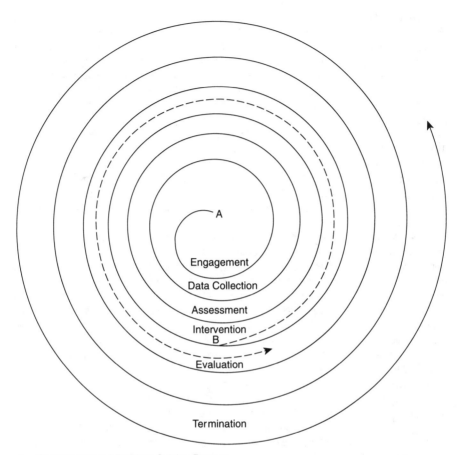

A = General Method-Problem-Solving Process

B = Advanced Intervention(s)

**DIAGRAM 5–3**    The Advanced General Method in Direct Practice

Combining general and advanced interventions in direct practice calls for a methodology that reflects complexity in thought and skill. Using entry-level and advanced interventions within the framework of the problem-solving general method, as symbolized in Diagram 5–3, may be referred to as the Advanced General Method. Further expansion of the method, as applied to indirect practice and holistic practice, will be developed later in this chapter.

The case of Mr. W. provides an example of the use of the advanced general method in direct practice.

## CASE EXAMPLE: THE CASE OF MR. W.

Mr. W. was unemployed and in the process of being evicted from his apartment. Although he had a degree from the University, he found it difficult to maintain a job. He was divorced two years ago and has monthly visitation rights, allowing him to take his two children for one weekend a month. After attending church one Sunday, he introduced his children to the pastor. As they talked about Mr. W.'s problems, the pastor encouraged Mr. W. to go to talk with the social worker at the diocesan office.

The social worker learned that Mr. W. had been renting an apartment on the second floor of a home owned by an elderly couple. They had recently sold the house and the new owner was not interested in renting the second floor. Mr. W. had to be out of the apartment in three weeks. There were not many apartments for rent in the town or surrounding areas. Mr. W. said he needed help finding one. He was currently receiving unemployment benefits and looking for work. In the course of working with Mr. W., the worker learned that Mr. W. was having trouble getting his children each month for a visit. He complained that they often were not ready when he arrived and that sometimes his ex-wife made other plans for the children on the weekends he was supposed to be with them. Mr. W.'s cultural background was Italian. The worker was a female of Irish ethnicity.

As the working relationship developed, and the worker and client moved through engagement and data collection, the worker could see that Mr. W. did not only need help with finding a place to live. She helped Mr. W. to begin to become aware of a pattern of broken relationships in his life. It became apparent that he had repeated problems with supervisors at several job sites. Although he had the abilities and credentials for employment in the field of computer technology, he had a history of difficulties with authority figures in different places of employment. As they began to plan and contract, at first Mr. W. was interested only in finding a place to live. Shortly after they began to work on this need, he agreed to begin psychotherapy for help with his problem relating to losing his jobs. The worker had developed extended knowledge and skill in psychotherapeutic intervention. She was the only diocesan worker for a large rural population, and she found that most clients who needed psychotherapy would not go the distance or pay the price for this treatment elsewhere. The contract with Mr. W., as found in Diagram 5–4, indicates the ongoing plans for obtaining housing and for psychotherapy. Later, as the problems regarding Mr. W.'s visitation with his children emerged, the worker and Mr. W. added this issue to the contract with planned interventions.

In assessing Mr. W.'s problems, strengths, and potential, the worker concluded that he could benefit from insight-oriented psychotherapy. She chose to use the time-limited insight-oriented psychotherapy as described by J.H. Weissberg:

> a treatment modality in which a single conflict underlying a patient's main complaint or symptom is focused upon actively and tenaciously during a series of weekly vis-à-vis sessions, usually numbering 12 to 20, with an upper limit of 30. Psychodynamic principles are used to understand and trace the focal conflict back to its origin. Transference attitudes and distortions related to the focal conflict are confronted actively as they arise.[11]

The worker assessed that Mr. W. met the following criteria developed by Marc Hollender and Charles Ford for this type of psychotherapy:

1. The capacity to establish a relationship with the therapist
2. An identifiable focal conflict
3. Adequate ego strength
4. Motivation
5. Psychological mindedness[12]

**DIAGRAM 5–4**   Contracted Plan

| DATE IDENTIFIED | PROBLEM/ NEED | GOAL | TASK | CONTRACT | DATE ANTICI- PATED | DATE ACCOM- PLISHED |
|---|---|---|---|---|---|---|
| 7/15 | Eviction notice | Locate hous- ing | 1. Check news- paper | 1. Mr. W | 7/15 | 7/15 |
| | | | 2. Find other sources of info. | 2. Worker | 7/16 | 7/16 |
| | | | 3. Discuss find- ings | 3. Worker/ Mr. W | 7/19 | 7/19 |
| | | | 4. Follow up (call, apply) | 4. Mr. W | 7/19– | 7/21 |
| | | | 5. Discuss | 5. Worker/ Mr. W | 7/23 | 7/23 |
| 7/19 | Can't keep job | To be able to work with au- thority figures | 1. Receive psy- chotherapy | 1. Mr. W./ worker | 7/30, weekly | 7/30 8/6, 13, 20, 27, 9/3 |
| 9/3 | Chn. not ready for visits | Chn. pre- pared for visits | 1. Discuss with Chn. mother | 1. Mr. W/ mother | 9/8 | 9/8 |
| | | | 2. Discuss with mother's social worker | 2. Worker | 9/15 | 9/15 |
| | | | 3. Take legal action | 3. Mr. W | 9/25 | |

In working with Mr. W., the worker moved through an insight-oriented process as illustrated in Diagram 5–5. Beginning with the problematic behavior of losing his temper and walking out at a job, they traced the behaviors back to the feelings that precipitated such actions. Mr. W. said that he was feeling "put down" and "embarrassed." They then focused on the experience, event, actions or words that triggered the feelings in Mr. W. Usually it happened when Mr. W. had a face-to-face encounter

**DIAGRAM 5–5**   Insight-Oriented Process

A = Process Leading to Behaviors ⎯⎯⎯⎯⎯

B = Process Leading to Insight  – – – – – –

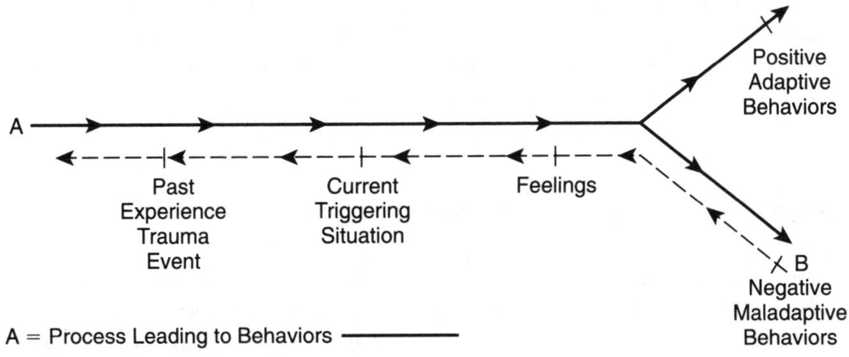

with a supervisor who found fault with something he had done. In time, Mr. W. and the worker were able to recognize that he was behaving in a similar way toward her whenever he felt she was critizing or reprehending him. As Mr. W. began to see a pattern in the way he responded to feeling "put down" whenever he was corrected, he was encouraged to try and connect such events with earlier experiences and feelings. In one session, he was able to say, "You remind me of my mother; I was never good enough for her." Mr. W. gained insight. He connected past experiences and feelings to current feelings and behaviors. The worker learned that Mr. W.'s father died when he was 3 years old. His mother, a school teacher, was very demanding, with exceptionally high expectations for her son. Mr. W. said he tried to be "the perfect child" but never could quite make it. All his life he seemed to be fighting the fear of being seen as a failure. He and the worker then moved into considering other more adaptive ways to handle his feelings. He began to be able to think more objectively about each situation as it arose and to accept the possibility that he could learn from each opportunity. He began to accept the fact that he did not have to be "perfect" to be "ok."

Mr. W. found work as a technician at the local high school. He would tell the worker about incidents at work that upset him and they were used as examples for practicing more adaptive behaviors. Even though Mr. W. eventually appeared to no longer need psychotherapy for his problem with authority figures, the worker continued to work with him as they moved into focusing on the problems surrounding his visits with his children. As shown in Diagram 5–4, Mr. W. attempted to work out the problem with his ex-wife himself. When this did not improve the situation, he and the worker agreed that she would try talking with his ex-wife's social worker to see if she could intervene. If this did not help, Mr. W. was going to take legal action. This was not necessary because the social services worker helped Mr. W.'s ex-wife see the need and value in cooperating with Mr. W. if she wanted to maintain her custody of the children with visitations as now dictated by the court.

During evaluation, Mr. W. and the worker reviewed the goals they had set to work on together. Since Mr. W. was able to locate housing, maintain his job, and was no longer having trouble with his visitations with his children, they agreed to move toward Mr. W.'s termination with the agency. He described himself as "now able to get on with his life."

In this case, the worker, an advanced generalist, used the advanced general method as she proceeded through the six-stage general process. She provided a variety of interventions in direct practice with the client. In addition to insight-oriented psychotherapy, the worker's general interventions included information and referral, case management, problem solving, and indirect intervention (contacting ex-wife's social worker).

## THE ADVANCED GENERALIST IN INDIRECT PRACTICE

Indirect practice, as defined earlier, covers a broad scope of roles and activities assumed by a worker that do not involve direct contact with client systems. Diagram 5–6 portrays a range of roles often expected of advanced generalists.

**DIAGRAM 5–6**  Indirect Practice Roles and Responsibilities

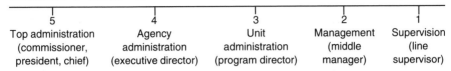

| 5 | 4 | 3 | 2 | 1 |
|---|---|---|---|---|
| Top administration (commissioner, president, chief) | Agency administration (executive director) | Unit administration (program director) | Management (middle manager) | Supervision (line supervisor) |

Although each interval on the scale in the diagram may not necessarily be equal, and not all types of indirect practice are identified, the extensive range of diverse roles and responsibilities found in indirect practice is indicated. In any of the indirect practice positions identified in Diagram 5–6, advanced generalists rely on the essential elements of generalist and advanced generalist practice. Their perspective and approach reflect their advanced ecological systems perspective, problem focus, open selection of theories and interventions, advanced research skills, awareness of international developments and policies (as well as their impact on service delivery), and the six-stage problem-solving general method. In addition, advanced generalists doing indirect practice may select supplemental tools, theories, and techniques to assist with goal accomplishment. Diagram 5–7 suggests some of the supplements that may be used.

### Problem Solving: The Advanced General Method in Indirect Practice

As an advanced generalist performs indirect practice roles, the stages, tools, techniques, and process of the general method are applied dynamically to different situations and systems with creativity, flexibility, and complexity. As stated, additional tools, techniques, and theories may be used to supplement and complement those found in the general method. Administrators, for example, may need to engage in data collection before attempting to engage a resistant system. They may need to develop a proposed plan (assessment) prior to engagement with a system. In selecting a program to be proposed, a costeffectiveness analysis may help to study possible alternatives. The six-stage general process serves as an open and adaptive guiding framework in supervision, management, and higher levels of administration. When a worker uses the general method in any of the roles of indirect practice, it may be called "the advanced general method."

**DIAGRAM 5–7**  Indirect Practice Theories, Tools, and Techniques

| | |
|---|---|
| Blanchard's leadership styles | McGregor's theory X and Y |
| Chemiss' symptoms of worker burnout | Ouchi's theory Z |
| Cost-effectiveness analysis | PPBS (planning-programming-budgeting system) |
| Herzberg's motivation-maintenance model | Ratio analysis |
| MBO (management by objectives) | Thomas' conflict management interventions |
| Mintzberg's typology (5-part organization model) | ZBB (zero-based budgeting) |

### Supervision

Advanced generalists often have the responsibility of supervising other employees. While in this position, they continue to reflect all the characteristics of advanced generalist practice. In the process of guiding, directing, training, supporting, and evaluating a supervisee, the advanced generalist may apply the six-stage problem-solving process. In the following case example, a supervisor recognizes emerging symptoms of burnout in a supervisee. She asks to meet with the worker in an effort to engage her in a collaborative problem-solving process.

### CASE EXAMPLE: MARY O., SUPERVISEE

Mary O. has been working in public social services for two years. Her current caseload is 50 families. She has a baccalaureate degree in social science. Recently, she has been failing to keep up with her recording, coming to work late, and avoiding discussion of her work with her supervisor. She frequently appears to be angry and resentful. Mrs. Smith, the advanced generalist supervisor, saw a need to talk with Mary not about her cases, but about Mary. The six-stage general method was used as a guiding framework in the process.

Phase I: Engagement

Supervisee:  You asked to see me, Mrs. Smith?

Supervisor:  Yes, come in Mary. I would like to talk with you about some concerns I have lately about you and your work.

Supervisee:  Sure. What's the matter? I thought I was doing ok.

Supervisor:  Over the past two years, you have been doing a fine job, Mary. Lately, though, you are getting behind in your recording, coming late to work, and often appearing upset about things. I wonder if I might be of some help.

Supervisee:  Oh (sigh), I don't know. I guess it's just everything. I guess I'm having a hard time with my caseload. Getting those extra five cases last week was probably the "straw that broke the camel's back."

Supervisor:  You are feeling somewhat overwhelmed by the size of your caseload—is that it, Mary?

Supervisee:  Yes, I used to feel like I was doing a good job. There was time to visit the homes of those clients who couldn't come in to see me. But lately, there just isn't enough time for anything.

Supervisor:  Yes, I'm sure that with fewer cases you were able to spend more time with your clients.

Supervisee:  Right, but now that my caseload has doubled, there just isn't enough time to make the contacts, keep up with the paperwork, and attend the necessary meetings. I try to take work home with me, but that just gets my husband upset.

Supervisor:  Having your husband upset at home doesn't help the situation.

Supervisee:  No, it sure doesn't. We are also having some problems at home with Billy, our son. We started going for counseling to see if it will help. That seems to be coming along pretty good, but I know it's just going to take time. I guess I'm just not able to keep up with all the demands I'm facing right now.

Supervisor: It sounds like you are under quite a bit of pressure right now, Mary. I hope that the counseling will help all of you. Is there some way I might be of help to you?

Supervisee: I guess it would be great if you could hold off from giving me any more cases for a while, or even find a way to lighten up my present load. I don't know if that's possible.

Supervisor: I can see that you are feeling pretty upset because of the pressures of home and at work right now, and you would like some relief to feel better about what is happening with you.

Supervisee: Yes, I sure don't want to get any worse.

Supervisor: You know, Mary, the problems at home I can't help you with. But what's happening with you here at work I would like to look at with you. Let's see if there might be a way to help you with your caseload so you can regain a sense of satisfaction with your job.

Supervisee: I'd really appreciate it.


Phase II: Data Collection

Supervisor: In order to work on the problem of your heavy caseload, Mary, I will need some information.

Supervisee: Sure, where do we begin?

Supervisor: Let's see, you came to work here about two years ago, right?

Supervisee: Right, it was in September.

Supervisor: And you have been doing an excellent job; you have high potential for advancement here. I'm wondering, Mary, when did you start to feel that you were slipping in your work and that the pressures were getting to be too difficult for you to manage?

Supervisee: I don't remember. I do love it here and want very much to do high quality work. Perhaps it was about two months ago, when my caseload was increased by 15 cases. I know that some of the other workers have been here even less than two years and they have even more cases than the 50 I have, but I just don't know how they are able to balance everything.

Supervisor: Did you come with any previous experience or professional education?

Supervisee: No, not really. I came right after graduation from college. My major was psychology.

Supervisor: Perhaps you know this, but some of the workers studied social work and caseload management in school, or they may have come with previous social work experience.

Supervisee: Yes, I don't want to lag behind, but I just don't seem to have the energy or the skill to handle such a large caseload. I wish I could learn how to do it.

Supervisor: Are you aware of the training opportunities that are available for employees? I can get you that information. Sometimes it calls for an overnight in a training location. Would that be a problem for you?

Supervisee: I don't really think so, but I would have to ask my husband to see what we could work out.

Supervisor: Well, let's both take some time to gather more information and to think about what possible ways might be helpful to you with your caseload. Should we plan to meet again on Monday?

Supervisee: Sure. Would it be at this same time?

Supervisor: Yes, it looks like that would be fine. I'll see you on Monday.

## Monday—Data Collection Continued

Supervisor: Come in, Mary. How are you doing?

Supervisee: Better, I'm glad we talked last week.

Supervisor: Yes, I am too. Did you think more about getting some training?

Supervisee: Yes, and my husband said he would take care of the kids if I had to go overnight.

Supervisor: Fine. There will be a session on Caseload Management in October. Here is the announcement with the application to be completed. Why don't you take it and see if you think it might help.

Supervisee: Great. I'll see what I can work out.

Supervisor: I also gave some thought to what else we might do to help you at this time. Another possibility is to hold off from adding to your workload for a while. Also, a worker from another unit is transferring here to have her field experience for her Master's degree. Perhaps we can assign some of your cases to her.

Supervisee: That would be great. I can think of some that I could easily transfer.

Supervisor: O.K., let's see if we can assess what we have here and spell out our plan of action.

## Phase III: Assessment

Supervisor: Based on what we have discussed, how would you assess the problem?

Supervisee: I guess I would say that I am having a problem with the pressures of a large caseload at this time due to the fact that I really have had no preparation for this job and that I am experiencing heavy home difficulties at this time also.

Supervisor: Yes, I would agree. Now to work on it, what is our plan?

Supervisee: Well, (1) I'll complete the application for training in caseload management.

Supervisor: Yes, and (2) I'll approve it and send it forward to get your name on the list.

Supervisee: And (3) I will look over my caseload and see which cases I would suggest for the new worker.

Supervisor: Yes, and if we are in agreement, (4) I will reassign them to the worker coming over into our unit for her field placement. Also, (5) I will hold off from giving you additional cases for a while. What timeframe should we put on this, Mary?

Supervisee: I think things are starting to get better at home. The counseling isn't easy but it's helping us to face things.

Supervisor: Let's see. You should be taking that training in October. Let's say that I will try to hold off on additional case assignments until November. That gives you a little over a month. How does that sound?

Supervisee: It sounds great. I really appreciate your understanding.

Supervisor: O.K. Let's plan to work on this and then meet again the first week of November to evaluate how it's going.

Supervisee: Thanks so much.

## Phase IV: Intervention

Planned activities were carried out with brief contacts and shared comments between worker and supervisor relating to the problem throughout October. Other needs or concerns of the worker and her clients were addressed in bimonthly group supervisory sessions.

## Phase V: Evaluation

Supervisor: Come in , Mary. It's difficult to believe it's November already. I'm glad to see you smiling again.

Supervisee: Yes, Mrs. Smith. That training was great. It takes time to organize your cases and systematically plan your weekly contacts, but it really helps. As they said, "You have to take time to make time."

Supervisor: Sounds like you got a lot from the training. How are you feeling about your workload now?

Supervisee: I really feel good about it. I know part of why I'm finding more energy to invest in my work is also because things are really better at home, too. Billy likes his counselor and I think he's doing better in school.

Supervisor: Fine, and our new worker seems to be moving along well with those cases. You did a nice job with the transfer process.

Supervisee: Thanks. She's really a nice person and brings a lot to the unit.

Supervisor: Are you ready to move on and take more cases?

Supervisee: Yes, I think so. I feel better about my work, and I'd like to get caught up.

Supervisor: O.K., I'd like you to look over these five new applications and let me know what you think.

Supervisee: Right. Should I plan to stop in later today?

Supervisor: No, give it a little more time to see how they fit into your caseload management system. Let's meet next week. If all looks well, we can move on and just plan to check up every now and then on how you're doing.

## Phase VI: Termination

Supervisor: Come in, Mary. How are you today?

Supervisee: I'm fine, thanks. Weekend went well, and things are moving along O.K.

Supervisor: That sounds fine. Well, are we ready to get back on track with your caseload?

Supervisee: Yes, I think so. I looked over the cases you gave me last week, and I don't think I'll have a problem. Some of them may develop into more serious situations, and I'll be sure to give them priority.

Supervisor: I'm glad to hear that, Mary. And, I'm glad we were able to talk about what was happening a few months ago when you were feeling all that pressure.

Supervisee: It really helped to talk about it with you. That training workshop helped a lot, too. It was good to get away and take some distance from everything, too. Things are really a lot better for me now—both here and at home.

Supervisor: You have come a long way, Mary. You know my door is open if you ever find that your work is becoming too much for you and you want to talk about it. And I'll see you at our bi-monthly supervisory meetings to get

an update on how you're doing. We value our workers, Mary, and want
to give you as much support as we can to keep you with us.
Supervisee: I can see that. I really appreciate your help.

In this case example, the supervisee does not present a problem with a particular case but rather a problem with the size of her caseload. The supervisor focuses, therefore, directly on the presenting problem and the worker's needs for effective problem solving. From an ecological systems perspective and with knowledge of cognitive theory, ego psychology, professional socialization, stress theory, and signs of burnout, the supervisor listens and responds with skill and sensitivity. It became apparent that the supervisee was being drained of energy and output due to increasing pressures and demands from her home and work environments. The worker was receiving little positive input and was struggling to find ways to regain a sense of balance and equilibrium. If the worker and her family had not been going for counseling, the supervisor could have used referral skills as part of her intervention efforts. Fortunately, the supervisee and her family demonstrated sufficient strengths to seek and use this help. The supervisor applied the six-stage general method and used task-oriented interventions effectively. Support and stress reduction were offered through decreasing caseload demands. The job training and family counseling provided additional opportunities for positive growth and management of stress. Using the six-stage process as a guiding framework in supervision demonstrates the advanced general method in indirect practice.

### Management

Middle managers and unit directors deal daily with a variety of issues and problems that could threaten the effectiveness of service delivery. They stand at the nexus of many different groups and social systems (Diagram 5–8) that often have conflicting interests or desires. Frequently, they are put in the middle to mediate between the two levels of top administrators and line workers. Advanced generalists in these roles call upon their "interculturalism" (Chapter 2) as they apply principles and ideas, experience feelings and engage in diversity. Henry Havassy describes the process of "engaging diversity" as:

> a complex process that includes interacting and meshing with different perspectives, accepting and dealing with the differences rather than trying to unify or gloss over them. It entails a commitment to maintain, master, and use the diversity of perspectives. Three interdependent factors jointly produce the ability to engage diversity: (1) considerable tolerance for ambiguity, (2) maintenance of multiple loyalties, and (3) cross-system translation.[13]

He defines "cross-system translation" as "expressing needs, expectations, and demands of one system in the terms and concepts of another system."[14] The

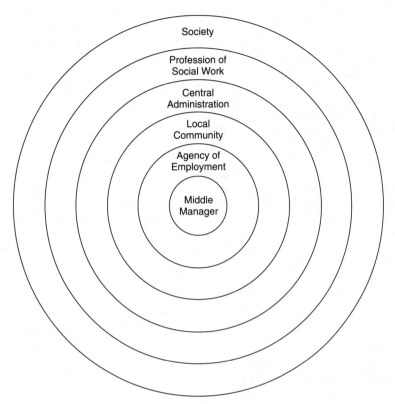

**DIAGRAM 5–8**   Systems Surrounding Middle Management

middle manager strives to find a common goal that would be acceptable to both opposing groups.

## CASE EXAMPLE: MIDDLE MANAGER

A manager of a unit office of a human service agency, for example, was asked by central administration to establish a drug rehabilitation program in her unit. The staff of the unit was resistant and unmotivated because they felt overworked, and they were inexperienced in this area of service. As unit manager, the advanced generalist saw the whole, focused on the problem, demonstrated interculturalism while engaging diversity, and applied the advanced general method.

During the engagement stage, the manager recognized and listened to the two major groups impacting the problem. She understood the pressures placed on administration by the legislature to do something about the emerging drug problem in the community. At the same time, the worker heard and understood the staff's frustration and limitations in developing a drug rehabilitation program. Appealing to the staff's professional values and commitment to serve the local community, the worker enthusiastically asked staff members to accept the fact that "we need to do this" and appealed to them to "create the best possible drug rehabilitation program." She assured them that she would do all she could to get them the information, training, and compensation needed to achieve this goal. When talking with central administration, she said that she and her staff would work to develop the best possible drug rehabilitation program, but certain demonstrated supports were needed from administration (e.g., time and finances for training, visitations to other programs, and additional staff).

During data collection, a community needs-assessment and a feasibility study were conducted. A contracted plan was developed by the manager, with input and agreement from staff and central administration (Diagram 5–9). Throughout the process, the resources of the staff and central administration were used. Jay B., for example, from central office told the manager about Dr. Gene R. of the School of Social Work who served on the agency's advisory board. Dr. R. had extensive practice experience and published research in the area of drug rehabilitation. The manager presented this information to the staff. One of the staff members said that he had studied under Dr. R. and would be happy to contact him to see if he would serve as a trainer/consultant for the staff.

As the contracted plan was implemented, the manager played a major role in mediating, reporting, and motivating the staff and central administration. Upon completion of the plan by the staff, it was sent to administration for discussion, modification, and approval. After receiving approval, the manager, staff, and central administration then evaluated the situation. They agreed that the problem of conflict between the two groups regarding the development of a drug rehabilitation program was resolved. The manager knew, however, that they had "only just begun." She and the staff needed to move on toward the goal of establishing and running the new program with the continued support of central administration. For this goal, the process would be revisited with a formulation of an extended contract.

In this case scenario, the manager advances in the six-stage problem-solving process and contracts with two major systems simultaneously. The methodology used may be called the advanced general method. It serves as a guiding framework for problem solving at all levels of administration.

## *HOLISTIC PRACTICE*

The practice of advanced generalists may be referred to as "holistic." The advanced generalist in any capacity (e.g., direct service provider, supervisor, manager, chief administrator) has the generic skills, theoretical perspective, and problem focus that allow for (1) looking at the whole and the interrelationship of its parts, (2) identifying and assessing the problem/need, and (3) responding (singularly or with multiplicity) in a variety of ways and roles. Even when partializing a situation for problem targeting and intervention, the practitioner continues to see the interrelated influences and resulting consequences on the whole system and its environment.

Often, an advanced generalist may be working directly and indirectly at the same time. In the case of Mr. W. (cited earlier), for example, it is possible that a new worker would be hired by the diocesan office and Mr. W.'s

**DIAGRAM 5–9**  Contracted Plan

| DATE IDENTI-FIED | PROBLEM/ NEED | GOAL | TASK | CONTRACT | DATE ANTICI-PATED | DATE ACCOM-PLISHED |
|---|---|---|---|---|---|---|
| 8/10 | Conflict staff/ admin. about drug rehab program | To agree on plan for drug program | 1. Discuss results of needs as. & feas. study | 1. Manager and staff | 8/10 | 8/10 |
| | | | 2. Locate model programs | 2. Manager and staff | 8/11–8/17 | |
| | | | 3. Select sites & visitors | 3. Manager and staff | 8/17 | |
| | | | 4. Author. funds for staff dev. | 4. Central administration (KL) | 8/11 | |
| | | | 5. Visit sites & report to staff | 5. Tom, Bo, Sarah | 8/20– | |
| | | | 6. Locate Trainer/consultant (Dr. R.) | 6. Pete | 8/18 | |
| | | | 7. Arrange training | 7. Training Committee | 8/20–8/30 | |
| | | | 8. Attend training | 8. Staff & Manager | | |
| | | | 9. Assign new staff position to unit | 9. Central Admin. (MH) | 8/17 | |
| | | | 10. Dev. job description | 10. Manager (with staff input) and agency personnel dir. | 8/20 | |
| | | | 11. Advertise position | 11. Personnel Office | 8/27 | |
| | | | 12. Discuss program to be proposed a. location b. services c. staffing d. time table | 12. Manager and staff | 9/2 | |
| | | | 13. Form a D. P. program planning committee | 13. Staff and manager | 9/2 | |
| | | | 14. Develop plan | 14. D. P. P. committee | 9/3– | |
| | | | 15. Present plan to staff and manager for discussion, modification, approval | 15. D. P. P. committee | 9/16 | |
| | | | 16. Present plan to administration for discussion, modification, approval | 16. Manager | 9/24 | |
| | | | 17. Mediate, reach agreement | 17. Manager with staff and administration | 9/25– | |

worker could be assigned as supervisor. To enhance the example, the new worker could be assigned to lead a support group for single males, to which Mr. W. could be referred by his worker. The result would be that Mr. W.'s original worker would be serving as direct service provider, supervisor, and team worker in service delivery for Mr. W., all at the same time. The diver-

**DIAGRAM 5–10**    Advanced Generalist Practice Range

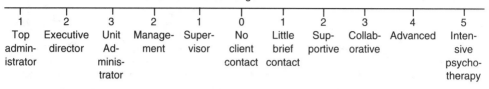

| 1 | 2 | 3 | 2 | 1 | 0 | 1 | 2 | 3 | 4 | 5 |
|---|---|---|---|---|---|---|---|---|---|---|
| Top admin- istrator | Executive director | Unit Ad- minis- trator | Manage- ment | Super- visor | No client contact | Little brief contact | Sup- portive | Collab- orative | Advanced | Inten- sive psycho- therapy |

sity in abilities needed would appropriately be expected of an advanced generalist. In this situation, the advanced generalist could find herself using the advanced general method concurrently in both direct and indirect practice. This ability to work on multiple problems/needs in direct and indirect practice roles at any given time may be described as "holistic practice."

The range of roles and interventions of a holistic practitioner is depicted in Diagram 5–10. Combining the direct practice roles and interventions of Diagram 5–1 with the indirect roles and practices identified in Diagram 5–6 helps illustrate the scope of abilities and expectations of advanced generalists. The scale also reflects the polarity of roles and contrasting competence in therapeutic relationship skills as compared to social systems operational skills.

Advanced generalists have sometimes been described as "God," because they appear to be able "to do all things." In some positions, particularly in remote rural areas or in public welfare offices, they are given such a diversity of duties and demands that they may, in fact, need "divine intervention" to accomplish all well. Recognizing the growing demand for nonspecialized social workers throughout the field of human services today, the profession of social work has begun to face the challenge with the introduction and development of advanced generalist practitioners. The key to effectiveness may lie in the central need for these practitioners to "know thyself." They need to know their strengths and their limitations, to be able to creatively stretch their knowledge and abilities as they "engage diversity," and to have the skill to mobilize other resources as needed in the extended environment. Knowing that they cannot be "all things to all people," they rely on their solid foundation, the clear identification of the scope of their abilities and limitations, and the belief that they can make a contribution to help others achieve greater harmony and wholeness in their lives.

## *SUMMARY*

In this chapter, the methodology of advanced generalists was explored. The range of possible direct and indirect practice roles and approaches found in advanced generalist practice was delineated. The methodology of advanced generalists is a skeletal guiding process of six dynamic stages applied creatively. It is often carried out with the use of complementary tools and techniques, theories, and approaches. When the six-stage process is used with advanced interventions such as psychotherapy, or when it is used during indirect practice such as supervision or management, it may be referred to as the advanced general method. The integration of the general method with a variety of theories, tools, and techniques and the use of the integrated method in one or many roles, individually or concurrently, in direct and/or indirect practice was presented and described as holistic practice.

Definitions, case examples, and a variety of diagrams were offered to clarify the methodology of advanced generalists. The need for advanced generalists to know what they can do and to accept their limitations was emphasized as essential for effective practice. Further exploration of advanced generalist practice in higher administration will be given in the following chapter.

## NOTES

1. Commission on Social Work Practice, NASW, "Working Definition on Social Work Practice," quoted in Harriet M. Bartlett, "Toward Clarification and Improvement of Social Work Practice," *Social Work* 3, no. 2 (April 1958): 7.
2. Allen Pincus and Anne Minahan, *Social Work Practice: Model and Method* (Itasca, Ill.: Peacock, 1973), p. 63.
3. Pincus and Minahan, *Social Work Practice*, p. 63.
4. James K. Whittaker and Elizabeth M. Tracy, *Social Treatment: An Introduction to Interpersonal Helping in Social Work Practice,* 2nd ed. (New York: Aldine De Gruyter, 1989), p. 221.
5. Alfred Kadushin, *Supervision in Social Work* (New York: Columbia University Press, 1976), p. 21.
6. Ibid.
7. Howard M. Carlisle, *Management: Concepts and Situations* (Chicago: Science Research Associates, Inc., 1976), p. 5.
8. Henry M. Havassy, "Effective Second-Story Bureaucrats: Mastering the Paradox of Diversity," *Social Work* 35, no. 2, (March 1990), p. 103.
9. Sue W. Spencer, "The Administrative Process in a Social Welfare Agency," in *Social Work Administration: A Resource Book,* Harry A. Schatz, ed. (New York: Council on Social Work Education, 1970), pp. 135–136.
10. Maria O'Neil McMahon, *The General Method of Social Work Practice: A Problem-Solving Approach,* 2nd ed. (Englewood Cliffs, N.J: Prentice Hall, 1990), p. 330.
11. J. H. Weissberg, "Short-term Dynamic Psychotherapy: An Application of Psychoanalytic Personality Theory" *Journal of American Academy of Psychoanalysis* 12 (1984): 101–113.
12. Marc H. Hollender and Charles V. Ford, *Dynamic Psychotherapy: An Introductory Approach* (Washington, D.C.: American Psychiatric Press, Inc., 1990), pp. 135–136.
13. Havassy, "Effective Second-Story Bureaucrats," p. 106.
14. Ibid.

# 6
# The Advanced
# Generalist Administrator

Sarah A. DeLancey and Nancy M. Hall

## *INTRODUCTION*

In this chapter, the authors describe and illustrate advanced generalist practice in administrative settings. The advanced generalist administrator is described as carrying out various roles and using the key elements that characterize advanced generalist practice: the advanced ecological systems perspective; the advanced general method; advanced knowledge of problem, person and triplex environment; international social work/welfare; advanced research; and ethical decision making.

The indirect practice of social work administrators identified in this chapter refers to the practice of advanced generalist administrators that does not involve direct work with client systems but rather involves work with staff, organizations, groups, and other large systems. The indirect practice of advanced generalist administrators includes agency administration, supervision, management, policy development, planning, and program development. Further description details leadership and managerial functions, roles, operational structures, and systems' impact. Diagrams illustrate the complexity of the roles and levels of involvement in various systems. Practice examples are provided to illuminate process steps as well as ethical and value conflicts. The advanced generalist administrator described in this chapter does not only operate in the upper echelon of a bureaucratic structure but connects with systems at multilevels, acting as a conduit, catalyst, and evaluator for the sharing and exchange of information, ideas, and issues. The advanced generalist administrator impacts the system at every operational level, focusing on the organization's mission, goals, problem-solving interventions, and outcomes. Most of the examples in this chapter are taken from the practice of administrators in public social services. A description of the function of a regional public social service office and of the duties and responsibilities of county and regional directors of public social services may be found in Appendix C.

## DEFINITIONS

The advanced generalist administrator enables, enhances, maintains, intervenes in, and evaluates the operation of multilevel systems by using a range of theories and practice interventions. The skill of advanced generalist administrators is highlighted in their ability to adapt and apply a theoretical approach and/or intervention and technique that may have been designed for one area of practice to another area of administration.

The advanced generalist administrator may be found in public and private and small and large organizations, with titles as varied as Section Chief, Director, Executive Director or Chief Executive Officer. The role becomes more complex with the expanding scope of the function and the multilevel target system. Regardless of the complexity, the six-level process of the general method is repeatedly used in problem solving.

The advanced generalist administrator works in a system whose boundaries touch numerous other systems (Diagram 6–1) that may share similar goals while serving similar segments of society. In the public domain, those systems are created by law, funded by tax dollars, and operated by a bureaucratic structure while being supervised by a higher level of government. For example, the state division of social services supervises the county department of social services, which administers a range of human services programs.

Private nonprofit systems are created because of an established community need. They may be funded by religious organizations, philanthropic foundations, or united community fund drives. Like public systems, they are administered by a director who is generally accountable to a board of directors.

The examples used in this chapter are from a state-supervised and county-administered social services system. Diagram 6–1 depicts the county social services agency as the center of a human services satellite system. A county department of social services operates in a complex multilevel system of state

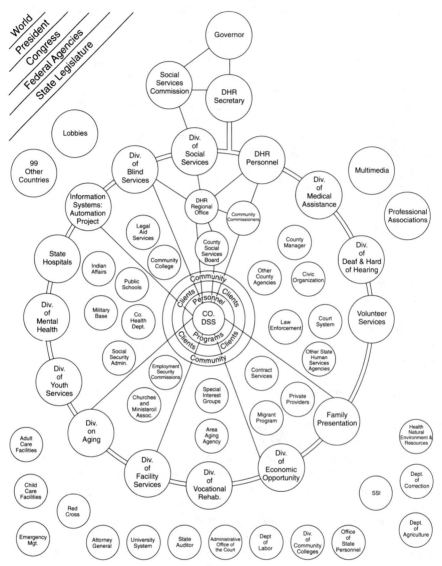

**DIAGRAM 6–1**   A County Social Services Agency in Relation to other County, State, Federal, and Private Interest Systems

and county governments. Actions taken by one level can have a ripple effect on many other levels. Private interest groups may attract attention and energy from several systems and levels at the same time. International events impact the operations of all levels of government and many private interest groups through funding, volume of work, and reduced manpower.

In some states' social services system, the county department of social services is county administered and state supervised. This means that the county agency administrator is charged with the responsibility for devising his or her own plan for administering mandated and operational social services programs while abiding by very specific state and federal laws, policies, and procedures.

The state receives federal funds and, through a complicated allocation process, distributes those funds to county agencies that provide county matching funds. To remain eligible to receive federal and state funds, a county agency must pass a state monitoring process that verifies the county's adherence to state and federal laws, policies, and procedures in its administration of the social programs. County agencies compete with one another for limited local tax dollars, and frequently it is the articulate administrator who is successful in receiving adequate or better funding. Political astuteness and negotiation skills are keys to success.

## ROLES OF THE ADVANCED GENERALIST ADMINISTRATOR

Today there is some discussion about whether administrators are leaders or managers. The authors also confronted this question. In the minds of some experts there is a clear difference between leaders and managers. Abraham Zaleznik describes leaders as creators using their imaginations to create a vision and managers as strategists focusing on problem solving.[1]

The authors concluded that the human services advanced generalist administrator must demonstrate both leadership and managerial attributes. Stephen Covey has written that to be successful one must "begin with the end in mind" or have a clear vision of what must be accomplished.[2] Management deals with how things are to be accomplished; leadership deals with direction. Renowned management experts Peter Drucker and Warren Bennis have both written, "Management is doing things right; leadership is doing the right things."[3]

The primary function and role of the advanced generalist administrator is to lead and manage work groups. Peter Drucker has identified three equally important and essential tasks that management must execute to enable an organization to function and achieve its purpose: (1) management activities must be congruent with the organization's mission or purpose; (2) work must be productive while fostering achievement among the workers; and (3) the administrator must manage social impacts and social responsibilities.[4]

The effective advanced generalist administrator has many roles and may operate out of one or several at the same time in the process of getting work done through other people, as illustrated in the roles of the advanced generalist administrator in Diagram 6–2.

In order for advanced generalist administrators to function in a complex, multisystem, multilevel environment, they must operate out of many roles and

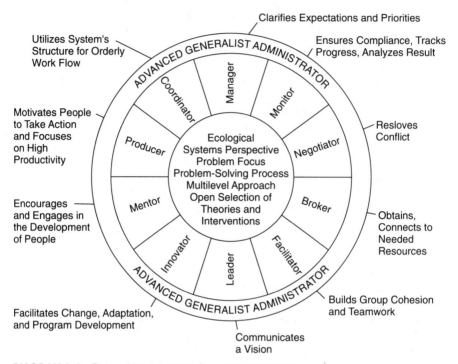

Clarifies Expectations and Priorities

Utilizes System's Structure for Orderly Work Flow

Ensures Compliance, Tracks Progress, Analyzes Result

Motivates People to Take Action and Focuses on High Productivity

Resloves Conflict

Encourages and Engages in the Development of People

Obtains, Connects to Needed Resources

Facilitates Change, Adaptation, and Program Development

Builds Group Cohesion and Teamwork

Communicates a Vision

ADVANCED GENERALIST ADMINISTRATOR

Coordinator · Manager · Monitor · Negotiator · Broker · Facilitator · Leader · Innovator · Mentor · Producer

Ecological Systems Perspective
Problem Focus
Problem-Solving Process
Multilevel Approach
Open Selection of Theories and Interventions

**DIAGRAM 6–2**    Roles of the Advanced Generalist Administrator

make easy transitions from one role to another. These roles (Diagram 6–2) are defined as the following:

*Leader:* one who communicates the organization's vision

*Manager:* one who provides clarification of work expectations and priorities

*Facilitator:* one who builds group cohesion and teamwork

*Coordinator:* one who utilizes the system's structure to achieve orderly work flow

*Innovator:* One who facilitates change and assists in the process of worker and program adaptation

*Monitor:* one who ensures compliance, tracks progress and analyzes results for effectiveness

*Producers:* one who motivates people to take action and focuses on high productivity

*Negotiator:* one who participates in conflict resolution

*Broker:* one who obtains, develops, and connects users to needed resources

*Mentor:* one who encourages and engages in the development of people

These roles will be evident in the following case examples and those found throughout the chapter.

### Examples of Roles of the Advanced
### Generalist Administrator

The advanced generalist administrator not only works with individuals to serve client populations but also mobilizes groups, organizations, and institutions to accomplish goals. The following example demonstrates the broker and coordinator roles of the advanced generalist administrator.

EXAMPLE 1: SPECIAL PROJECT DEVELOPMENT

A county department of social services received grant money to establish a *special project on aging.* Goals of this project were to (1) assess needs of the community's elderly, (2) identify existing resources for the elderly, (3) connect resources and the elderly together as needed, (4) create new services/programs, and (5) document unmet needs for future goals. The social work project director engaged in many different groups in the community, both public and private. Public awareness and community involvement with the elderly were essential if the goals were to be accomplished. After data collection and assessment, one finding was that there were many elderly and disabled persons in nursing and rest homes who were quite able and motivated to take trips outside the facility if some type of transportation could be made available to them. After brainstorming, the social work director made the following proposal: All residents of a county-sponsored nursing home will be given the opportunity to go into the city to a large department store to do some Christmas shopping and will then be given a festive meal in a restaurant. The social services director and the social work director were able to use their knowledge of resources, networking skills, and memberships in various community organizations to secure funding and sponsorship for the venture. A women's service club paid for the meal; the department store paid for the bus and driver while also furnishing corsages and boutonnieres for the women and men who were being treated. The project was a great success. The residents talked about the occasion for weeks. The ensuing publicity in the newspaper and on television satisfied the sponsors. The outing became an annual event coordinated by the social work project director. Residents of the home were motivated by the event to save their money, to ready their clothes and to take care of personal hygiene by taking baths and going to the beauty and barber shops. The cooperation between the business community, service club, and governmental agency served as a partnership model for meeting the unmet needs of the elderly and disabled.

EXAMPLE 2: UTILIZATION OF STAFF

The advanced generalist administrator is always alert to how people can be better served. This is especially true in times of greater service demands and shrinking resources. In the last five years one state agency has been testing some methods that counties can use to address the problem of better utilization of staff. Under an umbrella term of "resource management"[5] a number of counties have participated in identifying functions and tasks of the line workers in a given program. The worker activities were identified, tracked, timed, sequenced, and tallied for frequencies. This intense effort has yielded the following outcomes: (1) worker standards for timeliness, quality, and quantity, which are translated into a supervisory tool called the Performance Index Evaluation; (2) a job design that offers a method of work simplification; (3) function and task analysis that provides a basis for a competency-based training system; (4) workload standards for use in budgeting requests for staffing and for supervisory use in workload assignment and coverage; and (5) identification of the 20% tasks that consume 80% of the worker's time (Pareto's Law), which can be useful in training and supervision.

The advance generalist administrator primarily performs the producer, manager, innovator, and broker roles in the following case situation.

### EXAMPLE 3: AGENCY STAFFING PROBLEM

A County Director contacted the Regional Director requesting assistance to analyze and solve a problem regarding staff needs in her county. Her problem was that requests for additional staff were being questioned and denied by the County Manager and County Commissioners. The County Director requested that the Regional Director study and analyze the work being performed by the staff. The Regional Director arranged for the State Coordinator of Resource Management to make a presentation to the County Director, the local Board of Social Services, the County Manager, and the County Commissioners regarding the design and methodology to be used in the study as well as the anticipated outcomes. After the study was authorized by the County Commissioners, a similar presentation was made to line staff and supervisors. Regional consultants were then assigned to conduct the study. After the data were analyzed, staffing levels were recommended. The County Commissioners approved the recommendation for additional staff (including two supervisory positions) and upgraded computer equipment. The analysis also revealed the need for some realignment of staff.

In the above problem-solving example, the advanced generalist administrator's roles were producer, innovator, and broker. In these roles, the advanced generalist administrator implemented a new approach for organizational analysis that resulted in county commissioner–approved agency change. While new resources were added to the agency, existing resources were better used for greater productivity.

## THE ADVANCED GENERALIST ADMINISTRATOR AND THE KEY ELEMENTS OF ADVANCED GENERALIST PRACTICE

Because of the multiple roles and complexity of the environment of advanced generalist administrators, they must have a thorough knowledge of ecological systems, methodically examine all aspects of the problem, and focus on the highest priority of the problematic issue. Frequently, this process requires several important players from the various layers of the community power structure to become involved in the problem's solution. The advanced generalist administrator may have to use different approaches with each level of the power structure or with those who have a vested interest in the problem's solution. It is not uncommon for the advanced generalist administrator to play different roles with different levels of the problem-solving participants at the same time.

While enacting various roles, the advanced generalist administrator uses the following key elements: the advanced ecological systems perspective, the advanced general method, advanced knowledge, international social work/welfare, advanced research, and ethical decision making. The six phases of the general method and the other elements of generalist practice provide the base for advanced generalist practice administration. Although one element may be highlighted as central in a particular situation, all, in fact, are interdependent and used simultaneously in practice. Only the first five elements are discussed in this chapter; the use of advanced research and technology is explored further in the next chapter.

### Advanced Ecological Systems Perspective

The advanced generalist administrator must know the agency's client community and the entire community culture within the extended environment. Knowledge of community values, power structure, politics, and demographics enables the advanced generalist administrator to network and build spheres of influence that eventually result in developing resources and valuable alliances.

An advanced generalist administrator operates from the leader, innovator, and broker roles. He knows not only the interest of the power structure but who has a stake in solving the problem that would favor a solution congruent with his needs for additional resources.

## CASE EXAMPLE: REST HOME CARE QUESTIONED

The problem identified initially was that the community needed more rest home beds. A closer study revealed that a significant number of adults (disabled and elderly) needed assistance with activities of daily living (feeding, housekeeping, laundry). Some citizens along with some rest home operators believed that the solution to this problem was to increase the number of rest home beds; this would require legislative action. While there were some rest home beds available, some people described some of those beds as existing in "human warehouse" conditions. On paper, the rest homes could meet the adult needs, but in reality, one home provided minimal care; in addition, frequent community complaints were made about this home's quality of care.

What also began to emerge in the data collection stage was a value conflict. The question arose, "Should not elderly citizens have a right to a choice or alternatives in care—and quality care?" The course of least resistance and conflict would have been to claim that choice and quality care issues could be satisfied in the rest homes. But this was inaccurate and advocacy action was necessary.

Under the leadership of the advanced generalist administrator, environmental resources were mobilized. A coalition of Directors of the Department of Social Services, Health, Mental Health, Council on Aging, and Community Action agencies joined forces. Collectively, data were gathered and assessed, and plans and strategies were developed. The Boards and County Commissioners supported the proposed expansion of in-home and home health care services. Emerging outcomes were quite favorable: (1) reduced numbers of adults were placed in costly institutional care; (2) the cost of in-home care was less than institutional care and resulted in saving county funds; (3) over the span of a few years with continuous loss of residents, the questionable rest home improved its quality of care for those who wanted to avail themselves of that service; and (4) elderly persons and other adults had a choice among a range of in-home services.

Thus, the advanced generalist administrator stimulated a system's change and resolved a values conflict by expanding in-home services, offering a choice, and reducing the need for institutionalization by mobilizing the collective power of the appropriate community agencies. Not only did competition force the rest home to offer improved services, but a continuum of care was developed for the community's adult population.

The problem-solving process can be successful only if the problem is clearly identified and communicated to those individuals and groups who are the greatest stake-holders. Consequences of failure to take action (including any specifically required course of action) must be stated explicitly in order to offer a choice and gain commitment to the problem-solving process. Resources and problem-solving pathways emerge as a result. Frequently, political representatives of the local and larger community become involved in the problem-solving process as they have been vested with the power to fund and sanction through the democratic process. Awareness of the power structure and of the those who must be involved in the planning and decision-making process is essential to successful encounters in the ecological systems perspective of person and environment.

### The Advanced General Method

The advanced general method is a problem-solving process that is goal oriented and value laden and may be seen as reflecting the overall mission and vision of the individual organization. As stated earlier, the core of advanced generalist practice consists of the key elements of generalist practice and the six phases of the general method that are described below in breadth and depth from the advanced generalist administrator's perspective.

*Engagement*   Engagement is the act of one system joining and exploring mutual goals and interests with other systems. Each level of the system yields information regarding problems, issues, people, and their feelings and reactions, as well as the hopes and goals for themselves and others. The advanced generalist administrator engages as a means of taking the pulse or obtaining a barometric reading of people and the environment. Engagement occurs through system networking, and timing is a crucial element. There is a right time to reach out; existing circumstances are important. The use of empathy as a skill is just as important to the administrator as it is for the direct practitioner. In the words of Stephen Covey, "Seek first to understand, then to be understood."[6]

*Data Collection*   Data collecting takes place continually both formally and informally. The administrator is exposed to so much data that it can be overwhelming. One cannot deal with all of it; nor does one need to deal with all of it. Much of what the administrator knows is through intuition, that is, "being able to hear what is left unspoken"[7] and taking in emotional signals and making sense of them. The administrator has a system for dealing with the data. Some data can be delegated to others for processing; other data need more thought and individual attention. The administrator has mechanisms for receiving data; in the absence of such mechanisms, the administrator designs structures for information flow.

*Assessment*   Once data are collected, priorities must be established, since everything cannot be done at once. The rationale for decision making is based upon a specific set of criteria. Criteria are influenced by one's values, time frames, politics, and the severity, duration, and scope of the problem. Decisions are made. Planning and goal setting take place and agreements are finalized.

*Intervention*   In order to serve the client community, the advanced generalist administrator frequently intervenes in all levels of one or more systems. These interventions may take place sequentially or simultaneously. In this perspective, each level may become the administrator's target system. The administrator's interventions are the plans and solutions that have been agreed upon earlier in the goal setting and contracting stage. The types of broad interventions used by the administrator are (1) developing programs and resources; (2) mobilizing groups and organizations to provide a new service program; (3) becoming a team player; (4) delegating assignments to others; (5) arranging, accessing, and conducting training; (6) consulting; (7) developing resources; and (8) studying and analyzing work organization and tasks.

*Evaluation*   The evaluation process is characterized by revisiting the established goals and measuring the level of goal attainment or agreement. Such an examination reveals (1) appropriateness of solutions; (2) appropriateness of people involved; and (3) appropriateness of the problem solved, and, if not appropriate, identification of the real problem or barriers to the problem-solving process.

*Termination* Termination is the process of bringing closure to goal-directed activities and relationships. There are myriad feelings: pride, accomplishment, sadness, disappointment, or relief. Termination may also be the occasion for a system to reflect on its past status, its current status, and the future.

In the following example the six phases of the general method are described along with the advanced generalist administrator's roles as leader and innovator.

## EXAMPLE: COMMUNITY RESPONSE TO NEEDS OF THE AGED

*Engagement.* In one country, the social services director engaged with the other agency administrators whom she knew had an interest in addressing the problem of the community's aged and disabled. She joined forces with the Directors of Health, Council on Aging, Mental Health, and Community Action to discuss the community's elderly and disabled in-home services needs.

*Data Collection.* Several important facts emerged from the data collection: (1) There were insufficient numbers of beds and inadequate rest home care. (2) Many frail elderly persons expressed the desire to remain in their own home as opposed to being institutionalized. (3) Adult day care was needed to free care-givers to work or for respite. (4) Several elderly persons regularly attending the senior center required more attention and supervision than the Senior Center could provide. (5) By the year 2000, 46% of the country's population would be 60+ years old. (6) The cost of institutional care was escalating. (7) Adult protective services cases were on the rise.

*Assessment.* The group studied the data, then reviewed models of intervention that would best address the problem. A decision was made to select the adult day health/care model. The various boards of the above agencies were informed of these facts and agreed to support the development of an adult day health/care center. As part of the contract, the agency directors agreed that the county department of social services director should take the leadership role on this project due to this director's interest in and knowledge of resources and funding. Further, all these agencies would appoint a representative to serve on the center's board along with several other interested community persons.

*Intervention.* Implementation plans were carried out when grant proposals were written and submitted, and one was approved. State guidelines for the physical plant, operational structure, and funding were studied and implemented. Community, civic and religious groups were informed of the purpose, goals, and needs of the center;

and those groups and individuals donated furniture, equipment, and supplies for refurbishing the center. Once the goal had been set and the public made aware of it, other individuals and groups were attracted and wanted to become associated with the project. Thus, a youthful offenders program performed community service hours to clean, make minor repairs, and improve the grounds of the center.

*Evaluation.* The adult day center became operational within two years of the initial planning date. It clearly satisfied some of the community needs for its adult population. Evaluation of this project was continuous by the board of directors and the clients themselves. A more formal evaluation was conducted by the state licensing Division.

*Termination.* After two additional years of administrative support and training of the board and the center's staff, the center and its board became more independent and able to successfully manage personnel, policy, and funding issues without direct assistance from the department of social services. A developmental task in termination is to enable the system (in this case, the center and its staff) to consolidate the gains they had made in order to move on to other goals.

Indirect intervention by the advanced generalist administrator was achieved by forming an organization that would provide a specific service to meet current community needs as well as future needs of a growing elderly population.

Advanced generalist administrators usually do not deal with the client directly. As just illustrated, they use the indirect approach as they set plans in motion and establish or create structures and processes that ultimately enable the client population to receive a service or intervention. The administrator's main target is the environment in order to make it sustaining for the client. The above example illustrates an environment lacking in resources but filled with motivated people capable of responding. The advanced generalist administrator recognizes the elements of the situation and initiates action.

### Advanced Knowledge

The advanced general method provides for open selection of theories and interventions. Through experience in applying various management and clinical theories and after experimentation with adapting those same theories and interventions to administrative situations, the advanced generalist administrator develops mastery in performance of duties, roles, and responsibilities. The advanced generalist administrator's knowledge and versatility will be illustrated in the following examples.

### EXAMPLE: STAFF DEVELOPMENT

As a supervisor, the advanced generalist administrator has the responsibility for promoting the growth and development of staff. Alfred Kadushin in his work *Supervision in Social Work* clearly identifies educational supervision as one of three major functions of social work supervision.[8] Therefore creating opportunities for employee knowledge and skill development is not only a supervisory responsibility and wise management activity but also a demonstration of leadership. By this behavior, the advanced generalist administrator is clearly stating what is expected, what is needed to achieve the expectation, and that a commitment exists to creating growth and development pathways for employees to acquire knowledge and skills to meet performance expectations.

The advanced generalist administrator frequently is a mentor for staff in promoting their growth and development. The Regional Office of the Division of Social Services is a group of multidisciplinary human services consultants led by an administrator who not only has supervisory authority for them but also for the counties they serve. This is a highly skilled, professional group that does not always fully understand or appreciate its colleagues' unique skills and methods of work performance.

To gain a better understanding and appreciation of likenesses and differences, the administrator arranged for all staff to take the Myers-Briggs Type Inventory.[9] This instrument was interpreted and related not only to them individually but also to their role as consultant. Quickly the group began to understand why colleagues behaved certain ways in prescribed situations. Differences were appreciated when one ENFP said to an ESTJ, "Now I understand why you always want to know so many details and exactly what you are going to do all of the time;—and I really don't have a plan or care about all those details—and I might change my mind at the last minute."

All the consultants agreed to post their "type" on the bulletin board for easy reference. For months the consultants talked about their types and speculated about "types" of personalities that they worked with in counties. This Myers-Briggs Type Indicator was frequently used to identify "blind spots" that the consultant might have in his work with county officials.

In actuality this training in type had a twofold purpose: (1) to understand and appreciate oneself and (2) to understand and appreciate likenesses and differences in others. A side benefit was an increase in the consultant's self-confidence in learning to work with individuals whose behavior previously had been a mystery or had caused conflict.

The advanced generalist administrator is open to utilizing new methodologies and instruments that contribute to the competence of staff. One of the authors has begun to use an assessment instrument that measures the conative part of the mind. This is the willing, striving part of the mind that is distinct from the cognitive and affective domains. Results of the Kolbe Conative Index[10] indicate the distribution and intensity of mental energy into four Action Modes, and has the capacity to predict what a person will or will not do in a given situation. The KCI is proving to be useful to administrators in the following ways:

Serving as one criterion in hiring and placement of staff
Promoting team building
Reducing stress
Resolving conflict between staff and managers
Leading differential supervision
Designing training

## EXAMPLE: PROBLEM WITH CONSULTANT

In this brief summary of the manager role, the advanced generalist administrator must make every effort to understand the on-the-job behaviors of employees and assign work that is congruent with talent, temperament, and mental energy.

One administrator had a supervisor come to her with a concern about one of her consultants. The complaints were that the consultant never met deadlines; when he made presentations he usually ran out of time before he finished covering the material; when asked questions, he would give overly detailed answers; and, in defense of his point of view, he could be argumentative to the point of being tedious. Several counties had requested he be replaced with another consultant. The results of the Kolbe Conative Index indicated that his modus operandi was one of a researcher, one who probes for facts and details, one who works with complexity, needs to cover all angles and points of view, before making a decision. It seemed to others that he procrastinated. Once the supervisor and administrator learned that the consultant did not have a personality disorder and that he was acting according to his natural instinctual needs, they were able to be more understanding and tolerant. They also were able to assign him to those situations where thoroughness was important to the success of the assignment. He could be teamed to train with persons who would be able to keep the pace moving and not allow the time to run out before finishing what needed to be covered. The results gave the consultant an understanding of how he goes about problem solving and why others with a different profile would perform in different ways. The consultant was advised to affirm his talents and to meet any criticism with some humor. For example, the consultant might say, "Do you want the work completed now or do you want it done correctly?"

## EXAMPLE: DEALING WITH DEATH OF STAFF MEMBER

Another example illustrates an open selection of theories and provides an example of the advanced generalist administrator dealing with the termination process. For a variety of reasons, organizational composition changes over time. It is important for the administrator to acknowledge those changes whether they be of a joyous or sad nature. Retirements, maternity leave, promotions to new jobs, and so on signal a time for new adventures and hope. Regardless of the cause of termination, there are always issues of separation and loss. Occasionally, there is an unexpected loss, the death of a staff member. The administrator used Elisabeth Kübler-Ross's stages of death and dying[11] to help the staff recognize and feel the loss, grieve, and move on to picking up the pieces of work left by their colleague.

The advanced generalist administrator as a leader and facilitator created the opportunity and expectation that the staff would experience a termination process on the occasion of a staff member's death.

In a group of consultants who had worked together for many years, one of the experienced consultants died at home on a work day. All were saddened and several attended the funeral. After the funeral the staff went to a local restaurant to remember "Joe" with stories and a toast. At the staff meeting the next week, an empty chair with a helium balloon was placed in the circle to represent "Joe." The administrator asked everyone to think for a moment and to write down a word or comment that they would like to say to Joe. There were some verbalizations and a few teary eyes, but everyone wrote their comments and expressed fond memories of "Joe." At that point, the administrator asked everyone to tape their comments to the balloon ribbon. All went out to the parking lot (it was a sunny, windy autumn day), the group held the ribbon and upon releasing the balloon said, "Send this to Joe." For several minutes the group stood quietly watching the balloon fly above the tree tops and finally out of sight. The group felt closer to one another and at the same time felt closer to Joe by letting him go.

The advanced generalist administrator adapted the "there-and-then"[12] empty chair exercise that is sometimes used in Gestalt family therapy situations to acknowledge the absence of other members.

*Knowledge of Political Systems and Complex Boundaries*    Many advanced generalist administrators operate in multilevel systems, as shown in Diagram 6–3, a conoid that illustrates systems' levels and relationships. Due to the multilayered environment in which advanced generalist administrators work, they may need to answer a number of questions about the boundaries of what may appear to be a "boundaryless" terrain or zone. At each level there are key questions to ask:

1. "Who is in charge of what?" The Authority Boundary: How to lead but remain open to criticism. [And] [h]ow to follow but still challenge superiors.
2. "Who does what?" The Task Boundary: How to depend on others one does not control. [And] [h]ow to specialize yet understand other people's jobs.
3. "What's in it for us?" The Political Boundary: How to defend one's interests without undermining the organization. [And] [h]ow to differentiate between win-win and win-lose situations.
4. "Who is—and isn't—us?" The Identity Boundary: How to feel pride without devaluing others. [And] [h]ow to remain loyal without undermining others.[13]

At the top level or Level 1 of the conoid in Diagram 6–3, the advanced generalist administrator, in this case, the regional director, has responsibility for being involved in the creation and development of policies and procedures that directly apply to the operation of county departments of social services. The policies and procedures are based upon federal and state laws; however, values and ethics play a role in how conservatively or liberally they are written and interpreted. Frequently the incumbent political party influences the interpretation of laws, policies, and procedures and determines which programs will be funded and at what levels.

## EXAMPLE: BUDGET REDUCTION

In his role as manager, the advanced generalist administrator must sometimes make hard decisions based upon the political preferences of his superiors. This condition is frequently referred to as accepting "political reality."

In the fiscal year 1990–1991, state funds were extremely low and services and expenditures requiring state funds had to be reduced in order for state government to have a balanced budget. The division director met with all her key managers to decide

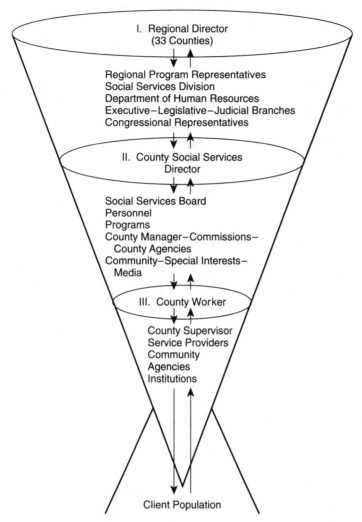

**DIAGRAM 6–3**  Regional Division of Social Services: A Systems Perspective

which budget items would be reduced or eliminated. Discussion centered around services not mandated by law that could be reduced or eliminated with the least amount of client harm or criticism at large. All the programs considered were purposeful and helpful. Staff reductions had previously been made, but other staff positions were discussed for possible elimination in the event program cuts were not sufficient to yield the division's share of the overall dollar reduction required by the Governor's Office of Budget and Management.

The advanced generalist administrator works closely with other human resources systems, the executive and legislative branches of state government, federal agencies, and congressional representatives (Diagram 6–3, Level 1). Frequently what is requested from these systems is information and verification of how counties are applying laws, policies, and procedures in the social programs for the citizens.

As Diagram 6–3 further illustrates, there are clear pathways for communication between and among the levels of the systems. The effective advanced generalist administrator uses those pathways, sharing the impact of specific laws, policies, and procedures with all entities in order that specified laws, policies, and procedures remain congruent with their intent or are changed to reflect their original intent.

The regional director works closely with county directors, as Level 2 in Diagram 6–3 illustrates, to assist with program development and monitoring for application and compliance with laws, policies, and procedures and to analyze agency operations. Frequently, a county director's Social Services Board becomes aware that one or more sections of the agency is problematic or dysfunctional and assistance is requested from the regional director to define the problem(s) and help design solutions.

The regional director leads a team of multidisciplinary program representatives who gather and analyze data from case reviews; interview the staff, administrators, and board; and study organizational structure and work methods. A full analysis of the problem situation along with recommendations are presented to the agency director and the board for their information and action. Occasionally, the regional director presents information to the county manager and commissioners when further support or clarification is needed or if there are other barriers that need removing. Ongoing consultation is provided to the county director as he applies recommendations. The regional director continues to evaluate the intervention design and implementation, revising the design with the director when necessary.

## EXAMPLE: PROGRAM RENOVATION

The advanced generalist administrator in his roles of manager, innovator, monitor, and facilitator works with a director of a county Department of Social Services.

A county director requested that the regional director help determine the extent of service delivery problems in his child welfare program, since this section had failed several routine monitorings for policy compliance. He believed that his staff was not adequately trained or supervised. He saw the supervisor as inept and believed that her removal from the position would solve the problem.

After the multidisciplinary team completed the data gathering and analysis process, their findings revealed the following: (1) significant areas of policy noncompliance; (2) low staff morale and high staff turnover; (3) crowded working conditions and low salaries; (4) one social work supervisor for 15 staff who administered 17 different programs; (5) high caseloads and workers who felt highly pressured to complete work on a tight time schedule; (6) staff's lack of clarity about agency goals and their involvement in the goal-setting process.

The following intervention plan was recommended to the director and the board: (1) Restructure the organization to create a separate child welfare unit and adult services unit with both units having separate supervisors; (2) add two additional social workers in child welfare to carry the high volume of work; (3) develop a corrective action plan for noncompliance areas; (4) continue efforts to complete building renovation that would relieve cramped quarters for staff; (5) involve all staff with administration in writing an agency mission statement and in creating a vision for establishing where they would like to see their agency in five years.

The regional director's presentation before the board and the director was successful in gaining approval for additional staff and for restructuring the organization. All that remained was helping the director, the board, and the staff develop a mission statement and establish a vision for their organization.

To assist the county further in solving the agency's staff morale problems, the regional director began a process with the agency director and staff to develop a mission statement by asking them to identify the purpose of the agency and to discuss their ideas in small groups. The small group reports yielded a list of ideas that would be discussed among the staff and in large groups for the next three months. This discussion culminated in a mission statement that all could identify with and agree upon. The mission statement was the following: "The County Department of Social Services is committed to improving the overall quality of life and to enabling individuals of our community to develop to their fullest potential." The primary goal of this exercise was to shift the staff focus from personality issues to the agency's reason for being and to identify and highlight their role in achieving the agency's purpose.

After the mission statement was completed, Joel A. Barker's video "The Power of Vision" was shown to all staff members. The staff was asked to write sectional vision statements.[14] This laid the groundwork for further stimulating and motivating the staff to put their energy into setting achievable goals for themselves and the agency and to feel a part of creating the overall direction that the agency would take in the next five years.

In the above example, the advanced generalist administrator intervened in the multiple levels of a county department of social services as follows:

*Agency:* The administrator deployed her consultants to go to the county and conduct a fact-finding process (manager's role).

*County director:* The administrator consulted with the director and made recommendations for corrective action, restructuring, and adding new staff. This plan of intervention was based on the data collection and assessment (monitor).

*County DSS board:* Because the nature of the recommendations needed the approval of the Board, the administrator made a presentation to the Board stating the recommendations and the rationale for them (innovator).

*County management team and representative staff:* With this group, the administrator took on the role of small group facilitator and trainer (facilitator).

### International Social Work/Welfare

Today events that occur thousands of miles away in another county impact the social services agency. We live in a global society. Some refugees from countries such as Cuba, Mexico, Haiti, and the Middle East view the United States as a desirable sanctuary from their tumultuous life of war, hunger, and political or religious oppression. Satellite communication and mass transportation systems deliver international problems and issues instantaneously and require prepared responses.

International social work is another complex element of practice for advanced generalist administrators. They often carry the role of manager, negotiator, coordinator, and broker in dealing with international issues. Federal agencies and officials from the Department of State and Immigration often have an interest or give specific direction in paper-processing activities as in the Kuwaitee refugee situation. However, the primary areas of conflict may come from cultural differences for which neither county administrative nor social work staff had been prepared.

## EXAMPLE: INTERNATIONAL IMPACT

The advanced generalist administrator's roles are manager, negotiator, broker, coordinator, and mentor in this case.

The 1990–1991 Desert Storm Gulf War had an international impact on some public service agencies. Not only had agencies temporarily lost staff to the military but they were called upon to settle (feed, clothe, and house) political refugees from Kuwait who were fleeing an aggressor, Saddam Hussein and his army, who not only captured the country's oil wealth and other resources but also killed many of the country's citizens.

The role that public agencies played in this relief effort was to facilitate the refugee's settlement process into this country, which included determining eligibility for certain government assistance programs and locating suitable housing, clothing, home furnishings, jobs, and job training.

Overall the relief and settlement efforts were quite successful; however, what neither the political refugees nor the public agencies were prepared for were the cultural differences. Many of those seeking asylum were accustomed to a more affluent lifestyle than what public assistance would pay for; and the refugees became angry and complained when certain amenities were unavailable to them. Not surprisingly, this behavior provoked frustration and anger from social workers who were already stressed and overworked due to their routinely bulging caseloads.

After some cultural diversity training, the social workers developed more acceptance and tolerance of the cultural differences. However, established policies and procedures for public assistance in the United States did not allow for such cultural differences—for example, the male family head speaking for the female or trying to negotiate benefit levels in Aid to Families with Dependent Children or food stamps. Both of these examples were powerful cultural differences. It remained difficult for Arab males to negotiate services with American social services females since they were used to talking about these matters only with males in their culture. In addition, social service workers were not prepared for one whom they perceived as an overtly expectant, aggressive client, as this was generally opposite from the presentation of self by the indigenous client population.

State and county administrators found themselves in the position of requesting local funds from an already burdened tax system to support these newcomers who were less than happy with their new country's accommodations. The administrators negotiated with state and federal officials to seek guidance in establishing policy to provide services that would meet these needs. Generally, county social services administrators and staff were left to design appropriate interventions for settlement and employment that ultimately resulted in satisfactory arrangements for most refugees.

The lesson that was learned slowly and painfully for some was that cultural differences must be learned, respected, and understood even in a crisis situation or the result will be greater frustration and confusion for all. All levels of staff must be prepared for specific cultural differences and the acceptance of those differences. The advanced generalist administrator must design mechanisms for social work crisis intervention that respect cultural differences and maintain the self-esteem of the vulnerable refugee.

### Ethical Decision Making

Because of the complexity of the environment in which the advanced generalist administrator works, every new project and problem challenges established goals, competes for resources, and presents opportunities for value conflicts. Difficult decisions must be made for the greater good not only of the client community but also for the multilevel stake-holders. The following example specifically underscores how the advanced generalist administrator's own personal and professional values impact the values of the client community and result in the creation and provision of a new service.

EXAMPLE 1: VALUE CONFLICT REGARDING BIRTH CONTROL FOR YOUTH

In this example, the roles of the advanced generalist administrator are the manager, the innovator and the broker. A new social work program director at a church-affiliated children's home discovered a values conflict and an ethical dilemma for herself and the home when the staff and teen-age population requested that birth control devices be made available at the campus infirmary. The conflict for the administrator was that to provide this service would appear to condone premarital sex, which was in violation of personal and professional beliefs as well as the home's policy.

In order to make an informed decision, the home's executive director appointed a committee composed of the minister, program director, school principal, social work director, and cottage parent representative to study this problem and to make recommendations to him and the board of trustees for a final decision. The committee learned that a significant number of teen-agers that the home had previously admitted were already sexually active, getting pregnant, and requesting abortions. Field visits were made by the committee to other child-care institutions to learn how they dealt with this problem of sexually active teen-agers. Not surprisingly, most programs did not have a policy to address the issue or denied that such a problem existed. At one sister institution, the social work program director learned from that administrator that sexually active teens were not a problem among their adolescent population. Disbelieving this response, the social work program director persisted in trying to learn what the administrator would do "if" they had such a problem. Finally, the administrator spoke rather harshly to the social work program director saying "JESUS did not say to the woman at the well, 'Go out and get birth control pills'." That ended the dialogue between the two administrators.

The committee continued its fact-finding process by searching the professional literature and compiling a list of the pros and cons of birth control for teens. In addition, other human services agencies in the community were contacted for their point of view and their suggestions. After many intense discussions, prayer, and citing of facts, the home's board of trustees decided to make birth control measures available to those teen-agers who had gained permission from their parents or custodian. A contract with Planned Parenthood was made to provide information and counseling to both staff and the children in cottages.

The groups affected by this decision were the children and their families, human services agencies (primarily the Department of Social Services, which was the chief referral source and legal custodian for many of the children), the staff who were divided between the "old guard" all-male administrative group and the younger child care staff and social work staff, the board of trustees of the western conference of the church, and the community at large.

There were two value systems into which the social work program administrator had been socialized: (1) the values of her family of origin and religion, which were in opposition to young people having sex before marriage for moral and developmental reasons and (2) her professional values, which espoused freedom of choice and respect for the individual. However, after careful evaluation of the facts and thorough discussion with the committee and house parents, the social work program director not only recommended but advocated to the home director that birth control devices be made available along with a counseling component. Her ethical dilemma was resolved by carefully weighing all the facts and placing a greater value on the principle of self-determination and on preventive service.[15] In addition to considering the underlying value principle for each option, the director considered the congruence of the values reflected in each option with the values and life consequences for the youth and for society. The chosen option was in congruence with the values of the youth involved and their parents as well as with the values reflected in society's services and laws. The director assessed that the chosen option could help to prevent adolescent pregnancy and premature parental responsibilities for the youth and, thus, contribute to the well-being of the youth and society. Although the director's personal and religious values were not in congruence with the decision, she did not choose to remove herself from the decision-making process.

## EXAMPLE 2: BOARD-DIRECTOR PROBLEM

In this case, the advanced generalist administrator is in the manager role resolving an ethical dilemma. The division of social services has supervisory responsibility over county boards of social services. Along with this, is the duty of supervising county departments of social services, which includes the county DSS director. Generally in this manager role, the regional director experiences no routine significant values or ethical conflicts in performing these supervisory duties. However, occasionally a situation arises when the board and director are in such serious conflict that the director's job is in jeopardy. The regional director must help both parties focus on following appropriate policies and procedures to resolve conflict while keeping in mind the mission or purpose of the agency.

In this case situation, the board of social services in a small, rural county with a small staff hired a new director to replace a person who had worked in the position for many years. The regional director's role was twofold: (1) to help the new county director get oriented to his role and function and to develop a training plan for him to learn his job and (2) to advise the board of their role in guiding and supervising the director.

The staff began complaining to some board members about the new director's treatment of them. What at first seemed like routine adjustment problems evolved into an awareness of the new director's unpreparedness for his role and responsibility. While he denied using threatening and heavy-handed tactics with staff, all but one staff member revealed statements that the director had previously denied making that were of a threatening nature.

The board consulted with the regional director about what action they should take while the new county director wanted acceptance of his statements of innocence of any wrongdoing. The regional director wanted to support both the board and the county director and advised both parties of the appropriate course of action. However, because the regional director could not agree with the county director's point of view and accept his protestations of innocence as fact, the director appeared to become mistrusting. The regional director advised the county director to comply with the board's requests and directives during the board's fact- finding process. Consultation with the board focused on clarifying and supporting them in their job of gathering facts, remaining objective, and at the conclusion of the fact-finding process, rendering a decision as to what action or remedy should be taken.

The regional director was careful to respect the confidence of the board and the county director and encouraged them to keep channels of communication open and focus on the process and the mission of the agency. In consulting with the board, the regional director encouraged them to compose open-ended questions and to be specific and uniform in all their interactions with employees. The chairman was advised to keep notes and to help the board remain objectively focused on the issues.

While the regional director wanted to give total support to the county director, he felt an ethical responsibility to remain objective and give careful nonbiased consultation to both the director and the board of social services. The guiding factor for the advanced generalist administrator was to stay focused on the mission of the agency, which was to serve the county's citizens rather than to provide employment for anyone. In addition, the advanced generalist administrator used the practice principles, the problem-solving process, and the duties of his role to stay clearly focused on helping both the director and the board to know the appropriate steps to follow in discovering the facts, conducting open meetings, and devising objective open-ended questions that could lead to the board's making a decision.

The advanced generalist administrator gave clear instruction on expectations to both sides, the board and the director, to resolve this issue. The tasks to be performed provided structure along with the practice principles that provided ethical clarity for the advanced generalist administrator. The regional director relied heavily on the principles of self-determination, acceptance, nonjudgmental attitude, confidentiality, and controlled emotional involvement.[16] Under the guidance of the regional director, the board and the county director were able to study the situation objectively and arrive at a mutual agreement.

## SUMMARY

The advanced generalist practice of social work administrators described in this chapter uses the key elements of advanced generalist practice: advanced ecological systems perspective, advanced general method, advanced knowledge of problem-person and triplex environment, international social work/welfare, and ethical decision making.

Indirect practice examples and diagrams provided illustrations of the advanced generalist administrator's multiple roles and use of the elements of advanced generalist practice. The six phases of the general method and the characteristic elements of generalist practice were presented as the core of the advanced generalist administrator. Values and ethical dilemmas were identified throughout the chapter, highlighting the advanced generalist administrator's use of the two basic values: (1) individual worth and human dignity and (2) a caring, participatory society as well as the NASW Code of Ethics[17] and the basic practice principles.

Advanced generalist administrators work in multilevel and international systems. They impact these systems at every operational level, focusing on the organization's mission and using problem-solving interventions and outcomes.

## NOTES

1. Abraham Zaleznik, "Managers and Leaders: Are they Different?" *Harvard Business Review* (March–April 1992): 126–135.
2. Stephen R. Covey, *The Seven Habits of Highly Effective People* (New York: Simon & Schuster, 1990), p. 101.
3. Warren Bennis and Burt Nanus, *Leaders* (New York: Harper & Row Publishers, 1985), p. 21.
4. Peter F. Drucker, *Management: Tasks, Responsibilities, Practices* (New York: Harper & Row Publishers, 1974), p. 40.
5. *The North Carolina Social Services Plan: A Road Map for Change* (North Carolina Department of Human Resources, Division of Social Services 1991), pp. 62–70.
6. Stephen R. Covey, *The Seven Habits of Highly Effective People* (New York: Simon & Schuster, 1990), p. 237.
7. W. Chan Kim and Renée A. Mauborgne, "Parables of Leadership," *Harvard Business Review* (March–April 1992): 126–135.
8. Alfred Kadushin, *Supervision in Social Work,* 2nd ed. (New York: Columbia University Press, 1985), pp. 139 and 140.
9. Isabel Briggs Myers with Peter B. Myers, *Gifts Differing* (California: Consulting Psychologists Press, Inc., 1986), pp. 1–16.
10. Kathy Kolbe, *The Conative Connection* (Reading, Mass.: Addison-Wesley Publishing Co., 1990).
11. Elisabeth Kübler-Ross, *On Death and Dying* (New York: Macmillian Publishing Company, 1970).

12. Michael Nichols, *Family Therapy Concepts and Methods* (New York: Gardner Press, 1984), p. 288.

13. Larry Hirschorn and Thomas Gilmore, "The New Boundaries of the 'Boundaryless' Company," *Harvard Business Review* (May–June 1992): 107.

14. Stephen R. Covey, *Principle-Centered Leadership* (New York: Summit Books, 1990), pp. 163–172.

15. Frank M. Loewenberg and Ralph Dolgoff, *Ethical Decisions for Social Work Practice,* 4th Ed. (Itasca, Ill.: F. E. Peacock Publishers, 1992), pp. 40–62.

16. Felix P. Biestek, S. J., *The Casework Relationship* (Chicago: Loyola University Press, 1957), p. 17.

17. Copyright 1979, National Association of Social Workers, Inc., "Code of Ethics of the National Association of Social Workers."

# 7

# Research and Technology for Advanced Generalist Practice

Linner Ward Griffin

## INTRODUCTION

As indicated throughout this text, advanced generalist practitioners exhibit and use the foundation elements and practice competencies attributed to generalist practice, but they do so in greater breadth and depth. Advanced generalist practice is characterized by the central concepts of (1) advanced ecological systems perspective, (2) international social work and welfare, (3) advanced theories and intervention models, (4) advanced general method, (5) ethical decision making, and (6) advanced research and technology. This chapter addresses the sixth concept, advanced research and technology.

Research, the systematic gathering of knowledge about activities in the here and now, often has been confused with or seen as an integral part of another entity, program evaluation.[1] Historically, research in the behavioral sciences stemmed from the emergence of psychology as a scientific discipline in the nineteenth century. As psychology matured, it developed a collection of methodologies and techniques borrowed from the physical and biological sciences, including principles of scientific inquiry, measurement, and data analysis—the latter incorporating many statistical models that were developed for agricultural applications. Anthropology, sociology, education, and other behavior-oriented fields added further adaptations to research methodology in these new areas. Social work was one of the last behavioral sciences to incorporate research to determine the effectiveness of helping strategies and to improve the profession. To clarify the distinction between research and evaluation as presented in this chapter, research, which has its origin in science, is interested in the testing and development of theories. Empirical research activity is illustrated while using the experimental method, in which hypotheses are logically derived from theory and tested under controlled conditions.[2]

Evaluation, on the other hand, has come from technology rather than science. Its focus is on mission accomplishment or on product delivery and not on theory building.[3] Evaluation is defined as the assessment of the overall effectiveness of a program in meeting its objectives—the objective, systematic, empirical examination of the effects of programs on their targets.[4] Research and evaluation are essential components of all social work programs and are a necessity for advanced generalist practice.

For many human service practitioners, research and evaluation have seemed mystifying, complex, anxiety producing, and virtually impossible to achieve. Research involved activities they regularly sought to avoid. This has been especially true in parts of the United States and other countries that are rural and isolated and that contain small human service agencies with very small staffs. The role of the advanced generalist in such circumstances is to be the researcher and/or to motivate line staff to make objective inquiry part of their practices. The advanced generalist encourages by illustrating that most people are involved in some form of research and/or evaluation almost every day of their lives and rarely find them to be complicated. For example, talking with a coworker about a new agency policy can be equated with nonstandardized interviewing and involves information sharing and data collecting, but such information sharing rarely is anxiety producing. The social worker who "matter of factly" inquires about a client's family also gathers information for use at a later time but experiences little anxiety. The goal of social research is to systematically and rigorously analyze "empirical data, collected by someone firsthand concerning the social or psychological forces operating in a situation."[5] Although the day to day activities of social workers may not involve conducting formal research studies, they are using some of the skills necessary to the research process.

The remainder of this chapter examines research and program evaluation, synthesizing available knowledge about both activities for advanced generalist practice. Distinctions are made between qualitative and quantitative research designs, and appropriate research methodologies are identified for specific types of problems and social agency data. Specific attention is directed toward hypothesis-generating models, empirical strategies, and experimental/quasi-experimental investigation and to the concepts and terminology applicable to these types of inquiry. The chapter also examines the sequential steps in social science research and in program evaluation. The final section of the chapter provides concrete examples of research in advanced generalist practice. A glossary of terms used throughout the chapter may be found in Appendix D.

## QUALITATIVE RESEARCH

In our society there is a tendency to show great respect for numbers and precision. Perhaps this tendency explains the great amount of interest and attention bestowed on quantitative research. It is surprising because qualitative measures often provide greater depth of understanding than one can derive from quantitative measures. "Qualitative research refers to the meanings, concepts, definitions, characteristics, metaphors, symbols, and descriptions of things."[6] Qualitative methods develop the notion of quality, i.e., "the what, how, when, and where of a thing—its essence and ambience."[7]

> Qualitative research . . . seeks answers to questions by examining various social settings and the individuals who inhabit these settings. Qualitative researchers, then, are most interested in how humans arrange themselves and their settings and how inhabitants of these settings make sense of their surroundings through symbols, rituals, social structures, social roles, and so forth.[8]

Ethnography, historical research, and interviewing are the forms of qualitative research that are discussed in this chapter.

### Ethnography

Ethnography, the work of describing a culture, is the type of research most frequently used by anthropologists. Its central aim is to understand another way of life from the *native* point of view. This method is concerned with both *explicit culture* (obvious and communicable information) and *tacit culture* or knowledge outside of one's awareness.[9] These same interests are of importance to advanced generalists, who specifically are concerned with understanding the meanings of experiences and interactions of individuals, families, groups, communities of different cultures and countries. Ethnography or participant observation is the only type of research that allows the researcher "access to . . . the subjective experiences under study."[10]

Ethnographers seek to learn meanings by looking at three aspects of the human experience. They examine what people do (cultural behavior), what people make and use (cultural artifacts), and what people know (cultural knowledge). These meanings suggest hypotheses, that may later be proven through quantitative measures; ethnography is a hypothesis-generating and not a hypothesis-testing research method.[11] Ethnographic research is a very natural activity for human service professionals who use observation as a part of their practices and are accustomed to recording those observations in case records.

The work of ethnography is accomplished through field work, which is the disciplined study of what the world or situational environment is like to people who have learned to see, think, hear, speak, and act in ways that are different from those of the researcher. Examples of research situations may include small isolated communities, group treatment centers, prisons, ethnic neighborhoods, and halfway houses. The process begins with questions and observations that address who, what, when, how, where, and why of the social situation being examined. The data collection part of field work is done by the researcher through participant observation and is recorded in field notes or a field work journal. Field notes are a record of the objective observations of the researcher in the language of the subjects or of the researcher. A field work journal is a subjective record of the problems, ideas, experiences, confusions, and feelings that arise during field work.

According to Spradley, information is obtained through five types of participant observation, which range from low to high degrees of worker involvement.[12] The five types of participant observation are (1) nonparticipation, (2) passive participation, (3) moderate participation, (4) active participation, and (5) complete participation.

The two most effective methods for analyzing ethnographic data are comprehensive content analysis and ethnographic narrative accounts. *Comprehensive content analysis* involves coding and categorizing "to reinforce the hypotheses or themes developed during the data-collection phase and generate new hypotheses and themes previously unrealized—in short, to ground themes and hypotheses to the data."[13] Spradley uses the inductive content method in his proposed four levels of analysis for field work data:

> *Domain analysis* seeks to recognize a category of cultural meaning that includes other smaller categories. The cultural categories are made up of three basic elements: a *cover term*, the *semantic relationship*, and *included terms*.
>
> *Taxonomic analysis* shows more of the relationships among the things *inside* the cultural domain. This type of analysis clarifies the way cultural domains are organized.
>
> *Componential analysis* searches for the attributes (components of meaning) of terms in each domain. It seeks contrasts and differences among terms, e.g., fruit may be oranges, apples, grapes, bananas, tomatoes, and so on.
>
> *Theme analysis* searches for the relationships among domains and examines their linkage to the cultural scene as a whole.[14]

To utilize *ethnographic narrative accounts* the researcher "must demonstrate various topics and patterns by presenting appropriate (and often lengthy) narrative textual accounts from the field notes."[15]

Writing an ethnography, a report of the research findings, is the final step in this research method. Written in an open-ended and exploratory manner, an ethnography is intended to create questions that can be answered by more traditional, quantitative research methods.

### Historical Research

In recent years, historical research has received less attention than ethnography or the quantitative methods. Many human service professionals believe the past is gone and no longer of any importance in our present scientific era. Other professionals see historical research as a way of enlarging their world of experiences and of developing an appreciation of and more insight into change and one's ability to change. They believe that a synthesis of knowledge about the past may help them make decisions about current problems with greater efficiency. Historical research, consequently, can help advanced generalists make informed decisions in context and become efficient problem solvers.

The purpose of historical research is to reconstruct the past systematically and objectively by collecting, evaluating, verifying, and synthesizing evidence to establish facts and reach defensible conclusions, often in relation to particular hypotheses.[16] It depends on data observed by others rather than by the researchers. Good data result from strong detective work that analyzes the authenticity, accuracy, and importance of source materials. One is incorrect to see historical research as easy. Much work claiming to be historical research is only an undisciplined collection of inappropriate, unreliable, and biased information.

Beginning researchers occasionally see little difference between historical research and the literature reviews that precede other forms of research. Indeed, some similarity exists with "reviews of the literature," but the historical approach is more exhaustive and involves seeking out information from a larger array of sources, tracking information that is much older than required by most reviews, and seeking unpublished materials not cited in standard references.

When undertaking historical research, the researcher engages in some activities that are common to all investigations. The activities include those described in the following paragraphs.

*Formulating the Problem*    Some event, development, or experience of the past is questioned. Typical concerns for investigation are stresses associated with scientific, political, or economic change such as the Great Depression, farm subsidies, the settlement house movement, international health initiatives, medical research in the area of AIDS, smallpox, and so on.

*Collecting Source Materials*    Historical research depends upon two kinds of data. *Primary sources* are those where the author is a direct observer of the recorded event. *Secondary sources* are those where the author is reporting the observations of others and is one or more times removed from the original event. *Records and remains* are another dimension of data useful to historical researchers. Records are source materials "that have been preserved with the conscious intent of transmitting information," i.e., legislative, judicial, or executive documents, newspapers, minutes of committees, etc.[17] Remains or relics "are handed down from the past without the specific intent of imparting facts or information".[18] Records and remains of the investigated period may be either primary or secondary sources and are sought as illuminating information or corroborating data. Primary sources carry more authority than secondary sources and have priority in data collection.

*Location of Source Materials*    The search for resources must be exhaustive and thorough, often requiring travel to the site of special collections or to the actual site being investigated.

*Criticizing Source Materials*    Two basic forms of criticism determine the value of the data. *External* criticism confirms the authenticity of the document; *internal* criticism examines the accuracy and relevancy of the document. The critical evaluation of the data is what makes true historical research so rigorous—in many ways more demanding than experimental methods.[19]

*Formulating Hypotheses*    Researchers formulate tentative hypotheses that explain the occurrence of events or conditions. They seek hidden connections, underlying patterns, and so on, that explain or describe the structural interrelations and/or phenomena under study. Examples of patterns or themes used by researchers to interpret historical events include:

> "Empathy theory" holds that the best way to understand the past is to get at the purposes in the minds of people in the past through the historian's own intuitive feelings and understandings. The "great man" theory . . . holds that important events or changes are caused by the presence, absence, or disappearance of forceful historical personalities. The "common man" theory holds that the average person of the age provides the best key to an understanding of past events. Some [researchers] hold that past events can best be explained from a theological view, within the context of the divine plan for creation and from the standpoint of the eternal.[20]

Still others researchers have proposed that economics, laws, or wars are the central themes that influence history and have used these ideological frameworks to interpret history.

*Reporting the Findings*    The final report is a well-organized report of the investigation. Within the framework of the hypothesis, data are patterned in some systematic order, i.e., chronological, topical, or a combination of these, to support or refute the researcher's hypothesis.[21]

### Interviewing

Interviewing is a method of data gathering that has many applications in advanced generalist social work research. Indeed, interviewing for the collection of data often comes quite naturally for most social work researchers. Social workers use interviewing to obtain information during the engagement and assessment processes of the generalist method and during case management, but there are differences between helping or treatment interviews and interviews conducted for research.[22]

Yegidis and Weinbach propose a standard protocol that researchers follow in the planning and implementation of research interviewing that involves the following steps:

1. *Develop an interview schedule,* including pilot testing of the instrument and conditions under which it is administered. Make revisions, as needed.
2. *Train interviewers,* or, if the researcher is to conduct all interviews, carefully think through and plan interviewing procedures.
3. *Select the sample* of subjects for study.
4. *Contact subjects* to gain permission to be interviewed.
5. *Schedule interviews* with research subjects.
6. *Conduct research interviews.*
7. *Check recorded data* for accuracy and completeness.
8. *Debrief subjects,* if required.
9. *Analyze data.*
10. *Write up and disseminate findings.*[23]

Gorden identified two dimensions of types of interviews: (1) scheduled and nonscheduled or (2) standardized and nonstandardized.[24]

The *standardized interview* is designed to collect precisely the same categories of information from a number of respondents about the same problem; and the answers of all respondents must be comparable and classifiable. Public opinion polls are prime examples of standardized interviews because every person is asked the same questions so that statements can be tabulated to reflect how many or what percent of the sample responded in a certain way to a specific question.

In contrast, the *nonstandardized interview* does not pose all of the same questions to all respondents, and there is no way the information can be statistically summarized to reflect the aggregate response of the group or to compare one individual's response with that of another person. An example of this type of interviewing would occur if a researcher were investigating the efficiency within a department of social services. The director/program chief might be asked about salaries. For example, are salaries high enough to attract qualified social workers? Supervisors might be asked about adequate office space and number of interviewing areas. Generalist social workers might be asked about average number and time of field visits per month.

Since the nonstandardized interview is essentially formless, the subtypes exist according to purpose, rather than form. The *preparatory nonstandardized interview* is done in order to prepare a more standardized interview. The researcher is free to explore such things as the vocabulary used by different respondents discussing the topic or to determine the qualitative or quantitative range of answers to establish reliable and valid answer categories. The *independent nonstandardized interview* is not preparatory to any standardized interview but has an independent function of its own. It is used in situations where there is no need either to compare one set of responses with another or to summarize the responses of a sample of respondents.[25] Neither type of nonstandardized interview is ever used in public polling or any other study where one needs to measure some attribute of each individual in a sample.

"The second dimension of a typology of interviews is the dichotomy between scheduled and nonscheduled interviews."[26] *Scheduled interviews* not only specify the questions in advance, they also use the same number of questions, with the same wording and in the same sequence, with each respondent. The degree of scheduling can vary. Interviews may be highly scheduled, as described above, moderately scheduled, or nonscheduled. The *nonscheduled interview* gives the interviewer some choice as to the order of the questions, freedom to attempt alternative wordings of the same question, and freedom to use neutral probes if the first response to a question is not clear, complete, or relevant. To keep within the requirements of a standardized interview, the nonscheduled interviewer must either initially record the responses on a standardized form or reduce the free flow of information to a standard form later by the process of content analysis. The content analysis allows comparison and statistical analysis of collected information.

*Advantages/Disadvantages of Research Interviews*  While interviews allow skilled researchers to collect data from respondents who might be unable to complete written data collection instruments, interviews have other important advantages. These include the following: (1) Interviews provide the researcher with an opportunity to probe and initiate discussions that allow subjects the opportunity to expand their responses and provide more in-depth information. This is especially important for exploratory research and attitudinal research, where it is important that researchers understand specific points and origins of attitudes. (2) Interviews permit the investigator to secure a high rate of completed returns. Few subjects agree to participate in interviews who do not complete them. (3) In-person interviews allow researchers to observe subjects' nonverbal behaviors while they are responding to questions. Nonverbal behaviors can indicate ease in responding, truthfulness in answering questions, and attitude about the interview.

On the other hand, there are three disadvantages of research interviewing: (1) It is impossible to eliminate the influence of the interviewer on subjects' responses in data gathering. How questions are posed, the interviewer's vocal inflections, the interviewer's appearance, and so on, all influence respondents; the amount of influence should be addressed and minimized as much as possible. (2) There is the potential for recording errors during interviews. Respondents may provide truthful information, but if data are forgotten, distorted or misinterpreted by the researcher, data may be sacrificed. (3) The final disadvantage of interviewing is the expense associated with this method of data collection. Interviewing can involve enormous amounts of time, salaries of interviewers, training costs, travel and related expenses, and telephone costs.

## QUANTITATIVE RESEARCH METHODS

Quantitative research is more familiar to all social workers. It is the type of research traditionally taught in undergraduate and graduate social work programs; it is also the type of research most often reported in newspapers and scholarly journals. Quantitative research involves a set of problem-solving activities; it is concerned with counting, measurement, and precision. Rubin and Babbie define quantitative analysis as "the numerical representation and manipulation of observations for the purpose of describing and explaining the phenomena that those observations reflect."[27] Stated another way, quantitative research methods describe and/or explain in numerical form what society wishes to confirm, reject, or better understand. There are several quantitative models of inquiry, and how a researcher determines which quantitative design to use is an important concern that must be addressed early on when planning a research project.

Researchers have different opinions about which factors influence one's choice of research design. Reid and Kidder supported the ideas of Selltiz, Wrightsman, and Cook, who proposed that research design is determined by the particular functions that the research will serve in knowledge building, e.g., exploratory, measurement, description, or explanatory.[28] Yegidis and Weinbach theorize that when there is little research information about a problem, i.e., there are many more questions than answers, decisions about which design to use are clear.[29] They suggest that group research designs "can be placed in a continuum reflecting the sequence in which they occur over time to build knowledge about a problem and its possible solution."[30] Although there are exceptions, Yegidis and Weinbach suggest that exploratory research designs are supposed to occur first and form a basis for descriptive designs. Descriptive designs precede explanatory ones, and explanatory research forms a basis for experiments.[31]

Following the analogy of human developmental theorists, researchers must develop or build a sufficient body of knowledge at each level (exploratory, descriptive, explanatory, experimental) before proceeding to the next level of research design.

Monette, Sullivan, and DeJong propose that "research in the human services focuses on one or more of the following goals: description, prediction, explanation, or evaluation.[32] Adams and Schvaneveldt identify two research designs, exploratory and descriptive, and note that the purpose or intent of a study defines the kind of research design that should be utilized.[33] Similarly, Babbie and Rubin and Babbie discuss three commonly accepted and useful purposes of scientific inquiry—exploration, description, and explanation[34] Either purpose or function can be a useful way to describe studies, but neither singularly constitutes a clear-cut basis for determining research designs. Most studies perform more than one function or address more than one purpose. Researchers rarely think in terms of exploring or explaining or describing a concern, but are more likely to see the purpose of a study as acquiring information or answering questions or testing hypotheses. Limiting a study to one function or one purpose may promote insensitivity on the parts of both researchers and consumers to other functions of a study.[35]

Two other concerns that affect a quantitative study's design are time and the lack of absolute control of samples or variables (quasi-experimental).

The remainder of this section presents the behavioral research sequence and, using an eclectic theoretical framework, examines the research designs most frequently found within the three major dimensions for quantitative models: (1) purpose or goal, (2) time, and (3) quasi-experimental designs.

### *Behavioral Research Sequence*

The sequence steps in social science research are systematic and procedural and are used in all types of quantitative research. The steps follow the scientific method; they also parallel the six-stage problem-solving paradigm of generalist practice as indicated parenthetically. Although the number of steps may vary, the essential activities remain constant. They include:

A. Define a research issue or problem (*Engagement*)
B. Undertake a thorough review of the literature available (*Data Collection*)
C. Formulate hypothesis(es). (*Assessment*)
D. Formulate the research methodology. (*Assessment*)
   1. Operationalize definitions in measureable, behavioral terms.
   2. Select an appropriate research design.

3. Identify the study population.
4. Select the research sample.
5. Design and validate the research instrument(s).

E. Collect data. (*Intervention*)

F. Analyze data. (*Evaluation*)

G. Determine conclusions based on analysis (es).

H. Write the research report using an accepted writing format, e.g., American Psychological Association (APA) (*Termination*).

### Purpose- or Function-Focused Research

*Exploratory Research*   The objective of exploratory research is to lay the groundwork for other knowledge building. Utilizing this design, a researcher explores that which is important about a problem and then describes it clearly and accurately.[36] Exploratory designs are based on the assumption that much more information is needed about a topic in order to begin to understand it. This formative design is used when the investigator may be unclear about which or how many variables relate to the problem being studied. In fact, two products of exploratory designs are the identification of variables relevant to the research and the development of a list of priority topics for future research.[37]

A goal of exploratory designs is to learn as much as possible about a problem or question. The studies seek to conceptualize broad constructs, to illuminate the forms the constructs may take, to identify their components, and to identify recurring relationships and variables.

Exploratory designs do not test hypotheses; they generate hypotheses that can be tested in later, more rigorous investigations. The design often is used because of small sample size, which limits the representativeness of the results. However, exploratory studies are very valuable to advanced generalists because such studies help the practitioner-researcher examine "new interest[s], when the subject of study is relatively new and unstudied, or when a researcher seeks to test the feasibility of undertaking a more careful study or wants to develop the methods to be used in a more careful study."[38] Exploratory research requires a sense of purpose and flexibility. It encourages ingenuity and cleverness by researchers to devise ways to acquire the greatest degree of understanding about the research problem with the least expenditure of resources.[39]

*Descriptive Research*   Once sufficient insights and useful information have been obtained about a problem, descriptive research can be undertaken. Descriptive research seeks to address the question, "what exists," i.e., what is the present status of a phenomenon. This type of quantitative research systematically describes the facts and characteristics of a given population or area of interest, factually and accurately. Its "main goal is to portray an accurate profile of persons, events, or objects."[40] Public opinion surveys during elections, community surveys about proposed improvements, and test score results are examples of descriptive research.

Descriptive research is sometimes called survey research. It focuses on events that are in process or have already taken place. Using a schedule or list of questions, survey research is the accumulation of a data base that is solely descriptive. But, descriptive designs involve more than merely gathering and analyzing data. They involve interpretation, contrast, classification, and integration of findings. They do not necessarily seek to explain relationships, test hypotheses, make predictions, or clarify meanings or make implications, although they can support these purposes.

The quality of a descriptive study, i.e., its validity and reliability, and the generalizability (size and representativeness of the sample) of the study's results are important concerns of descriptive researchers. Descriptive studies can be broad or narrow in scope. They can use verbal descriptions or numerical descriptions. Verbal descriptions require that the investigator use the right words and a clear writing style to establish validity. Numerical descriptions obligate the researcher "to present an accurate profile of the situation with descriptive statistics (typically measures of frequency, central tendency, and dispersion)."[41] Descriptive studies make a descriptive assertion about some population, discovering the distribution of certain traits or attributes. The researcher is not concerned with why the observed distribution exists, but merely what the distribution is (e.g., age and sex distributions of the census, attributes about early prisoner release, or sex education in the schools).

*Explanatory Research*   A shift in focus occurs in knowledge building when enough is known about a problem to warrant the use of explanatory designs. "Exploratory and descriptive designs primarily seek understanding of the extent of a problem and factors that are associated with it."[42] Explanatory surveys describe the problem and the population but have the additional objective of asserting why a description is true. It begins the process of identifying and understanding the causes of a problem and projecting what can be done to resolve it. Explanatory research designs test hypotheses to identify relationships among and between specific variables, which have been identified through previously conducted exploratory and descriptive research. Care is taken to control the influence of intervening variables and to ensure that the samples are representative in order to generalize the study's findings. This type of research uses statistical analysis to test hypotheses, and almost always requires multivariate analysis—the simultaneous examination of two or more variables—to determine the significance of its results.

Occasionally, psychologists and sociologists conduct "basic (or pure) research" because their immediate purposes are to advance factual knowledge of human behavior with minimal concern for practical benefits.[43] Explanatory research by advanced generalists is more likely to be "applied research" because it is "designed with a practical outcome in mind and with the assumption that some group or society as a whole will gain specific benefits from research."[44] This type of study seeks to ascertain *why* persons who have been abused are more likely to become perpetrators of abuse, *why* some people are unemployed and others are not, *why* some parolees return to prison and others do not.

> Explanatory research seeks to identify relationships that exist between variables, but it does it within certain methodological limitations. Specifically, it does not introduce the presence of independent variables; it studies their possible effects ex post facto (after the fact). It tries to reconstruct what happened and to understand how and why it happened, but it does not make it happen.[45]

*Experimental Research*   A researcher wishes to investigate the effects of a drug counseling program on the attitudes of convicted drug offenders in Anytown, U.S.A. Another researcher, an advanced generalist, wishes to investigate the effects of two methods of counseling intervention with truant students in two junior high schools in a rural district. A third researcher, an advanced generalist practitioner, seeks to learn the impact of a newly adopted computer software package among a state's mental health agencies. The three researchers plan to use experimental research designs involving randomly selected experimental groups and control groups. They devise strategies that insure that the nine steps of the social science research sequence are employed to provide thorough, systematic, and defensible products.

Experimental designs require rigorous and methodical management of experimental (independent, intervening, dependent) variables and conditions either by direct control/manipulation or through randomization. Typically a control group is used as a baseline against which the behaviors of the group receiving treatment are compared. The first objective of this quantitative methodology is *internal validity,* or determining if the experimental manipulation in the study really makes a difference. The second objective is *external validity,* or determining how representative the findings are and if the results can be generalized to similar subjects in similar situations.[46]

Although desired by most researchers, *true* experimental research is extremely difficult for human service workers. Experimental research seeks to investigate possible cause and effect relationships by exposing one or more experimental groups to one or more treatment conditions and comparing the results to one or more control groups not receiving the treatment. In experimental design, all variables are held constant except a single treatment variable that is deliberately manipulated or allowed to vary. Denying potentially helpful treatment to members of a control group raises important ethical issues for advanced generalist practitioners. The need to deny treatment (independent variable) to control group members is but one reason many advanced generalists have elected to use quasi-experimental methods, which will be presented in the next section.

While the experimental approach is the most powerful design because of the control it allows over relevant variables, it is also the most restrictive and artificial. The restrictiveness and artificiality are major weaknesses in applications involving human subjects in "real world" situations, since human beings often act differently if their behavior is artificially restricted, manipulated, or exposed to systematic observation and evaluation.[47]

Purpose- or function-focused research efforts, like other quantitative investigations, follow the social science research sequence presented earlier in this chapter. Data are analyzed using measures of central tendency (arithmetic mean, mode, or median), measures of association (chi-square, lambda, Pearson's $r$ or Yules $Q$), and tests of statistical significance ($t$-test or test of variance) to illustrate the strength of the relationships identified by the data. Upon completion of appropriate analytical tests and measures, an objective report of the study's results is written using an acceptable writing format, such as that of the American Psychological Association.

### Time Dimension

The time dimension examines interrelationships of phenomena and changes that take place as a function of time. This dimension allows advanced generalists to investigate patterns and sequences of growth and/or change as related to time. This type of quantitative research focuses on the study of variables and their development over a period of hours, days, months, or years. It asks, "What are the patterns of growth, their rates, their sequences, their directions, and the interrelated factors affecting these characteristics."[48]

There are two major categories of quantitative studies that are defined in relation to time: cross sectional studies and longitudinal studies. A *cross-sectional* study is one that is based on data collected at one point in time from a sample selected to describe some larger population at that time. Cross sectional studies have been called snapshot studies because theoretically all variables are measured simultaneously or as close in time as possible. They are both cheaper and faster to complete than longitudinal studies. Examples of cross sectional studies can include a study of the unemployment rate at a particular time or a study of the relationship between completion of high school and success.

A *longitudinal* study design involves the collection of data at different points in time; it uses multiple measurements of the same variable(s). Data, collected at different points in time, are analyzed and used by the researcher to report changes in descriptions and explanations based on the documented differences.

There are three types of longitudinal studies: trend studies, cohort studies, and panel studies. *Trend* studies draw a sample of subjects on several different occasions from a group of potential subjects that tend to vary in composition over time. For example, a study of social workers' salaries conducted over five years would be a trend study if salaries of masters level social workers new to the field were surveyed each year. The investigator would learn if there were a change (trend) toward higher or lower salaries over the five-year span. *Cohort* studies involve a population of potential research subjects that does not change, but the cases selected for study may differ during stages of data collection. Using the same example of social workers' salaries, investigators could annually survey the masters of social work (MSW) class of 1994 to learn how salaries change between 1994 and 1999. The population, 1994 MSW graduates, would remain constant, but individual subjects might differ over the five-year period. *Panel* studies use the exact same group of research subjects over time, with sample changes resulting only from attrition.[49] In the earlier example of social workers' salaries, each of the 60 members of the 1994 MSW class from a particular university (panel) would be surveyed annually for five years. The investigator would learn how salaries changed among this specific group of MSW graduates.

Illustration of patterns is the most obvious advantage of longitudinal research. Expense, loss of subjects, and study coordination are clear disadvantages of longitudinal research.

### Quasi-Experimental Research

Most studies of social issues such as delinquency, domestic violence, smoking, and client satisfaction concerns, where strict control and manipulation are not always feasible, are appropriate topics for quasi-experimental research. This quantitative design seeks to approximate the conditions of the true experiment in a setting that does not allow the strict control and/or manipulation of *all* relevant variables e.g., antecedent variables or intervening variables.

Often it is impossible or impractical to randomly assign subjects to experimental and control groups to test hypotheses. Experimental research, which requires the deprivation of an intervention to a randomly selected control group, is sometimes considered unethical, fiscally undesirable, or prejudicial to certain clients by practitioners, administrators, or consumers. Additionally, opportunities to randomly designate service recipients as control or experimental group members rarely occur within the clinical arena. Practitioners and administrators have been encouraged to create and implement alternative research designs that are congruent with social work ethics and that provide medium support for causal inferences, but recognizably have less external validity than experimental research. This creative alternative is commonly called quasi-experimental research, and its most obvious deviance from experimental research is the absence of a randomly assigned control group. The process steps of quasi-experimental research are the same as those previously described for true experimental research.

There are two commonly used types of quasi-experimental research: nonequivalent control group and single subject design. A *nonequivalent control group* design involves the use of an already existing "control group" that is similar to but has not been randomly selected from a common pool with the experimental group. The nonequivalent control group typically is called a "comparison" group and functions as a control group in comparing the effect of practice strategies.[50] An example illustrates the appeal of this design for the advanced generalist practitioner. Consider for a moment a MSW program that offers two sections of a research course in its curriculum. Students in the two sections, which are taught by two different professors, are similar in age, ethnicity, physiological functioning, overall grade point average, socioeconomic status, and so on. The professor in section A decides to initiate weekly computer laboratory sessions throughout the semester to reduce students' anxiety about using computers. The professor in section B does not schedule weekly activities in the computer laboratory, but instead continues the practice of recent years (i.e., scheduling three sessions in the lab during the last month of school). The independent variable in the example is the weekly computer laboratory sessions experienced by section A. The instructors agree to examine student anxiety (dependent variable) about computer use through a pretest-posttest of the experimental group (A) and the comparison group (B).

*Time series/single subject design,* the more popular type of quasi-experimental research, is particularly appealing to generalist and advanced generalist social work practice because it is relatively uncomplicated and may be conducted within the context of a case record, a program's clientele, a hospital wing, or an entire wing, or an entire system. Time series designs are studies of processes occurring over time, specifically ascertaining the effectiveness of some phenomenon. Single subject designs apply the logic of time series design to the evaluation of the impact of an intervention or policy change on individual cases or systems. It is important to note that single subject research can only examine the relationship between *one* type of intervention and changes in *one* type of behavior; the researcher must be able to specify exactly what change was sought and what single method was used to attain it. These methods involve obtaining repeated measures of a client system with regard to particular outcome indicators of a target problem.[51]

> The assumption underlying the use of single subject research designs is that if the intervention makes a difference, [one] should be able to demonstrate that the presence or absence of intervention will produce measurably different results. The behavior that is the target of the intervention should fluctuate when the intervention is introduced or removed, or shortly thereafter.[52]

The phase of repeated measures that occurs before the intervention is introduced is called the *baseline* or "A" phase. The baseline data serve as the control phase or dependent variable of the study. Data collected during the baseline (control) phase are compared with data collected during the intervention (experimental or "B") phase and later. The researcher looks for shifts in trends or patterns in the dependent variable that can be attributed to the intervention. The four most common types of measurement of the target population are the following:

1. Frequency: the number of times a subject exhibits a behavior
2. Interval: the measured lengths of time between a given behavior
3. Duration: the length of time that a given behavior lasts
4. Magnitude: the degree of severity of a given behavior

"Single subject research design consists of one or more pre-planned baseline (A) phases and one or more treatment (B) phases."[53] These phases are mixed and sequenced differently given the stated purpose of the study. Some common design alternative are AB design, ABA design, ABAB design, BAB design, ABCD design, and Multiple Baseline design.

The researcher plots the data on a histogram and looks for distinct visual patterns, which can be termed increasing, decreasing, flat, cyclical, or unstable, depending on the trends displayed by the target population. Undergraduate level generalist social workers examine the effectiveness of interventions in their practices. Advanced generalists also are concerned with intervention effectiveness, but they may be more concerned with program effectiveness, agency change, and broader system changes.

## *PROGRAM EVALUATION*

Stufflebeam distinguished evaluation from research by suggesting that the purpose of evaluation is to *improve,* not to *prove.*[54] More recently, Rutman, as cited in Monette, Sullivan, and DeJong, described program evaluation as "the use of scientific research techniques to assess the results of a program and evaluate whether the program as currently designed achieves its stated goals."[55] Still more recently, Hornick and Burrows defined evaluation as "the systematic study of the operation of social action, treatment, or intervention programs and their impact."[56] The stated definitions illuminate the basic difference between research and evaluation. Evaluation focuses on service delivery or mission accomplishment. Its purpose is to provide feedback leading to a successful outcome defined in practical, concrete terms. Evaluation has functioned informally since the beginning of time. A more formal version coincided with the advent of the computer and gave rise to the development of man-machine systems in the 1950s and to today's "systems approach."[57]

> The focus on *improving* service delivery suggests that: a judgment must be made regarding what constitutes worth or value. . . . The term evaluation typically is associated with how effective or ineffective, how adequate or inadequate, how good or bad, how valuable or invaluable, and how appropriate or inappropriate a given action, process, or product is in terms of the perceptions of the individual who makes use of information provided by an investigator.[58]

The steps of program evaluation can be identified as the following:

1. Identify and rank the goals of the program.
2. Devise measures and measurement instruments to describe progress toward these goals.
3. Identify the target group or recipient of services.
4. Specify the nontarget groups or control groups.
5. After the program has begun, using measurement instruments, measure the program's effects on the target and nontarget groups over as long a period as possible.
6. Identify and measure the direct costs of the program.
7. Identify and measure the indirect costs of the program.
8. Draw conclusions (effectiveness, efficiency, and so on).
9. Write a report describing items 1–8.[59]

As presented, program evaluation is a complex process involving many steps and considerations, but more simply stated, it merely involves (1) deciding what objectives are to be accomplished, (2) determining how they will be accomplished, and then (3) finding out whether, in fact, they were accomplished.

In the "real" world of agency or institution operation, program evaluation most often manifests itself in one of two ways: (1) accountability and (2) feedback. *Accountability* can be an activity of the funding monitor who checks the client records, service frequencies, and the books to determine whether or not there is an acceptable balance across the original expectations, final accomplishments, and associated cost-effectiveness considerations. *Feedback* is analogous to the agency supervisor skillfully conveying information that shapes and refines the performance of an individual or a department toward continuing improvement.

### Purpose of Evaluation

Numerous models of program evaluation have been developed, and many are discipline specific. Rubin and Babbie identify three broad purposes of social work program evaluation:

1. To assess information needed in program planning and development. This purpose is addressed through formative evaluation, which provides information through a needs assessment that is useful in planning a program.
2. To assess problems in how programs are being implemented. This also is determined through formative evaluation, which obtains information that is helpful in improving its implementation.
3. To assess the ultimate success of a program. Ultimate success is determined through summative evaluations, which are concerned with decisions about whether a program should be continued or even begun initially from among several alternatives.[60]

Evaluating the need for programs is most frequently performed through a needs assessment. A needs assessment typically defines the problem of concern, describes the actual and desired conditions, identifies unmet needs, and diagnoses the obstacles that prevent needs from being met and opportunities from being used.[61] The advanced generalist is a natural for conducting a needs assessment because of the skills required, which include:

1. The ability to process vast amounts of often conflicting information drawn from many sources and to perceive the total picture accurately
2. The services of a researcher who knows how to gather information from a variety of sources using different methods
3. Someone who knows and understands the behavior of individuals, communities, and other social systems
4. A researcher who understands the political processes that affect the success of social programs and services.[62]

Evaluating program implementation involves obtaining information about the program's functioning, to determine it if is operating as it was intended to operate. Sometimes called process evaluations, these evaluations seek to generate suggestions for improving the program and most often produce three kinds of information:

1. Information designed to help program planners learn about he management of program activities
2. Documentation that the program is operating
3. Information about defects in the program's design and unintended and undesirable results of the program.[63]

Evaluating program outcomes involves determining whether a program achieved its objectives and satisfied its mission.

> This kind of evaluation often involves a dual-focused emphasis on program effectiveness (achievement of objectives) and program efficiency (the relationship of outcome to expenditure of efforts and resources). Examining either one of these criteria independent of the other would provide insufficient information to program decision makers. A program may be achieving all of its objectives but at an extremely high price. Or, a program may be only marginally achieving objectives at a much lower cost.[64]

Advanced generalist social workers, who function as program evaluators, typically are required to assess the following activities: client gains and losses, the coincidental effects/consequences of the program, and the social, psychological, and economic costs of operating the program. Such activities necessitate that they rely on the knowledge, skills, and values of their profession.

Periodically social workers may be called upon to conduct three other types of program evaluation that have very specific uses. Although frequently criticized, cost-benefit analysis, analysis of program impact, and analysis of program structure continue in use as evaluation methods.

1. Cost benefit analysis attempts to identify the pluses of a program, both tangible and intangible, and the direct and indirect costs of conducting the program. It seeks to identify the return that society reaps from its investment in a program in the form of a ratio of benefits to costs. Critics note that results of social programs may not be immediately evident or may be impossible to quantify.

2. An analysis of program impact seeks to determine if programs have resulted in permanent desirable change. Data for this analysis are pulled from program outcome studies and must be carefully presented, for advanced generalists are aware that many intervening variables may influence the outcomes of long-term programs.

3. Analyses of program structure examine outcome measures in relationship to the education of its personnel, the absence/presence of particular desirable equipment, the range of services offered, the amenities of the work environment, and so on. Analysis of program structure evaluations have been criticized for excessive use of program resources to upgrade the area that are the focus of these evaluations, while neglecting other important program areas.[65]

### Determining Who Conducts Program Evaluation

One of the critical concerns in program evaluation is determining who will conduct it. Below is a list of acceptable evaluators ranked in order of preference by agencies/programs:

1. Agencies and their clients prefer that evaluation be done by the agency or by an organizational representative of its clients. This source is most likely to produce favorable results.

2. Agencies can contract with a private firm for an "outside" evaluation. Any firm that seeks a continuing relationship with the contracting agency or any other agency will rarely produce a totally negative evaluation.

3. Agency and program administrators and staff believe that total outsiders may not understand their work or their clients' or patients' problems. For that reason they fear evaluation conducted by an outside, independent office such as the Congressional Budget Office, the General Accounting Office, state human service office, or a state treasurer's office.[66]

Recognizing that even under the best circumstances, some negatives can surface during an evaluation, it is most helpful for all personnel to be clear and creative about program goals, short- and long-range effects of the programs, limitations of the research design, and possible bias on the part of the evaluators.

### Common Ways of Performing Program Evaluation

Government agencies that provide funding for many human service, health, and mental health initiatives make an effort to assess the utility of their expenditures. Many private local programs do the same. These efforts take one or more of the following forms according to DiNitto and Dye:

*Public Hearings*   The most common type of program review is through public hearings. Agency administrators, interested community persons, and program recipients frequently are encouraged by legislative committees to provide formal or informal testimony about the accomplishments of their programs. The program's "annual reports" are shared with legislators and interested citizens as "public information" during the hearings. Reports from program administrators and client testimonials are not as effective as objective forms of evaluation because they tend to minimize the costs of programs and magnify the benefits. Public hearings as a type of evaluation occur most often near budget time.

*Site Visits*   Site visits or field visits frequently are made to agencies or programs by legislators, federal and/or state officials, and/or expert consultants (or any combination of the three groups) to get a *first-hand view* of the program being evaluated. Members of these teams interview inmates/clients and workers, observe agency operation, and occasionally review client records. They develop impressions about fluidity of activities, competency of staffs, and satisfaction of recipients with program services.

*Program Measures*   Information developed by agencies generally describes program measures, which can include the number of recipients of program services, the number of beds available, the number of persons treated, and so on. The numbers are program measures; they are informative, but they do not indicate their *impact* on the service community. The numbers do not show the problems encountered by sexually abused children in adulthood or the conditions of life confronting the aged and the disabled.

*Comparison with Professional Standards*   Some professional associations have developed their own set of "ideal" standards of services and benefits. For example, the National Association of Social Workers (NASW) may have determined the maximum number of cases a worker can handle effectively or developed a salary guide citing average incomes for workers based on education and experience. Actual program statistics can be compared with these ideal standards. Such standards focus on the ideal, not on real service delivery or on conditions that may exist in some of our smaller or larger communities or on the impact of program activities on its target and nontarget groups.

*Formal Designs*   Experimental, quasi-experimental, and single-subject/ time series research designs are the most objective methods for evaluating policies and programs. The three strategies, as previously noted, use an experimental group and a control group or baseline, which are similar in every way except the intervention or service has been applied only to the experimental group. As presented in the previous discussions of the three strategies, differences after the intervention are carefully measured and changes in the experimental group are compared with changes in the control group or baseline data. These traditional methods allow researchers to estimate changes that can be directly attributed to helping programs.[67]

## INFORMATION TECHNOLOGY

Advanced generalists researchers, as researchers from other disciplines, have come to depend on information technology as provided by computers to conduct investigations. Information technology is especially important to researchers for two activities: information retrieval and data analysis.

Since the mid-1970s, researchers have been able to conduct bibliographic searches utilizing computers. This innovation allowed efficient and sophisticated searches of the literature catalogued in a number of national and international data bases to be conducted within university libraries and public libraries or with personal computer terminals. Data obtained through computer searches greatly reduced the time and effort required to develop a thorough list of references for a research effort.

> The computerized data bases . . . are frequently the computerized counterpart of printed indexes and abstracting services. Many of these indexes and abstracting services are prepared for machine use in original format. Other data bases are constructed from the printed copies, and the information is then adapted and loaded onto magnetic tapes (microfilm, microfiche) which then may be accessed from computer terminals with the aid of a librarian.[68]

Library staff are available and will explain which indexes and abstracts can be accessed, the foci and capacities of the different indexes, how to identify key terms to access data, costs of searches, and so on. This is information that can prove invaluable for advanced generalist social workers, who see research as a necessary part of their professional presence.

After data have been collected and coded, the advanced generalist researcher uses the computer in a different way. He/she uses either a mainframe computer available in most universities and large organizations or a personal computer capable of analyzing massive amounts of data. The advanced generalist enters the coded information into a computer statistical software program for analysis. The data necessarily *must be checked for accuracy* after it has been entered into the software program to ensure the correctness of the results. There are numerous statistical software programs, but five of the more commonly chosen ones for personal computers include SPSS[X] and SAS, for IBM formatted computers, and SYSTAT, JMP-IN, and Statview-SE for Macintosh computers.

> Once data have been entered into a computer hundreds of different statistical analyses can be performed in a matter of seconds. The researcher can quickly and painlessly apply many different types of complicated mathematical computa-

tions. Statistical tests that would have been outside the mathematical competence of many researchers . . . are now possible for anyone with reasonable competence in the use of personal computers.[69]

If a computer is used to analyze data, the advanced generalist will need to exercise care in choosing the correct statistical test. Decisions about statistical
tests rest upon three concerns: independent or related sampling, number and
type (independent/dependent) of variables, and levels of measurement for
each variable. After these concerns have been addressed completely, one is
more likely to pick an appropriate statistical package for data analysis.

A computer does not solve all of a researcher's problems, however. It
does not tell a researcher if a specific statistical analysis has been used correctly; it cannot ensure that a researcher is able to interpret the results of the
analysis correctly and apply the results appropriately to the hypothesis or research question; and it does not automatically develop sophisticated presentations of data. Effective use of the computer requires that the advanced generalist practitioner be computer literate and able to use the computer as an
information processing tool.

## TYPICAL STUDIES IN THE CONCEPTUAL AREAS
## OF ADVANCED GENERALIST PRACTICE

This chapter has focused on advanced research and technology for advanced generalist practice. The ideas and tools identified may be applied to complex situations involving multiple theories and geographic locations. The central concepts
that characterize advanced generalist practice, such as international social work
and welfare, advanced theories and intervention models, advanced general
method, and ethical decision making, are fertile areas for research in advanced
generalist practice. In the final section of this chapter, typical research efforts are
described that reflect the advanced ecological systems perspective and diverse approaches to research found in advanced generalist practice.

### Ethical Decision Making

"The Sibling Who Can Donate—But Doesn't" by Griffin and Bratton
used a hypothetical case situation to present a historical examination and a
thorough review/synthesis of the literature surrounding organ donation, specifically kidney transplantation.[70] Medical research has documented longer
survival for recipients of organs from living-related donors than for recipients
of cadaveric organs.[71] Much social research has addressed the emotional concerns of patients awaiting new organs.[72]

The dilemma confronting a newly wed sister (a near perfect, six-antigen
tissue match) whose husband is adamantly opposed to her donating a kidney

to her brother presents an excellent base from which the advanced generalist can address basic social work concepts. The sister is feeling indescribable pressure from her family of origin, her brother's family, and friends to contribute one kidney and provide her brother a chance for "life." There is pressure from her husband to retain both her kidneys until after the birth of their children, which is known to produce stress on the female urinary system. The authors conclude that the social worker's "real" client is the sister facing the ethical dilemma and not the brother awaiting a transplanted kidney. The potential donor invariably has to face words and concepts like rights, obligations, responsibilities, oughts, interests, and values. The social worker can aid by clarifying issues and supporting any decision made by the sister.

Gains and losses for significant others (including family and medical personnel), for the potential donor, and for the generalist and advanced generalist practitioner are essential considerations for the donor and the social worker. Autonomy, self-determination, informed consent, confidentiality, privacy, moral human rights, freedom, and well-being are issues that are examined in the research.

### International Social Work and Welfare

"Women's Health Care and Related Matters: A Cross-Cultural Perspective in a Social Welfare Context," by P. Gibbs and Y. Kim focused on and analyzed women's health care needs, practices, values, and issues in three countries: the United States, Korea, and Japan,[73] The analysis of health care practices in the three countries provided a foundation for identifying changes that need to be made in health care systems to humanize them and to make them more responsive to women's needs and women's cultures. The research concluded by examining the roles and functions of social workers in the health care arena as they relate to both health care in general and women's health care in particular.

The authors noted that in Korea and the United States, women's overall health and health care are linked to area of residence (urban vs. rural) and to financial status. Both factors relate in an economic way directly to quality of care and availability. Health care in Japan differs because economic factors have less importance in determining whether people are able to receive quality health care. Japan has a national health insurance that provides medical coverage for all its citizens. Yet, given these broad generalizations, overriding cultural values still determine the acceptable alternatives for women's health care, ways for women to seek care, and much of what is unspoken about women's care.

Gibbs and Kim used the conventional model of American health care for women, the traditional-authoritarian health care world, to reflect America's broader societal values. The seven characteristic features of the model provided a base to examine health care in the three countries. (Diagram 7–1).

**DIAGRAM 7-1**    Traditional Authoritarian Health Care Model

1. Woman's health care focuses primarily on reproductive functions, and these normal processes are viewed as illnesses requiring intervention.
2. Women are viewed as essentially family-oriented, and health care applies moral values based on society's stereotyped view of women when dealing with procreative issues such as reproductive freedom and abortion.
3. Women's physical complaints that have an organic origin are often diagnosed as psychogenic conditions of an emotional origin—a view that attributes much of women's distress to difficulties in accepting their stereotypical role in society.
4. Women are subjected to a myriad of iatrogenic (treatment-induced) disorders as a result of contemporary medical intervention—disorders that are often more serious (sometimes even lethal) than the condition that warranted the original intervention.
5. Women are viewed as other than competent adults capable of making health care decisions.
6. Women are expected to acquiesce and relinquish control to the doctor. "Scare tactics" are appropriate means to make women submit to physician authority.
7. Women are treated in myriad ways as impersonal objects by the health care system, all of which violate the universal values of enlightenment.[74]

The authors summarize:

> It seems that women everywhere are vulnerable to the practices of orthodox health care models. The high-tech approach to health care, the methodological and pharmacological experimentation on women, the unnecessary and all too common use of invasive measures, the disease-care focus, the lack of participatory influence, the professional regulation of practices and procedures related to health care, the paucity of solid health care information, the assignment of causality when dysfunction occurs, and the exclusion and rejection of alternative healers are the primary ills that plague the medical establishment, to one extent or another, in all three countries. . . . Korea's health care, in some respects . . . is the most palatable approach to health care, as it is medicalized to a lesser extent and accepts alternative healers. Yet the findings . . . underscore the point that the health care systems in all three countries have an array of problems that warrant a change of agenda.[75]

### *Advanced Theories and Intervention Models*

P. A. Brunson investigated the impact of a reading group on the depression level of a group of chronically mentally ill patients who attended a day treatment program.[76] She hypothesized that the depression levels of subjects (members of a mental health day treatment program in a mid-sized agricultural community) would decrease as a result of participation in the reading group. The researcher used a single subject design (ABA) on the total population of the day hospital. The subjects in this study (n=24) were atypical of their home community in that 67 percent were African-American, they ranged in age from 30–50 years of age, were unemployed, and had attended or graduated from high school.

Demographic data (e.g., race, gender, educational level, number of years unemployed, and age) were obtained from each subject. "In addition, diagnosis for each member was noted as being subsumed under one of three classifications: affective disorder, schizophrenia, and 'other'."[77] The reading group intervention was conducted over an eight-week period for one hour each week between October and December 1991.

The Beck Depression Inventory was administered to participants before and after their participation in the reading group to determine any differences in depression levels.[78] Additionally, a follow-up questionnaire was administered two months after the reading group concluded to ascertain additional information about the impact of the intervention. In the follow-up questionnaire, subjects were asked to rank order their subjective enjoyment of the reading group based on three categories: content of reading material, attributes of the reader herself (caring attitude, and so on), and style of the reader (soothing, animated, and so on). "The purpose of the follow-up study was to detect any change in reading habits a well as to detect the possible presence of the Hawthorne Effect."[79] The Hawthorne Effect refers to changes in the behavior of subjects caused by the presence and attention of researchers.[80]

The *t*-test for paired data was used to determine significance of the results. Frequency distributions were used to analyze responses from the follow-up questionnaire. The results showed no significant decrease in depression in the group's members that could be attributed to participation in the reading group. Findings also revealed that affective disorders were slightly more receptive to the intervention. Also of some importance was the high drop-out rate among the subjects (22%), which suggests a need for further studies of interventions aimed at this population.

The study has obvious limitations in its generalizability, but it does provide an excellent example of advanced generalist research investigating a promising intervention with a small and very difficult group of clients. Knowledge from this study can be used by workers in mental health day treatment centers and by other professionals within the field who seek to learn from the experiences of earlier researchers. The study advances the knowledge base.

### Advanced General Method

In an article, "Adult Day Care Centers and Adult Protective Services," Griffin seeks to determine to what extent adult day care services and adult protective services overlap in meeting the needs of chronically ill adults and to identify how to best meet the sometimes multiple needs of this population.[81] Toward that end, the study examined the presenting problems and progress of five randomly selected adult day care recipients (n = 56) who were admitted to a 19-person social/health adult day care program in rural western Massachusetts between 1985 and 1988. Utilizing a hospital model community-based system of care, adult day care services were available to all adults regardless of their social or economic levels. [82] To provide the hospital's group of services to nonhospitalized adults in the community, cooperative ventures (i.e., hand-shakes, letters of agreement) had been entered into with other health and social service providers, eg., adult protective services, area agency-on-aging–sponsored transportation, home health agencies, and so on.

The five randomly selected subjects presented chronic and ongoing con-cerns that necessitated immediate and competently delivered solutions with long-term capacity. Their presenting problems were typical of other partici-pants in the adult day care program. Each of the five client situations was ex-amined in relation to the presenting problem (i.e., physical and/or mental-emotional disabilities), available social supports, functioning within their immediate environments, level of endangerment, and progress after admis-sion to adult day care. Content analyses were performed on data obtained from adult day care patient records, in which client service utilization and health status data were regularly recorded. These recorded data included daily progress notes and assessments by the program nurse, social worker, physical therapist/occupational therapist/speech therapist, and quarterly assessments by the physician. This type of data, while not completely objective, provided insight into program supports, family supports, and changes in patient func-tioning.

Findings revealed the two programs (adult day care and adult protective services) to be complementary. Specific adult protective service patient prob-lems, e.g., isolation, poor health, mental confusion, depression, and func-tional disabilities, have been handled very effectively in the adult day care set-ting, with the added advantage of providing hand-on daily contact with patients. The findings also raised questions at the indirect level about duplica-tion of effort that exists in the case management process used by many agen-cies. Adult day care, adult protective services, mental health/mental retarda-tion, home health, Medicaid, and so on provided services to the five study subjects; each program was involved in assessment, case planning, arranging for services, follow-up/monitoring, and reassessment, which are the steps of case management. The reader again is reminded of the similarities between the case management process and the General Method (engagement, data collection, assessment, intervention, evaluation, termination). Although all of the agencies professed to be part of a coordinated community long-term health care system, the individual service agencies necessarily repeated case management evaluations for their own third-party reimbursement. They each attended the other's case management meetings as well as their own for the same clients.

The redundancy was clear. The researcher suggested that one joint plan-ning meeting per client convened quarterly or biannually could eliminate four other individual agency meetings about a given client within the same time span. Such a change would reduce service delivery costs, stress of multiple meetings on workers, and stress on service recipients caused by the current duplication efforts. The researcher also proposed that adult day care serve as the coordinating agency for "service" management when their clients were involved. The change was proposed because adult day care has daily contact with both clients and family, necessary physical examination requirements, and an optimal vantage point for observation of patient behavior.

Other "indirect" service provider needs/issues of the subjects, such as evening adult day care, a lack of adult day care programs in many regions of the country, problematic third-party reimbursement, and the tendency for members of adult day care programs to remain in the programs over long periods of time—often until death—were also addressed in the study. This study clearly focuses on the concerns of advanced generalist practitioners about direct and indirect systemic issues.

### Comparative Study: Multiple Theories and Locations

An unpublished study by Allen R. Katz entitled "A Comparative Study of the Allocation of Federal Health Grants and the Politics Surrounding Grant Distribution" provides an excellent example of a complex, comparative study involving diverse theories, policies, and geographic locations.[83] The study examined various theories of distributive allocations of federal monies for health block grants-in-aid to five North Carolina counties/cities with populations in excess of 50,000 persons.

Beginning with a historical overview of grants-in-aid, the researcher also examined the consolidation of 21 categorical programs into four health block grants in the 1980s as Congress sought to shift the decision-making responsibilities for allocations to the states and local communities. The four health block grants—maternal and child health, preventive health and health services, alcohol, drug abuse and mental health, and primary care—also involved spending cuts of approximately one billion dollars that reduced health spending by about 25%.[84] The loss of funding was to be replaced by the states and local communities.

The study, which followed a historical research model, identified four theories of policy distribution: Congressional politics, the political business cycle, bureaucratic politics, and grantsmanship. The investigator sought to determine if any causal relationship(s) existed between the theories of policy distribution and the three special concerns of the study:

1. *Political influence* was seen as positive (p) or negative (n) and was determined by whether the county had voted for the current chief executive (President, governor, and so on) in the last election, whether the county's senators and representatives were members of the majority parties in Congress, and if elected members of Congress were member of any relevant committees.
2. *Community needs* were aggregate numbers determined by Census indicators (numbers of population below the poverty level, per capita income, population

aged 25 and over with a high school education, unemployment rates, families on public assistance, infant mortality rates and number of live births).

3. *Local demand and administrative capacity* was determined by whether the counties received funding and if they had a lobbyist who advocated and publicized their assets and needs.

The three special concerns also served as the independent variables of the study. The dependent variable(s) was (were) the amount of federal aid (in thousands of dollars) received in 1978–1979, 1984–1985, and 1989–1990, pivotal years in the evolution of health block grants. Data were analyzed using content analysis to identify patterns among the voluminous details.

Findings indicated the following:

1. Influence of Indicators of Political Influence: There did not appear to be any "proof" that the indicators were significantly related to the funding measures in any of the time frames.
2. Influence of Local Demand and Administrative Capacity: The characteristics of the indicators used were essentially the same. Available data did not reveal how often grants were applied for or any relationship between the number of applications filed and the amounts of awards received. Most simply stated, the findings indicate that "where grants were applied for, funding [was] received."[85]
3. Influence of Community Need: Study findings consistently demonstrate that, within the limits of this study, funding was allocated on established and accepted indicators of level of need. In nearly all instances, counties exhibiting the greatest need, as determined by the study's variables, received the greatest amount of funding.

This research revealed that the myths about political aims overshadowing social needs cannot be supported. The study also provided insight into health policy issues at various levels of agencies and government. It developed a model of analysis that can be used again and again to examine future policies and the impact of the policies upon service delivery and the general population. Finally, the study indicated that social workers can conduct commendable research on important social work policy issues.

## CONCLUSION

Changes occurred rapidly and dramatically in human service agencies during the 1980s. The ability to seek answers to puzzling questions or to promote efficiency within one's practice or within one's program has been equally desirable. The determination of efficiency and effectiveness also requires the systematic and objective examination of both individuals and programs, or what is commonly called research. Research and evaluation are necessary activities in the workplaces of the 1990s.

The advanced generalist practitioner conducts research within the field of social work as an ongoing professional activity. He or she also models behavior and activities for general practitioners. Most important, the advanced generalist utilizes the research methods presented in this chapter to promote accountability in practice and to enhance the current knowledge base of the social work profession.

## NOTES

1. Earl R. Babbie, Survey Research Methods (Belmont, Calif.: Wadsworth Publishing Co., 1973), p. 5.

2. Steven Isaac and William B. Michael, *Handbook in Research and Evaluation*, 2nd ed. (San Diego, Calif.: Edits Publishers, 1982), p. 184.

3. Ibid., p. 6.

4. Diane M. DiNitto and Thomas R. Dye, *Social Welfare—Politics and Public Policy*, 2nd ed. (Englewood Cliffs, N.J.: Prentice Hall, 1987), p. 273.

5. Duane R. Monette, Thomas J. Sullivan, and Cornell R. DeJong, *Applied Social Research: Tool for the Human Services* (New York: Holt, Rinehart and Winston, 1990), p. 5.

6. Bruce L. Berg, *Qualitative Research Methods* (Boston: Allyn and Bacon, 1989), p. 2.

7. Ibid., p. 2.

8. Ibid., p. 6.

9. James P. Spradley, *Participant Observation* (New York: Holt, Rinehart and Winston, 1980), pp. 7–8.

10. Monette, Sullivan, and DeJong, *Applied Social Research*, p. 234.

11. Louise H. Kidder, *Selltiz, Wrightsman and Cook's Research Methods in Social Relations*, 4th ed. (New York: Holt, Rinehart and Winston, 1981), pp. 102–103.

12. Spradley, *Participant Observation*, pp. 58–62.

13. Berg, *Qualitative Research Methods*, p. 76.

14. Spradley, *Participant Observation*, p. 33.

15. Berg, *Qualitative Research Methods*, p. 77.

16. Isaac and Michael, *Handbook in Research and Evaluation*, p. 38.

17. Deobold Van Dalen, *Understanding Educational Research: An Introduction*, 4th ed. (New York: McGraw-Hill, 1979), p. 353.

18. Ibid., p. 354.

19. Ibid., pp. 256–360.

20. Ibid., p. 368.

21. Ibid., pp. 351–381.

22. Alfred Benjamin, *The Helping Interview: With Case Illustrations*, (Boston: Houghton Mifflin, 1987), pp. 111–128.

23. Bonnie L. Yegidis and Robert W. Weinbach, *Research Methods for Social Workers* (New York: Longman Press Publishing, 1991), p. 194.

24. Raymond E. Gorden, *Interviewing: Strategy, Techniques and Tactics*, 4th ed. (Chicago: The Dorsey Press, 1987), pp. 42–48.

25. Raymond E. Gorden, *Interviewing: Strategy, Techniques and Tactics*, 3rd ed. (Homewood, Ill.: The Dorsey Press, 1980), pp. 46–47.

26. Gorden, *Interviewing: Strategy, Techniques and Tactics*, 4th ed., p. 44.

27. Allen Rubin and Earl R. Babbie, *Research Methods for Social Work* (Belmont, Calif.: Wadsworth Publishing Co., 1993), p. 701.

28. William J. Reid and Audrey D. Smith, *Research in Social Work (New York: Colum-*

*bia University Press, 1981), pp. 67–79;* Louise H. Kidder, *Selltiz, Wrightsman and Cook's Research Methods in Social Relations,* pp. 83–100.

29. Yegidis and Weinbach, *Research Methods for Social Workers,* pp. 74–80.
30. Ibid., p. 75.
31. Ibid., p. 75.
32. Monette, Sullivan, and DeJong, *Applied Social Research,* p. 5.
33. Gerald R. Adams and Jay D. Schvaneveldt, *Understanding Research Methods,* 2nd ed. (New York: Longman, 1991), pp. 103–114.
34. Earl Babbie, *The Practice of Social Research,* 5th ed. (Belmont, Calif.: Wadsworth Publishing Co., 1989), pp. 80–82; Rubin and Babbie, *Research Methods for Social Work,* pp. 106–108.
35. Reid and Smith, *Research for Social Work,* p. 79.
36. Adams and Schvaneveldt, *Understanding Research Methods,* p. 103.
37. Yegidis and Weinbach, *Research Methods for Social Workers,* p. 76.
38. Rubin and Babbie, *Research Methods for Social Work,* p. 107.
39. Yegidis and Weinbach, *Research Methods for Social Workers,* p. 76.
40. Adams and Schvaneveldt, *Understanding Research Methods,* p. 106.
41. Ibid., p. 107.
42. Yegidis and Weinbach, *Research Methods for Social Workers,* p. 77.
43. Monette, Sullivan, and DeJong, *Applied Social Research,* p. 6.
44. Ibid., p. 6.
45. Yegidis and Weinbach, *Research Methods for Social Workers,* pp. 77–78.
46. Isaac and Michael, *Handbook in Research and Evaluation,* p. 59.
47. Ibid., p. 53.
48. Ibid., p. 47.
49. Yegidis and Weinbach, *Research Methods for Social Workers,* pp. 86–87; Monette, Sullivan, and DeJong, *Applied Social Research,* p. 92.
50. Rubin and Babbie, *Research Methods for Social Work,* pp. 280–281.
51. Ibid., pp. 257–275.
52. Yegidis and Weinbach, *Research Methods for Social Workers,* p. 128.
53. Ibid., p. 130.
54. Daniel L. Stufflebeam, Walter J. Foley, William B. Gephart, Egon G. Guba, R. L. Hammond, H. O. Merriman, and Malcolm M. Provus, *Educational Evaluation and Decision-Making* (Itasca, Ill.: F. E. Peacock, 1971).
55. Monette, Sullivan, and DeJong, *Applied Social Research,* p. 8.
56. Joseph P. Hornick and Barbara Burrows, "Program Evaluation," in R. M. Grinnell, Jr., ed., *Social Work Research and Evaluation,* 3rd ed. (Itasca, Ill.: F. E. Peacock, 1988), p. 402.
57. Isaac and Michael, *Handbook in Research and Evaluation,* p. 2.
58. Ibid., p. 2.
59. DiNitto and Dye, *Social Welfare—Politics and Public Policy,* p. 273.
60. Rubin and Babbie, *Research Methods for Social Work,* p. 545.
61. Blaine R. Worthen and James R. Sanders, *Educational Evaluation: Theory and Practice* (Belmont, Calif.: Wadsworth, 1973), p. 136.
62. Yegidis and Weinback, *Research Methods for Social Workers,* p. 115.
63. Worthen and Sanders, *Educational Evaluation,* p. 136.
64. Yegidis and Weinbach, *Research Methods for Social Workers,* p. 118.
65. Ibid, 119.
66. DiNitto and Dye, *Social Welfare—Politics and Public Policy,* p. 281.
67. Ibid., pp. 275–278.
68. Adams and Schvaneveldt, *Understanding Research Methods,* p. 69.
69. Yegidis and Weinbach, *Research Methods for Social Workers,* p. 210.

70. Letitsha Bratton & Linner W. Griffin, "The Sibling Who Can Donate—But Doesn't," *Social Work in Health Care* (pending).

71. Margaret Strong & Carson Strong, "The Shortage of Organs for Transplantation," *ANNA Journal* 12, no. 4 (1985): 239–242.

72. Marilyn R. Bartucci & Peggy R. Bishop, "The Meaning of Organ Donation to Donor Families," *ANNA Journal* 14, no. 6 (1987): 369–371; Karen Y. Roberts, "Black American Attitudes Toward Organ Donation and Transplantation," *Journal of the National Medical Association* 80, no. 10 (1988): 1121–1125.

73. Patty Gibbs and Younock Kim, "Women's Health Care and Related Matters: A Cross-Cultural Perspective in a Social Welfare Context," in *International Symposium on Social Welfare and Culture: Universal Values and Indigenous Cultures* (Kyoto, Japan: Bukkyo University, 1989), pp. 332–389.

74. Naomi Gottlieb, "Woman and Health Care," in Naomi Gottlieb, ed., *Alternative Social Services for Women* (New York: Columbia University, 1980), pp. 61–110; Naomi Gottlieb, "Women's Health and Health Care," in Diane S. Burden & Naomi Gottlieb, eds., *The Woman Client: Providing Human Services in a Changing World* (New York: Tavistock, 1987), pp. 32–34; Catherine K. Reissman, "Women and Medicalization: A New Perspective," *Social Policy* 14, no. 1 (1983): 3–18; Sheryl K. Ruzek, *The Women's Health Movement: Feminist Alternatives to Medical Control* (New York: Praeger, 1978), p. 234; Hilary Salk, Wendy Sanford, Norma Swenson, and Judith Luce, "The Politics of Women and Medical Care," in the Boston Women's Health Book Collective, *The New Our Bodies, Ourselves* (New York: Simon & Schuster, 1984), pp. 555–597.

75. Ibid. , p. 365

76. Patricia A. Brunson, "The Effects of a Reading Program on the Depression Levels of a Group of Chronic Mentally Ill Patients in a Day Treatment Program," Unpublished professional paper, School of Social Work, East Carolina University, Greenville, North Carolina, April 1992, p. 3.

77. Ibid., p. 19.

78. Aaron T. Beck, J. Erbaugh, M. Mendelson, J. Mock, and C. H. Ward, "An Inventory for Measuring Depression," *Archives of General Psychiatry* 4 (1961): 561–571.

79. Brunson, "The Effects of a Reading Program on the Depression Levels of a Group of Chronic Mentally Ill Patients in a Day Treatment Program," p. 21.

80. Babbie, *The Practice of Social Research,* p. G3.

81. Linner W. Griffin, "Adult Day Care Centers and Adult Protective Services," *Journal of Gerontological Social Work* 20, nos. 1/2: 115–133.

82. Richard H. Fortinsky, "The National Eldercare Systems Project: A National Study Comparing Successful Community-Based Systems of Care for Older People," Presented at East Carolina University, Greenville, North Carolina, May 21, 1991.

83. Allen R. Katz, "A Comparative Study of the Allocation of Federal Health Grants and the Politics Surrounding Grant Distribution," Unpublished professional paper, School of Social Work, East Carolina University, Greenville, North Carolina, June 30, 1991, pp. 1–68.

84. A. R. Markusen, A. Saxenian, and M. A. Weiss, "Who Benefits from Intergovernmental Transfers?" *Publius* 11: 5–35.

85. Katz, "A Comparative Study of the Allocation of Federal Health Grants and the Politics Surrounding Grant Distribution," p. 51.

# 8

# Social Policy for Advanced Generalist Practice

Elbert Siegel

## *INTRODUCTION*

Consider the following case example:

Laura is an experienced social worker who practiced as a direct (clinical) practitioner for a number of years. She recently took on employment at an immigrant resettlement agency, and within a three-month period was promoted to district supervisor, where she supervised the professional activities of seven social workers.

Laura begin to notice that the caseload of one worker in a particular geographical location kept increasing. Service requests included additional money for support and medical services. Upon further investigation with the social worker she observed that this situation did not match the demographics of the caseload of the other social workers within the district. Speculation and discussions at staff meetings suggested a number of reasons that could explain this difference. Further retroactive examination of worker monthly statistics revealed that this pattern had existed for a number of months.

Laura and her immediate supervisor, the agency director, hypothesized that the caseload increase might be due to insufficient family incomes. How to validate this speculation now became important. The agency director recommended a survey of all the households within the defined area that would provide data that could be utilized for the development of policy that might address this situation.

Laura responded that she was not trained for this activity; that she was first and foremost a clinical practitioner. Furthermore, she suggested that a consultant be engaged to do this work, since she did not have the time to carry out the tasks that were necessary. Laura and the agency director had many lengthy discussions in which she was told that this was a vital and crucial aspect of everyday practice and that in order to advocate for any new or additional client services, the agency, through its personnel, had to be familiar with and "own" the information needed to convince decision makers.

Although very anxious and unsure Laura agreed to carry out this task. The agency director agreed to hire a consultant to assist in the development of a survey instrument with data analysis. In order to make this a regional endeavor, Laura elicited the aid of all the regional social workers in various aspects of the survey.

The survey results showed that in the defined geographic area there was indeed a lower percentage of two-family wage earners. The main reason was insufficient day care arrangements for children, which prevented a significant number of people from pursuing employment and becoming economically self sufficient.

Learning this, the director and Laura began to develop strategies for ways to effect a change. They decided that they would focus on the development of a child care center that would service children of women who chose to work.

Laura and her supervisor decided to make this a joint project. They immediately understood that this project would be time consuming and that there was no guarantee that they would be successful once they began. They also understood that they were entering areas that they would need to learn a great deal about in order to be able to influence decision makers about this situation.

Armed with their data they began to lobby the municipality, private funders, and their own department to provide the necessary funding to open such a center. This process took an inordinate amount of time because of the complexities involved in dealing with large-scale political systems, the complexities of convincing the targeted systems of the need to invest funding in this venture, and the coordination efforts needed to ensure that the agreements reached among the three parties would not break down. After a period of time they were able to get all three to agree to fund a child care center and finally contracted with an experienced private day care operator to operate the center.

Laura and her supervisor agreed to monitor the program, the services provided by the day care center, and the caseload numbers. After three months a sampled follow up showed an increase in the number of mothers who chose to become employed in the defined area, through their use of the day care center. Concurrently, there was a decrease in the caseload in this defined area, presumably caused by an increase in family income.

What is often indicated by social workers is precisely what Laura indicated to her supervisor: that she was not prepared to conduct a policy-related practice activity and that she did not have the training for it. Moreover, students and practitioners alike often say that they have no interest in policy; their main interest is to learn how to become clinicians and work with families, individuals, and perhaps groups. Policy is considered to be something esoteric, carried out by people other than social workers who may not have an interest in client problems. Often the practitioner is not able to see the relationship between practice with clients and the role social policy plays in this interchange. When faced with a professional task that would require interventions in the policy process, most social workers tend to avoid it, claiming that they do not have sufficient knowledge or training that would enable them to carry out such an activity.

The modern social worker must possess the knowledge base and skills consistent with the mission and goals of his or her place of work to handle a myriad of client-related issues in daily practice. Unlike his or her counterpart of a century ago when the profession was in its formative stages, or even as late as a generation ago, today's professional social worker may handle a variety of client issues and problems that range from the interpersonal to the effects of large-scale systems upon clients' daily lives, from teen pregnancy to street violence, from generational conflict to group competition for societal resources, from agency change initiatives to family violence. In other parts of this text social work practice issues and skills, using the advanced generalist perspective, are discussed and elaborated. These skills range from individual, family, and group counseling to research skills, from being cognizant and knowledgeable of ethics to administrative functions in everyday practice.

This chapter discusses and elaborates on the role of social policy for advanced generalist practice. It assumes a context of practice that is founded in agency-based public social services (i.e., the not for profit sector) and not necessarily private practice. This is not to say that the following discussion does not have implications for private practice. Access for service by clientele of private practitioners is also affected by social policy decisions enacted by large-scale entities such as insurance companies who provide third-party payment and the regulatory bodies of government. This has elicited an active lobbying effort directed toward the legislative process by clinical societies in order to ensure their market share in social work and counseling services.

Today's social worker can no longer brush aside policy as an aspect of practice because a great portion of our daily professional activities is affected by current social welfare policies enacted by various levels of government, by service agencies regardless of size, and even professional organizations. How these policies are developed, planned, articulated, and implemented have direct impact on our clientele. For example, current discussions regarding "welfare reform," most often a code word for reduction of benefits for public assistance clientele, will seriously affect the status of clientele who bring their problems to social workers for help in resolution. It is no accident that among the people who are actively engaged in influencing political decision makers in this particular issue are social workers who have had to develop the knowledge and skills to participate in social policy decisions.

What social workers are able to provide as part of a service package for their clientele is partially dependent upon decisions—oftentimes with the input of individual social workers—made elsewhere in the social welfare enterprise system. This provides a cogent argument for our further involvement in public social policy issues in order to maximize benefits for our clients. It also fulfills the ethical obligations of a professional social worker to ensure that unmet needs and opportunities for increasing the quality of life of clients are met.

The rationale for the social worker's involvement in policy may even go beyond national boundaries to include an international perspective that would sensitize the worker to the growing array of client problems and issues that can cross international boundaries and may involve human rights issues. The treatment of abandoned children in Romania, hunger in Somalia, or the treatment of women in India or Saudi Arabia brings out individual and sometimes group activism.

This chapter presents the role of the advanced generalist practitioner in social policy. It begins with a discussion of a number of definitions of social policy pertinent to the advanced generalist. This is followed by a consideration of professional skills necessary to implement and carry out social policy practice. The chapter concludes with a discussion of an international perspective necessitated by recent global trends that are beginning to affect social work practice.

Herein the role of social policy in advanced generalist practice is presented as a "new" way to conceptualize professional service delivered by social workers. For the advanced generalist, the discussion does not cultivate different territory but suggests concepts, frameworks, and strategies that can guide practice in policy and can create an awareness of possibilities that both enhance our practice and affect the lives of our clients. It is an area of professional activity that is continuously evolving and redefining its roles, tasks, and boundaries of responsibilities.

## SOCIAL POLICY FOR THE ADVANCED GENERALIST PRACTITIONER

Over the past decade and a half a number of scholars have reconceptualized the notion of social policy in order to make it amenable for practice. Policy was no longer seen by this group of writers as strictly policy analysis or comprehensive or incremental policy planning but rather a function of normal professional practice with a practical knowledge base for use as needed. The concurrent rise of the development of a "generalist" social work practitioner helped demystify the notion of policy as a practice issue by defining its scope and role as part of everyday social work practice especially for the entry-level practitioner. Graduate schools have begun to provide in the curriculum either specific courses or content interspersed in the general curricular framework that make students aware of and ready for opportunities for policy intervention that emerge in usual practice situations.

There are a number of definitions of social policy, each conveying a separate focus for practice purposes for various levels of generalist practice. Robert S. Magill views social policy as a series of concerns for "social goals and the programmatic means to implement these goals."[1] Even though these goals may be in conflict, they are resolved through the political, research, and negotiation activities of decision makers. No less important to Magill is the perspective and knowledge of social workers to impact on these decisions.

Policy, according to Robert Moroney, is a "process of decision-making" that results in the selection of an action-oriented activity. It includes four elements: what should be done, what can be done, what must be done and who should do it.[2] Moroney suggest that, in order to carry out these elements, one must have a knowledge of the political and economic processes and forces that affect policy. Furthermore, a recognition of an historical perspective needs to be added.

A second feature of Moroney's perspective is the recognition that policy involves deciding among various options in order to decide on the optimal choice for the issue or problem to be addressed. Decisions regarding choices can center around allocation of resources, distribution of resources, service delivery issues, implementation strategies, and, finally, evaluation strategies.[3] All these policy tasks involve an action-based framework that takes professional social work activities away from merely passively studying the historical antecedents of policy (undeniably important as part of the learning process that lends the background and framework for conceptualization) and forces the professional to actively engage in concrete tasks and activities that can bring about changes in the social environment for the betterment of the client or to take corrective measures that would eliminate the negative unintended consequences of policy decisions.

Tropman[4] in the 1987 edition of *The Encyclopedia of Social Work* draws upon the work of Pierce,[5] Jansson,[6] and DiNitto and Dye[7] to posit the notion that policy is firmly rooted in social work practice. He uses the term "policy practice" to denote the "mobilization of ideas at each stage of the policy process and the guidance of these ideas through the process. . . . Policy practitioners should be directly involved in the policy process and should seek to improve the quality of policy decisions through that involvement, in the same sense that interpersonal practitioners seek to improve the quality of a client's life."[8]

More basic to advanced generalist practice is Pierce's position that knowledge of policy and the skills necessary to accomplish or affect policy are essential for professional practice and should be part of a practitioner's everyday basic skills. Moreover, he suggests that this skill begins with the ability to ascertain and identify those policies that directly affect generalist practice. To Pierce, policy is "a guide to achieve what people value."[9] As a guide, policy "is sometimes subject to change, that directs a person's actions in . . . meeting needs, or in explaining and justifying such actions, or in restraining or limiting the actions of permissible behaviors."[10]

Jansson further elaborates these positions. In 1984, by coining the term *policy practitioner,* he set in motion a trend that would place the concept of policy squarely in the midst of ongoing social work practice rather than the usual mystical policy roles. Moreover, he extended the notion of policy activity from strictly legislative activity and positioned it within general professional practice, giving the social worker an additional professional task that would enhance direct service and administrative roles.[11]

In a recent monograph describing generalist practice, Carolyn Wells cogently argues that "it is policy that makes practice possible and that shapes the directions it take."[12] She further illustrates how organizational rules, procedures, and regulations define the parameters of practice and hence the nature of services that can be delivered. This mandates social workers to be knowledgeable of policy from an organizational perspective and to be aware of the necessity of proposing and implementing policy changes if needed. She ends with the positive note that practitioners can affect needed change; it should not be alien to their practice even with associated risks.[13] In a sense it is a statement of empowerment and confidence building.

Finally, Day, Macy, and Jackson suggest that "no action taken by a social worker is outside the field of policy. By being employed, working within the guidelines of an agency, working with clients, you are involved in *implementing* policy."[14] In other words, social workers' practice is squarely dependent on the parameters imposed by social policy decisions and their employment situation.

Social workers are in the central position to influence and impact policy decisions that affect their client population. The social worker's unique position as the central person between the client and the agents of service provision compels him or her to assume a proactive stance. In this sense it is incumbent upon the worker to consistently monitor the horizons of the environment for those forces that would impact on the needs of our clients, to be current on recent policy trends (local and national), and to seize the opportunity to influence decision makers that would consequently have an impact on policy decisions affecting clients and the nature of the social welfare policy system.

In summary, social policy for the advanced generalist may be defined as an action-oriented series of professional skills, processes, and activities designed to improve and enhance client services that is part of everyday professional functioning. These are implemented by the social worker who is also known as a "policy practitioner." These individuals are most often agency-based social workers who function in indirect social service roles as supervisors, managers, administrators, researchers, and sometimes social policy planners and analysts.

## POLICY KNOWLEDGE BASE FOR ADVANCED GENERALIST PRACTICE

In addition to having mastered the six-stage process outlined earlier in the text, the effectiveness of advanced generalist social workers is enhanced with the acquisition and mastery of knowledge and awareness of policy specific to their positions and identified tasks in their chosen agency of employment. For the purposes of this chapter, the term *agency* is used in a broad sense and denotes any place of employment where a social worker is engaged in professional activities. However, at this level of practice, the social worker is often exposed to complex political situations that require skills to analyze client issues and situations, assess complex political situations, evaluate and formulate policy, and use power and authority in an ethical manner to bring on policy changes while at the same time assisting staff or coworkers to develop a sense of empowerment through supervision or consultation. Finally, new national and international circumstances require the advanced practitioner to have a "world view" perspective in order to begin to assess social policies that affect practice with a diverse clientele that hails from many parts of the globe.

### The Ecological Perspective

Essential to understanding the role of the social worker as a generalist practitioner is the use of the ecological perspective as developed by Carel Germain and Alex Gitterman.[15] This framework views the person from the perspective of the environment, allowing a broad systems outlook that will afford the opportunity to interact with many systems that affect the client. For the advanced generalist this framework affords a viewpoint to perceive the interplay and interaction between relevant systems that can help in choosing points of entrance to affect social policy decisions.

The framework is applicable to various systems. For example, if one chooses to alter or impact agency policies, this framework immediately views agency structure not in terms of a horizontal or vertical entity but as clusters of smaller systems that continuously interact and have a significant effect on clients. These systems are composed of, but not limited to, the client system, the professional staff, the nonprofessional staff, administrators and managers, funders (grantors, legislative, private contributors, and so on), sometimes legislative bodies, and boards of directors or trustees. Entering into a mode that would bring on agency change requires a knowledge of the influence of these systems and the values—economic and political—that the individuals who compose these systems bring to bear on the defined decision. Employing an ecological perspective allows us the freedom to move toward systemic solutions to client problems through the policy process rather than depending wholly on client-centered modalities of treatment. For example, to reduce isolation among the elderly residents of a housing site, congregate meals are served to maximize group contact. This solution is chosen in preference to exploring potential social outlets on an individual basis through counseling.

### Policy Change Within the Agency

Very often the advanced generalist practitioner must focus attention on agency policies that impede client development. In order to systematize a possible change in agency policy, Brager and Holloway[16] have presented us with a useful analytic framework that provides the practitioner with a systematic manner to conceptualize, organize, and order information that is important for affecting agency policy decisions. This framework is briefly outlined below. The brevity of this discussion should not detract from its high degree of usefulness as an agency-sensitive tool that can inform us of the many issues surrounding agency policy change. It also helps practitioners focus on the organization as a system and forces us to consider relevant sources of input and influence on the organization.

This author strongly recommends a thorough reading of the Brager and Holloway text for a fuller understanding of the usefulness of this framework. In this chapter, the purpose is to inform the reader of the existence of this framework and its applicability as a structured analytic tool for the advanced generalist practitioner. In short, the five-stage framework encompasses the following elements:

1. Initial assessment: assessing and analyzing readiness for change
2. Pre-initiation: heightening awareness of the problem and creating an appropriate climate
3. Initiation: introducing the change, developing the necessary alliances and coalitions, and preparing for adoption
4. Implementation: actualizing the change and heading off unanticipated actions
5. Institutionalization: implanting the change within the organization[17]

One begins by assessing the problems or issue that will become the unit of attention. The practitioner then assesses the "readiness" of the agency to deal with such a change and identifies the critical actors relevant to the change goal. Often one may decide not to carry out or advocate for a change because the environment is not considered to be hospitable to an innovation.

Once the environment is considered to be conducive and receptive to change, an assessment is made of the problem/issue and a statement is made on the focus of the issue. The practitioner then must begin a deliberate process of study to reveal the pushing and pulling forces—the "field of forces" as they are appropriately referred to—within the agency that will affect the movement of that change situation and to consider the relevant forces from outside the agency that can influence the change activity.

Engagement in this particular stage of the change process puts the practitioner squarely in the middle of the political issues within the agency and the interpersonal politics that surround most agency-based issues. Navigating this particular stage requires that the practitioner utilize interpersonal skills such as communication, negotiation, bargaining, persuasion, networking, educating, and coalition-building skills. No less important is the acknowledgment that one is being recognized as an expert. In addition, the practitioner must be knowledgeable about issues of power and authority and must be able to exert and apply these in an appropriate and ethical manner.

Upon completion of an assessment of the pushing and pulling forces and the receptivity of the organization to the change, the practitioner then decides to move forward, wait, or cancel. If the decision is made to proceed, the practitioner begins to set the stage for the introduction of the change by increasing the awareness of the problem and creating an organizational climate of "receptivity."

The next stage is to formally introduce the goal of change. Once this decision is made, the social worker needs to, once again, assess the pushing and pulling forces within the agency in addition to the relevant external forces that would directly bear upon and affect the proposed innovation or change. The worker needs to influence the critical actors, build coalitions, and neutralize or win over opponents.

The most critical stage is implementation. According to Pressman and Wildavsky,[18] this is the stage when many agreements go awry. It is the stage in which careful attention should be paid to maintaining the change initiative and the intensity of the relationships that are needed by relevant actors in order to achieve agreement on the focus of change. Often the people that were initially supportive may not be so at this juncture. This requires the practitioner to reestablish the political ties that were first used to build alliances of support.

The final phase is to anchor the policy change in the organizational system so that it becomes linked to the service elements of the agency.

Although designed for organizational change, Brager and Holloway's framework is very useful for general application in many different macro systems, including legislative and governmental interventions. This is believed to be true because of the growing need to intervene as professional social workers in this arena. This systematic framework provides the social worker with the ability to assess the "geography" (or "turf") of a given environment so that one can decide to move forward, wait, or cancel the proposed initiative. It also provides the opportunity to consider many different aspects of a given system in appraising and decision making.

As an advanced generalist, a major portion of one's work at the agency or with associated systems involves advocacy for client services, which is often informed by a policy perspective.[19] Gaps in service, illogical social policies, unanticipated consequences of planned services and policies, inordinate numbers of rules and regulations, and unethical or inappropriate treatment of clients become matters of consideration for intervention by each practitioner as part of daily professional practice. Because of the unique administrative position in the organization or because of special knowledge, prestige, or skill, the advanced generalist can and should affect these issues. The perspective just outlined provides one source of knowledge to effect needed interventions.

### Power and Authority

A second area of knowledge is concerned with the issues of power and authority. Knowledge of the uses of power allows the advanced generalist to become empowered and helps one understand both the breadth and the limitations of power.

Sanction by the agency—whether this agency provides direct service or acts in a policy capacity—to be a supervisor, administrator, social planner, or other managerial person gives the practitioner the authority to function and carry out certain responsibilities regarding policy. Often social workers enter new roles without a clear understanding of the limits of their authority. Job descriptions ought to delineate this. If authority is inherent in the new role, it is expected by both agency personnel and staff that this authority (and expertise) will be exerted in the policy issue initiatives that begin to emerge.

Although agency sanction through the provision of authority may appear to be sufficient on the surface, the advanced generalist must develop an understanding of power and must be comfortable with this knowledge as the means to implement this authority. It becomes even more crucial to have a comfort level and a clear understanding of the role and notion of power as an appropriate tool for influencing policy through political and legislative interventions.

A major aspect of the use of power is that it can be employed in both positive and negative ways. Although it may be assumed that power is used in a positive manner, the social worker must be cognizant of the ways power can be used in inappropriate, unethical, and destructive ways.

Power is derived from a number of sources. According to French and Raven,[20] power comes from the ability to reward or coerce people, from our personal or professional expertise, from our mandated or appointed positions (called "positional" power) in an organization, or from being perceived as someone to be looked up to either because one is charismatic or because one has certain attributes that are perceived to be attractive. This now classic explication by French and Raven is a useful and simple way to view power. When engaged in a policy event, the advanced practitioner is often called upon to use one or more of these power sources in combination; and to use them effectively the practitioner must be comfortable, aware, and confident.

The power to reward people, and conversely to coerce, requires that one must have a sufficiently recognized position within the organization that will allow individuals to be persuaded to understand that inducements will be carried out by the person in power. One must have the appropriate and sufficient organizational mandate and authority to be able to carry out the promises (or threats) made for this to be effective. Agency personnel must have the perception that administrators, supervisors, planners, and analysts within the agency do have the mandate to reward (and sometimes coerce) when necessary and appropriate. Failure to provide this within the parameters of job descriptions usually brings on confusion and can impede policy initiatives.

Positional power refers to the "position" or rank one has within the defined organization. Conventionally, we tend to understand that a supervisor, an administrator, a board president, or a unit coordinator has a certain degree of sanctioned authority to carry out policy activities and to influence, compel, and sometimes coerce others to act accordingly because of their rank in the hierarchy of the organization. This is often taken for granted—rightly or wrongly.

Other sources of power—"referent" and expertise—are earned. This distinguishes them from reward, coercive, and positional sources of power, which tend to be distributed through one's rank in an organization. A practitioner achieves recognition from peers, the organization, the agency, or the political process when one is able to project knowledge, skills, and information that are vital for policy initiatives. Very often scholars are defined in this manner and are sought after by legislative bodies to provide input into decision making. Often advanced generalist practitioners employed by agencies are recognized in this manner as well. This occurs when individuals are able to demonstrate success in policy initiatives or have been recognized to possess sufficient experience, expertise, or knowledge in their chosen field of practice. As a result they are called upon to present seminars to identified groups or to inform and educate public decision-making bodies (such as boards of directors, community groups, or legislators) or professional peers who can influence policy decisions.

A former student who wrote an evaluation research of an agency program for her master's thesis was requested by her agency to testify at legislative hearings. The purpose of the hearings was to gather information to decide whether funding for the affected agency program would be restored. Her research was the basis of her testimony and was instrumental in having funding restored.

In our opening example, Laura was able to influence three major organizations to jointly fund a day care center because she was perceived to have expertise as an advocate for child care. Having this expertise provided her with status among her peers and recognition among policy decision makers. Recognition emerged from this experience and she was engaged as a consultant by other social work agencies.

In addition to these power sources, the advanced generalist must also consider two other forms of power: procedural power and process power. Jansson[21] suggests that the policy practitioner must have extensive knowledge of the organizational procedures that affect the movement of a policy initiative. Legislative procedures provide a good example. In order for legislation to be enacted, a rather complicated process is set into motion. Usually legislative budgeting is complicated procedurally and politically and reflects compromises that sometimes do not make sense.

What may appear simple in graphic form becomes a tangled web of processes and procedures (and sometimes intrigues) that often appears complicated even for the experienced legislator.[22] Issues regarding legality, interest groups' behavior, legislative norms, parliamentary procedures, legislative tactics and strategies, and knowledge of relationships among and between policy makers are among many issues that require study.

Process power, as presented by Jansson, occurs when practitioners—in this situation advanced generalist practitioners—"take actions or make statements to shape the tenor, tempo, or scope of conflict of these processes in a manner that they believe will help them secure policy preferences."[23]

It would appear that timing, opportunity, and the intensity for the issue are crucial determinants for process interventions. For example, Presidents Ronald Reagan in 1981 and William Clinton in 1993 floated trial balloons to determine the degree of support and public receptivity for various aspects of Social Security in order to determine the feasibility for possible budget cuts in this entitlement program. Various interest groups, influential individuals, and experts voiced concerted concern and mobilized public pressure. Both presidents interpreted the public reaction as being too costly politically and retracted these budget-cutting initiatives.

### Legislative (and Political) Interventions

In recent years social workers have been called upon to involve themselves in policy issues at legislative and executive levels of government (in addition to advocating and promoting change within their own agencies). A number of reasons account for this activity: to lobby for funding to develop services as new social problems emerge (e.g., AIDS); to protect current resources and levels of funding during periods of budget rescissions; to further professional interests (e.g., vendorship agreements, licensure, and certification); to enhance agency services for the community (e.g., bringing mental health clinics closer to the neighborhoods they serve); or to act as a "lobbyist" to inform, educate, and influence decision makers when the opportunity is presented. Finally, an increase in social litigation has resulted in court-mandated services to thwart abuse and neglect of children and the elderly and additional services for the developmentally disabled and for children in the foster care system.

These events required that social workers enter the process to present their particular professional point of view, their knowledge of the social problem, and their expertise as advanced generalist practitioners. While an understanding of both legislative and governmental processes is crucial in order to effectively intervene in policy matters, a thorough understanding of the issue is equally important. Furthermore, understanding one's own personal and professional strengths is important, even though one may be considered to have power as an expert or as a charismatic professional.

In addition to having a well-grounded knowledge base of the problem that is being considered for intervention, the advanced generalist practitioner must know how social policies are developed and ultimately enacted. This involves learning about the working of the political process at either the local, state, or national level, depending on where one chooses to intervene. This is necessary for three reasons. First, as informed citizens this should be part of daily awareness. Second, professionals ought to be following and closely monitoring those decisions from law-making bodies because ultimately their decisions (and discussions leading to decisions) impact on agency policies affecting clients. Monitoring provides early warning and alerts us to a shift in the thinking of decision makers. Third, a full understanding of this process provides the knowledge and information needed if one chooses to intervene in this process.

The process of legislative enactment at either local, state, or national levels tends to be similar and is relatively simple—on paper.[24] First a proposed policy is introduced either as part of a general social agenda (usually welfare reform or changes in social entitlement programs or in an employment/training program begin this way) or as a reaction to a societal event (for example, the Brady Bill restricting handweapon sales) by either the executive branch of government or through a specific lawmaker as a response to the wishes of a constituent body or as a personal agenda item. Bills can also gain introduction from the administrative offices of governmental bureaucracies, especially those required to enact or implement policy procedures.

A bill is introduced to either house of the legislature, where it is given a number and forwarded to the appropriate committee for discussion, analysis, and consideration. Usually the bill is forwarded to a subcommittee, which is charged with the above scrutiny tasks.

After it passes scrutiny by the committee(s), it is sent to the originating legislative chamber with committee recommendation. Those bills that are favorably reviewed are forwarded to the full chamber for a vote. If approved, the bill is sent to the other chamber, where it is moved through the system in much the same manner and voted upon if recommended by the appropriate committee(s).

Differences in versions of the bill between legislative bodies are reviewed by establishing a joint conference committee to reconcile differences and to report out a compromise bill. The bill is sent back to both houses for ratification. If approved it is forwarded to the Chief Executive (President, Governor, Mayor, County Executive) for signature into law. The chief executive may veto the bill if it is objectionable. The legislative body has the legal authority to override this executive veto, but this is difficult to achieve.

The process does not end here, however. Effective policy legislation is dependent upon the implementation process. Usually legislative bodies do not spell out how a law is to be implemented, leading to gray areas that often result in action by the courts for disposition.

Another element of policy knowledge for the advanced generalist practitioner is understanding implementation theory for practice. This is as important as possessing alertness to the political process itself. Brager and Holloway describe implementation as a subprocess in the change model that is akin to "holding a tiger by the tail."[25] Pressman and Wildavsky alert us to many problems that can emerge at this juncture that can impede implementation. They point out that political disagreements among relevant actors and organizations, poorly conceived funding patterns, inadequate agreements among affected parties, faulty definitions of the issue, too great a time gap between passage and implementation of the policy, and a change in key personnel are among the problems that can prolong or cease implementation even in the best of times.[26]

If the role of advanced generalists is to participate in policy interventions at the macro or governmental level, interventive skills—policy practice skills—are needed to achieve this. Presented here is a list of skills, by no means complete, that can assist in policy interventions. The author invites readers to add to this from their own personal experiences:

1. Presenting information based on personal research, agency-based research, or anecdotal practice material to professional groups, community groups, or legislative bodies.
2. Formal testimony as a representative of a professional group or social agency.
3. Formalized "lobbyist" activities that could include telephoning decision makers, testifying, and initiating letter-writing campaigns to decision makers.
4. Editorial page letters to newspapers, professional journals, and newsletters.
5. Contacting media talk shows for time to present views, opinions, and general information regarding the issue.
6. Contacting and befriending politicians, officers, or members of boards of directors or other relevant policy makers. The purpose is to build political ties that would be needed to impact on decisions and to open the door to directly influencing the decision-making process.
7. Monitoring the organizational bureaucracies in order to determine what changes are being proposed. Bureaucratic employees, often of the same profession, can become part of an extended network of potential allies who can provide information through the research and analyses carried out by these organizations.

8. Developing strategies for coalition building.
9. Helping and supporting identified people to become elected to political office. This provides access to decision making and political influence.
10. Running for and being elected to political office.

A fuller treatment and analysis of these issues, along with a cogent rationale for involvement by social workers in the political process, is presented by Haynes and Mickelson. According to them,

> The most obvious advantage is the accumulated potential for creating progressive social policy to deal with unmet needs, resolve social problems, or ameliorate unjust or inequitable conditions in society . . . to amass political strength for the promotion and protection of professional standards for human-service personnel.
> Finally, because the majority of social work programs are publicly funded, a politically effective profession can be a positive influence on human-service funding during the budget allocation process.[27]

Furthermore, they suggest that, as resources shrink, influencing policy by agency administrators is becoming a more significant and important aspect of their daily jobs. In fact, they further suggest that agency administrators are more likely to define advocacy as part of their professional roles than micro practitioners. Moreover, their tendency to belong to organizations that take stands on public issues brings them into contact with others who are experiencing similar resource problems or have similar points of view on policy issues.[28]

### Program Planning

An aspect of policy for the advanced generalist practitioner at the agency level that is often overlooked because of its overlap as an administrative aspect is furthering agency service goals by developing appropriate programs to serve clients. This task is necessitated by the social problems that are recognized by agencies as being potentially within their constellation of services for their identified clients and as a way of responding to community need.

Program development is herein defined as a process that translates social policy issues (agency or societal) into agency-based services. The advanced generalist practitioner is the professional agent that is authorized by the agency to carry out this function. It is assumed that this individual has or will develop the skills and the ability to do so. Agencies have generally responded with community programs addressed to social problems and issues. New economic and political realities suggest that they will need to carry out this responsibility in a different manner, namely, that in the proposal development process, program funders will need to be convinced that the agency through its professional staff can address the issue and can provide evaluation of the program to justify initial and ongoing funding. The same rationale is being expressed by the budget and finance committees of individual agencies.

To develop and implement a new agency program requires knowledge about policy antecedents and the effects of the issue to be addressed by the new program as well as the skills to bring it through the organization. In this sense, Brager and Holloway's framework again is useful. "Agency" in this discussion is used to mean any organization concerned with social services, whether it is a local multi-service community center, a family service agency, a government-operated service agency (e.g., the VA system), a policy research organization, or a government bureaucracy that makes service decisions or is a direct service provider for clients.

If the advanced generalist practitioner must carry out program planning tasks, a useful and functional framework must be developed. Most analytic frameworks for program development tend to be joined to policy analysis frameworks because of an assumed similarity of analytical tasks or are seen as useful for the community or societal level[29] rather than being specifically for agencies. Although program development is recognized as an important administrative activity—and certainly part of the advanced generalist framework—it is rarely treated as part of the administrative or policy activities of the advanced generalist at the agency level.[30] And yet, advanced generalist practitioners spend a significant portion of their work time proposing, developing, and choosing programs for clients and pursuing funding. An example may help to focus this point:

> In response to a growing number of refugees from Southeast Asia, Catholic Family Services decides to establish a resettlement unit within the agency to plan services for this group of potential clients. Being familiar with this population, the social worker is requested to assess the need and plan a program, if necessary, that would offer resettlement services to the newcomers. In order to carry out this task, the social worker conducts a needs assessment in order to ascertain the extent of need and a justification for expending agency time and ultimately budget to accommodate this group. The social worker then defines what the focus of attention will be and assesses structural, personnel, and budgetary issues as they impinge on the proposal. Having assessed these variables, the worker now needs to develop a plan for implementation, which can include building supports and coalitions within the agency, leading to a service structure to begin to provide social services for the refugee group.

In the absence of appropriate frameworks for agency program development, a conceptual framework developed by Kammerman provides a useful tool.[31] She identifies three stages:

1. Planning: Action is taken to document need, determine the scope of the problem, specify objectives, choose interventive goals, design a structure, and search for funding.
2. Initiation: Following a decision to proceed, mechanisms must now be allocated

to translate the elements of the plan into an action mode by matching the plan to the mission and goals of the agency; establishing the organizational mechanisms and structure, which can include hiring staff and volunteers; appointing advisory personnel; establishing interventive strategies; and beginning the provision of services.

3. Implementation: At this point the plan is activated, services are set into motion, and efforts are directed towards achieving program objectives within the agency's mission. Additionally, measures are taken towards heightening community visibility, ensuring accessibility of client participation, and developing recordkeeping procedures.

It should be added that devices for program and practice evaluation need to be added for quality control, justification for funders and boards of directors, and to help ensure program continuation.

### Supervision

As an advanced generalist practitioner, an agency supervisor is at the interface with line staff as they begin to assume policy roles at the agency. Their position in the structure of the agency often thrusts them into the complexities of formulating, revising, or evaluating policy either through their own personal initiatives or through those of their supervisees. Line staff tends to maintain that supervisors carry up to administration their wishes for policy changes affecting a myriad of agency issues, while administrative personnel, to whom supervisors report, often require that supervisors transmit, translate, and implement policy decisions made elsewhere to staff. In addition, supervisors are expected to assist staff members if and when they engage in policy change activities.

A major function of the social work supervisor is to create an atmosphere in which staff can develop as professionals and learn those skills necessary to function as an advanced generalist practitioner. Kadushin has delineated three major aspects of social work supervision: administration, education, and support.[32]

This framework provides a useful manner to guide supervisory practice when the practitioner decides to embark on a policy initiative. As an educator, the supervisor helps the practitioner learn new policy practice skills and assists in applying different macro policy theories that will allow professional interventions targeted toward the defined social problem. The supervisor also provides additional information about the terrain and helps the worker learn about the particular social problem. As an administrator, the supervisor assists the worker by opening doors to higher administration or assisting in the removal of agency barriers. The supervisor helps and instructs the worker to manage the associated tasks involved in the policy initiative in an efficient and orderly fashion. Finally, the supervisor provides a supportive atmosphere that allows the supervisee to test out different analytical and interpersonal skills before engaging the larger system and is the sounding board for environmental feasibility and agency receptivity.

### Research and Evaluation

Consideration of policy roles by the advanced generalist practitioner would not be complete without a few words on the relationship between policy and research. Generalist practice today subscribes to the notion that research is important as a means to evaluate one's professional practice and to assist in systematically ordering information and data one needs in order to carry out professionally related functions. Developing a research framework also helps alert the practitioner to changes in policy and program, to the changing nature of client problems, to unmet community needs, to underserved clientele, or to justify an increase in budget, staff, or resources. Very few daily professional activities in the agency can escape being scrutinized by agency funders or the business offices. Therefore, social workers are called upon to justify many aspects of their work for accountability, quality control, management of departmental costs, and creation of more efficient service structure.

The advanced generalist is therefore "required" to keep current by reading appropriate professional reports and agency statistical reports and reviews. Moreover, agency trends need to be analyzed and reviewed via effectiveness studies or impact analyses. Occasionally, internal audits—agency and departmental—need to be conducted for monitoring purposes. Advanced generalist practitioners need to monitor government reports and new research within their chosen field of expertise to maintain currency.

Finally, the advanced generalist practitioner must acquire research skills in order to develop agency programs or policies. In the opening example, Laura learned to apply her knowledge of research to generate data that could be used to convince decision makers to underwrite a new client program.

### AN INTERNATIONAL PERSPECTIVE

Most specialists in social development, including social workers engaged in international development, believe that the 21st century will be a "global century," i.e., a century in which the most critical issues on the work agenda will emanate from *global* rather than national forces.[33]

Modern technology will be one of the reasons why this prediction will probably come true. The world seems to share the same social problems, and technology brings these problems to our doorstep for scrutiny, for information sharing among scholars and professionals, and for the pursuit of a common resolution. If our indicators are accurate, then we must look beyond our borders and expand our professional horizons for help in resolution.

Technological advances permit us to transcend national and international boundaries. Geographic barriers, time, and distance no longer impede our associations and interactions with professionals who reside beyond our national boundaries. Our ability to acquire knowledge and information is no longer limited to our particular region of the world. Our ability to receive and process information about international social events, professional information, and knowledge is enhanced through FAX machines, E-mail Internet systems, television, radio, and even newspapers and journals. Within a short span of time—sometimes mere moments—we witness international social and political events.

We can communicate instantly with fellow professionals, social workers, and colleagues in many parts of the globe. We are able to share and provide information, resources, practice technologies, and research. We can mutually provide assistance in our quest to solve social problems.

Although an international perspective may offer attractive possibilities for the advanced generalist practitioner, it also can pose some difficulties in that cross-cultural and cross-ethnic issues may lift up their hard edges, namely intergroup conflict, to complicate communication. Nevertheless, new insights are being developed that could allow us to study and analyze different social welfare systems, different formulations for social policy interventions, and different innovations and options for programs and services.[34]

Coupled with this rise in technology are the equally dramatic social, cultural, economic, and political changes occurring in Eastern Europe, Southeast Asia, parts of Latin America, and on the African continent. Some of these events have created a refugee (or immigrant) group that seeks entry into other nations that they see as more stable or where they already have family and friends. Many of these people seek to reach the United States, legally or illegally, in spite of the dangers involved—to feel safe or in the hope of bettering themselves economically. Many bring with them social problems that are similar to those we already experience, causing some to conclude that refugees and immigrants unduly exacerbate our already strained social service system.

As social workers, we can trace our professional roots back to the social and economic developments of the late 1800s. Urbanization, industrialization, and immigration in the United States were the antecedent conditions that fostered the growth of the profession and brought it to the forefront. In the late 1900s we appear to be faced, once again, with conditions that require professional interventions and services that would enhance human development and address the needs of immigrants and refugees. One difference, however, is that over the past century we have developed professional practice frameworks and skills that guide our helping processes. Designing policies and services and ensuring a sense of empathy and quality have become major tasks for the profession. Our frameworks for "ethnically sensitive," holistic practice will prove to be useful not only for interventions on the micro level but also for the design and implementation of social policies.

Many of the social problems addressed through social policies and delivery systems in the United States are similar to those being faced by other nations. Services for refugees and immigrants, poverty, child welfare issues, family violence (including child, elderly, and spousal abuse), disabilities, hunger and malnutrition, AIDS distribution of health resources and coverage, violence and public safety, employment, homelessness, and aging may require a global perspective for their improvement. For the advanced generalist practitioner, use of comparative policy analysis will provide us with "imported" service and practice options to consider in our attempt to resolve social problems and meet human needs specific to that identified population. For example, the propensity for reliance on friends for help and the suspicion toward agency-based and government services during resettlement by immigrants from the former Soviet Union need to be built into an overall service menu for this group.[35]

In order to interact on an international level, advanced generalist practitioners will need to develop the knowledge and understanding of international events as they affect their area of knowledge and expertise. The methodologies and skills developed as a policy practitioner, administrator, planner, supervisor, or agency-change expert will also be called upon in the international arena. What needs to be added is a knowledge base that encompasses an understanding of the specific historical context and development of policies and the role of culture in that identified nation. An inability to develop a framework to understand a society's culture or to move from the parameters of an ethnocentric position will result in a failure to impact on global problems.

It has become rather fashionable for social work educators from the United States to circle the world and provide consultation about social welfare policies, services, and delivery issues for newly emerging democracies and societies. Many schools of social work have some association with another country—some stronger than others—in the hope of establishing social work as a viable professional entity with accompanying training and education centers. Others act in a consultative capacity to help governments establish social welfare policies that address human need. The American social work profession has become an "exporter" of knowledge and expertise. But we must remember that what we produce can only serve as options for consideration in a dialogue, just as the social welfare knowledge we import from other nations or societies is an option to be considered for enactment by us. For example, under strong consideration today is the Canadian model of health care coverage as an approach for a health care service delivery system in the United States.

The social work profession, originally developed as a response to international events, once again is involved in helping to resolve problems brought on by international events. Our knowledge base, the historical development of social work as a profession, our professional values, ethics and practice skills, and most recently our leadership skills that express an international flavor, position the advanced generalist practitioner in the forefront of international social welfare activity.

### SUMMARY AND CONCLUSIONS

To function as an advanced generalist practitioner in social policy, the social worker must develop a broad systems framework for social policy practice that encompasses a political economy outlook. A broad-based outlook—an ecological perspective—provides the practitioner with the holistic underpinnings of general practice. Agency, societal, and even international problems are varied and complicated. Client groups are culturally and ethnically diverse and present a variety of problems, some brought on by faulty, inoperative, and inhumane policies and sometimes brought to the forefront by personal behaviors. This places policy issues squarely in the middle of professional practice. The advanced generalist cannot practice without policies, nor can policies be appropriate without the input of practice realities.

The author has attempted to show that policy problems occur at all levels, from the personal to the international, and that there is a need for social workers, particularly advanced generalists, to develop both analytic and interpersonal skills in policy practice activities. They need to become comfortable with issues of power as a tool for use and to develop a point of view that can be defended by research data. There is a need for them to be, as Jansson states, "flexible and adaptable."[36]

Knowledge and use of policy by the advanced generalist practitioner should not be viewed as standing alone in isolation. It should be viewed as one part of a total package, whereby the policy practitioner takes from the various elements of social work knowledge: our knowledge and application of research skills and outcomes provide us with data and a methodology to systematically assess their meaning *vis à vis* professional activities; practice skills enable the practitioner to empathize with client problems and to find ways to intervene; knowledge of human behavior provides the theoretical perspectives of the human condition and the framework from which to perceive the influences of a client's environment; educational institutions help instill a sense of ethics to guide the practitioner's activities; and, finally, the understanding of social policy should help create human social welfare policies that address human need.

Embarking on yet another practice area to be mastered, the advanced generalist must realize that the road to success is not level. Participants bring with them differing amounts of power resources and differing access to decision makers. Often the values and the philosophic position one is attempting to bring forward is not consistent with those exhibited by current decision makers. Results of interventions in policy are rarely instantaneous. Most often outcomes are not realized for many years. It took Senator Christopher Dodd (D, Connecticut) 10 years of persistence to realize passage of his Family Leave Act.

## NOTES

1. Robert S. Magill, *Social Policy in American Society* (New York: Human Services Press, 1984), p. 10.

2. Robert M. Moroney, *Social Policy and Social Work: Critical Essays on the Welfare State* (New York: Aldine De Gruyter, 1991), p. 2.

3. Ibid., p. 2; see also Neil Gilbert and Harry Specht, *Dimensions of Social Welfare Policy* (Englewood Cliffs, N.J.: Prentice Hall, 1989).

4. John Tropman, "Policy Analysis: Methods and Techniques," *The Encyclopedia of Social Work*, 18th ed., vol. 2 (Silver Spring, Md.: NASW, 1987), pp. 268–283.

5. Dean Pierce, *Policy for the Social Work Practitioner* (New York: Longman, 1984).

6. Bruce S. Jansson, *Theory and Practice of Social Policy: Analysis, Processes and Current Issues* (Belmont, Calif.: Wadsworth Publishing Co., 1984).

7. Diane DiNitto and Thomas Dye, *Social Welfare: Politics and Public Policy* (Englewood Cliffs, N.J.: Prentice Hall, 1983).

8. Tropman, *Encyclopedia*, p. 269.

9. Pierce, *Policy for the Social Work Practitioner*, p. 29.

10. Ibid.

11. Bruce Jansson, *Social Welfare Policy: From Theory to Practice* (Belmont, Calif.: Wadsworth Publishing Co., 1990), pp. 13–19.

12. Carolyn Cressy Wells, *Social Work Day to Day: The Experience of Generalist Social Work Practice* (New York: Longman, 1989), p. 131.

13. Ibid, pp. 131–132.

14. Phyllis J. Day, Harry J. Macy, and Eugene C. Jackson, *Social Working: Exercises in Generalist Practice* (Englewood Cliffs, NJ: Prentice Hall, 1984), p. 116.

15. Carel Germain and Alex Gitterman, *The Life Model of Social Work Practice* (New York: Columbia University Press, 1980); see also Carol Meyer, *Social Work Practice: A Response to the Urban Crisis* (New York: The Free Press, 1970).

16. George Brager and Stephen Holloway, *Changing Human Service Organizations* (New York: The Free Press, 1978).

17. Brager and Holloway, *Changing Human Service Organizations*, pp. 154–155. The authors provide a good summary of the pitfalls that occur during implementation.

18. The classic analysis by Jeffrey L. Pressman and Aaron Wildavsky, *Implementation* (Berkeley: University of California Press, 1973) discusses the "Murphy Laws" that surround implementation and what to do to avoid them.

19. For an overall description see Michael Sosin and Sharon Caulum, "Advocacy: A Conceptualization for Social Work Practice" *Social Work* 28 (Jan.–Feb., 1983): 105–110.

20. John R. French and Bertram Raven, "The Basis of Social Power," in Dorwin Cartwright and Alvin Zander, eds., *Group Dynamics: Research and Theory* (New York: Harper and Row, 1968), pp. 259–269; see also Yeheskel Hassenfeld, "Power in Social Work Practice," *Social Service Review* 61 (September 1987): 475–486.

21. Jansson, *Social Welfare Policy: From Theory to Practice*, pp. 143–144.

22. Ibid.; see also Andrew W. Dobelstein, *Politics, Economics and Public Welfare* (Englewood Cliffs, N.J.: Prentice Hall, 1986), Chapters 2, 3, 4; Andrew W. Dobelstein, *Social Welfare: Policy and Analysis* (Chicago: Nelson-Hall, 1990), Chapters 2 and 3; Howard J. Karger and David Stoesz, *American Social Welfare Policy: A Structural Approach* (New York: Longman, 1990), Chapter 3.

23. Jansson, *Social Welfare Policy: From Theory to Practice*, p. 146.

24. My intent is not to "homogenize" this process. Although there are many common elements to the legislative process at each level of government, there are also many differences. There are many excellent sources that describe the legislative process in greater detail. For a good outline see Ronald B. Dear and Rino J. Patti, "Legislative Advocacy," *The Encyclopedia of Social Work*, 18th ed., vol. 2 (Silver Springs, Md.: NASW, 1987), pp. 34–42. Probably the best analysis and description is Dobelstein, *Politics, Economics, and Public Welfare*, Chapters 2 and 3. Dobelstein informs us of these complexities (though fascinating and challenging) in the process at each step. Understanding the complex nature of this process will help us intervene more effectively. Willard C. Richan, *Lobbying for Social Change* (New York: The Haworth Press, 1991); John P. Flynn, *Social Agency Policies: Analysis and Presentation for Community Practice* (Chicago: Nelson Hall Publishers, 1985); and Karen Haynes and James S. Mickelson's analysis, *Affecting Change: Social Workers in the Political Arena* (New York: Longman, 1991) also alert us to the tasks, skills, and issues that need to be mastered for political involvement.

25. Brager and Holloway, *Changing Human Service Organizations*, pp. 206–207.

26. Pressman and Wildavsky, *Implementation*, pp. 125–163. See also Eugene Bardach, *The Implementation Game: What Happens After a Bill Becomes a Law* (Cambridge, Mass.: MIT Press, 1977).

27. Haynes and Mickelson, *Affecting Change*, p. xvii.

28. Haynes and Mickelson, *Affecting Change*, p. 55.

29. There have been many texts written in an attempt to show the connection between social work practice and social planning. These are all legitimate attempts, growing out of the realities of the social policies of the 1960s and 1970s. It is not my intent to list or review the many texts that emerge, but the following two have been proven to be useful for a general understanding of the concept of "planning," some of which can be applied to our thinking of agency based program planning: Alfred J. Kahn, *Theory and Practice of Social Planning* (New York: Russell Sage Foundation, 1969); Armand Lauffer, *Social Planning at the Community Level* (Englewood Cliffs, N.J.: Prentice Hall, 1978).

30. Robert R. Mayer, *Policy and Program Planning: A Developmental Perspective* (Englewood Cliffs, N.J.: Prentice Hall, 1985). Much of this text contains valuable information for the advanced generalist who is engaged in program planning; however, it is geared to the large-scale organizations such as government social services.

31. Sheila B. Kammerman, "A Paradigm for Programming: First Thoughts," *Social Service Review* 49 (September 1975): 412–420.

32. Alfred Kadushin, *Supervision in Social Work Practice* (New York: Columbia University Press, 1985). His theme, where he explicates these three areas of supervision, was originally in the first edition in 1976 but is carried forward in other books written about social work. See also Michael J. Austin, *Supervisory Management for the Human Services* (Englewood Cliffs, N.J.: Prentice Hall, 1981); Carlton E. Munson, *An Introduction to Clinical Social Work Supervision* (New York: Haworth Press, 1983).

33. Richard J. Estes, ed., *Internationalizing Social Work Education: A Guide to Re-*

*sources for a New Century* (Philadelphia: University of Pennsylvania, School of Social Work, 1992), p. 2.

34. Martin B. Tracy, "Cross-National Social Welfare Policy Analysis in the Graduate Curriculum: A Comparative Process Model," *Journal of Social Work Education* 28 (Fall 1992): 341–352.

35. Elbert Siegel, *The Use of Mutual Aid by Russian-Jewish Immigrants in Two Connecticut Communities: An Analysis of an Informal Helping System,* Columbia University, unpublished dissertation, 1988.

36. Bruce Jansson, *Social Welfare Policy: From Theory to Practice,* p. 433.

# 9

# The Field of Advanced Generalist Practice: Changing Practice Needs

Marilyn A. Biggerstaff, Frank R. Baskind, and Cary Jensen

## *INTRODUCTION*

Advanced generalist practice is a relatively recent development in the conceptualization of education for social work practice at the MSW level. The framework of advanced generalist practice is based on the assumption that the practice of social work requires a generalist foundation of five components—purpose, sanction, knowledge, values, and method—that are generic to all practice.[1] These components define the uniqueness of social work and differentiate social work practice from that of other professions. The focus of the debate within the profession about specialization during the MSW advanced practice education is whether there are distinctive practice specializations with clearly identified and mutually exclusive knowledge and skills that underpin specific tasks and activities and that distinguish one specialization from another. Specialization "rests on extended study and experience from which true expertise develops"[2] and is multidimensional rather than having a single focus.[3]

Advanced generalist practice is posed as one alternative for organizing an advanced concentration, or specialization, in social work education. Some of the traditional concentrations are method (e.g., family treatment, group work, direct practice, supervision, social planning, and management), intervention (e.g., behavior modification, social skills training, advocacy, and structural family therapy), setting of practice (e.g., mental health, child welfare, and health care), and social problem (e.g., substance abuse, interpersonal violence, and mental retardation). The advanced generalist model calls for the social worker to develop advanced knowledge and skills for multiple levels of intervention with diverse social problems across a range of settings.

Is the advanced generalist model a valid method for organizing advanced concentration study in social work education for MSW practitioners? Verification of any conceptual framework for practice is necessary for the framework to be useful as an organizing principle for social work education. A framework must be valid in order for its concepts and guiding principles to accurately inform the practitioner in defining practice roles and activities and making practice decisions. In order for an advanced concentration to have merit in preparing social worker practitioners, it must have an identified body of knowledge and skills that can be transmitted to practitioners, have evidence of empirical verification, and be evaluated for effectiveness in eliciting change in the target group, organization, population, or social problem area.

This chapter explores two questions: What are the roles and activities of the advanced generalist practitioner? What knowledge, skills, and values must be acquired through the process of professional education to prepare the social worker for those roles and activities? Qualitative research, using focus groups, is used in describing the advanced generalist framework. The research was conducted without superimposing the advanced generalist framework as a guiding principle.[4]

The study of curriculum needs was conducted at Virginia Commonwealth University in the Fall of 1992 using focus groups. The purpose of the study was to engage social workers, from their perspectives as practitioners and supervisors or administrators, in the process of identifying in their own language the knowledge, skills, and abilities that are necessary for practice in a wide range of social work practice settings in the public, not-for-profit, and private practice arenas. The research was useful in analyzing what may be advanced generalist in the practice of social work in both the urban, nonmetropolitan, and rural areas of Virginia. The authors believe that the diversity in the practice of social work reported by study participants and the range of cultural, economic, and social forces affecting the clients served by social workers in the regions of the state provide a basis for generalizing participants' responses to the practice of social work in other parts of the country.

## THE CHANGING NATURE OF PRACTICE
## AND THE PROFESSION

The nature of social work practice is changing. This is a result of changes in the composition and complexity of our society, social and economic conditions affecting its members, recognition of the importance the physical and social environment of the world has on well-being, and advances in the knowledge available about human beings and their biological, psychological, and social components.

The profession of social work is changing. From its inception, members of the profession have held differing views about the nature of social work practice, its specialized areas of expertise, the sources of knowledge for professional practice, and the roles appropriate for social workers in relation to clients, service delivery organizations, and the society that sanctions its services. While the mission of the profession has been stated in various terms, it is generally accepted that the mission of social work is to "ameliorate suffering, alleviate distress, ameliorate poverty and injustice, take care of people, and alleviate social problems."[5]

Throughout the recent history of the profession an ongoing debate has taken place between those who hold the position that the primary function of the profession in meeting its mission is societal and institutional change and others who believe that the primary purpose of social work is to deliver direct services to clients, altering social problems at the individual, family, or group levels. Among those who emphasize direct service as a primary focus, there is not a consensus regarding the type of services, the targets for change, and particularly the conceptual framework that guides social work practice.

There are, however, common themes in defining the practice of social work that have become institutionalized as the foundation of social work education.[6] The work of Harriett Bartlett defined the practice of social work as comprised of essential elements including values, purpose, knowledge, sanction, and methods.[7] Further, in defining social work by fields of practice, Bartlett identified the following characteristics of a particular field of practice for social work: problem (or condition) of central concern; system of organized services; body of knowledge; values and methods; sociocultural attitudes; characteristic responses and behavior of persons served.[8] Meares added to this framework: forces of change.[9]

The history of the social work profession points to a recurring theme of "generic and specific" formally identified at the Milford Conference in 1929.[10] Since that time, discussion in the professional literature has focused on the knowledge, skills, and values necessary for social work practice. The emphasis on fields of practice as an organizing framework for the profession, particularly in discussions of MSW educational curricula, has predominated. The emphasis on fields of practice, or a conceptualization of professional social work as primarily guided by the system in which organized services are delivered to address social problems,[11] is a theme that may not fit the changing nature of the profession of social work nor the changing nature of agency practice. In addition to a conceptualization of practice based on fields or agency function, social work practice has been viewed as guided by social units of concern (individuals, families, small groups, communities) social technologies (family therapy, clinical social work with individuals, group work, community development), social problems (poverty, delinquency, oppression, interpersonal violence, substance abuse), and the context of practice (urban, nonmetropolitan, rural, international).[12]

## THE CHANGING NATURE OF AGENCY PRACTICE

The arena of social work practice is changing. Social agencies and institutions providing services can no longer be neatly categorized as public, not-for-profit, and proprietary. There is a blending of the funding sources among agencies and, concomitantly, different accountability for services to those in need. The reduction of funding for services during the Reagan and Bush presidential administrations has led to financial burdens and a reduction in the level of services that may be provided. In addition, cost savings and cost benefit mechanisms introduced by Medicaid and Medicare programs are now the norm in establishing guidelines for units of services provided and the length of time that services may be provided. An emphasis on multidisciplinary approaches and cross-agency practice in communities has further changed the nature of social work practice as well as the practice of other professions.

The fee-for-service model and the public versus private models of practice result in changes in the traditional social work agency and social work services. A movement toward privatization in human services is taking place as a result of decreased federal funding and the federal government's purchase-of-service contracts with private agencies.[13] The growth of private and proprietary practice and the growth of for-profit organizations employing social workers in the delivery of health and mental health services is a trend that has been called privatization[14] and corporate welfare.[15] The 1980s can be characterized as the era of commercialization of human services. The distinctions between the public, proprietary, and voluntary sectors in social services have become blurred. The increasing availability of vendorship for third-party reimbursement of social work services has altered the ways in which social work services are offered and are reimbursed, as well as increasing the sources of accountability for social work services.

## WHY OUR PERCEPTIONS OF PRACTICE MUST CHANGE

The changing nature of social work practice and the organization of service delivery systems call for redefinition of the practice of social work. The place of specialization in social work education and the organization of concentrations for education at the advanced level of social work practice are at issue in the design of curricula for the MSW degree. An advanced concentration is comprised of specific knowledge and practice skills, informed by the liberal arts base of education, and foundation knowledge, skills, and values that inform the professional practice of an MSW social worker in agency practice. The advanced practitioner must be prepared to enter a world of practice that requires the social worker to be capable of practice in an ever-changing environment. The structure of this new environment of practice includes multiple roles for the practitioner that cannot as easily be categorized as the specific roles identified for social work practice in the past (e.g., case work, group work, community organization, management, supervision, and clinical social work). Nor does the structure of this practice reinforce a conceptualization of practice oriented to specific institutional or agency-based services (e.g., mental health, hospitals, public social services, juvenile justice, family practice, and child welfare). The clients served by social workers in all settings necessitate preparation of the social worker in assessment, intervention, practice effectiveness, and program evaluation that have multiple components. While social workers practice primarily within an environment in which services are designed and delivered—the agency—clients enter those systems from a variety of cultural and social contexts that may be similar or dissimilar to the contextual world of the service delivery system. The social worker must have the ability to make rapid shifts in the context for understanding human behavior and the social and cultural environment-of-origin of the client.

The rapid expansion in the biological component of the biopychosocial framework, widely accepted by social workers as an organizing construct for integrating variables, forces rapid acquisition and use of new knowledge about genetic and biochemical causation of problems clients bring to the social worker. No longer does grounding in ego psychological theory and the social work practice principles derived from this knowledge-base adequately or accurately inform the social worker dealing with an autistic child and his or her family, an individual diagnosed with bipolar disorder, or the client with a serious mental illness whose primary diagnosis is schizophrenia.

A multicultural perspective is required of social workers in all regions of the United States. The demography of communities throughout the country is fluid. Immigration to the United States from all parts of the world and the increase in mobility of people from one region to another requires a multicultural perspective as a guiding principle of social work practice. This perspective must include a knowledge base that informs practice with various family forms, the values of cultures different from the culture of origin of the social worker, and an openness to learn from the client different ways of expressing emotion and feeling, as well as "starting where the client is."

## REALISTIC SOCIAL WORK EDUCATION

Education and practice are part of a whole, or system, that must interact in a transactional relationship for continuous change and renewal. It is essential that the content and organization of the learning experience within social work education respond to the realities of the practice of the profession. The Curriculum Policy Statements for BSW and MSW programs adopted in 1992 emphasize the responsibility of social work education programs to maintain communication with social work practitioners and groups and organizations involved in policy development and social work services.[16]

## ASKING SOCIAL WORKERS FOR THEIR PERCEPTIONS OF PRACTICE

There are at least four approaches for obtaining information from practitioners to inform decisions about the design of curriculum and its content. These methods vary in structure and underlying philosophy of science perspectives. The purpose of each of these approaches is to determine whether concepts and constructs of practice are relevant to the world of everyday knowledge, thought, and experience of the social work practitioner.

One method, the task or job analysis,[17] is reported in a variety of research projects in the social work literature.[18] The job analysis approach has been used to develop the content validity of employment and credentialing examinations in social work and other professions.[19] The research instrument lists tasks assumed to be associated with social work positions and asks social workers to indicate the importance of the task to the job. Tasks are defined as discrete units of work and are considered to be the logical and necessary steps in the performance of a duty with an identifiable beginning and end. A variation on the task analysis also reported in the research literature lists specific knowledge, skill, and value areas presumed to be associated with the role of a social worker. Respondents are asked to indicate the importance of each knowledge, skill, and value area to the role of the social worker.[20]

A second approach, the nominal group method,[21] is a need identification approach for understanding "the views of the population that one is trying to serve."[22] This technique is based on the principles of interaction from small group theory.[23] The assumption underlying the nominal group approach is that consumers of a service can articulate their needs.[24] The use of the nominal group, in contrast to the discussion group, allows for receiving input from all group members rather than just the more vocal or articulate participants.[25] The use of the nominal group to identify student interests by proposing course content, specific problems in field instruction, and program development was reported by Zastrow and Navarre.[26]

A related approach, the Delphi Technique,[27] was used by Griffin and Eure in their analysis of the ideal curriculum content for the foundation curriculum in BSW programs.[28] Schatz and Jenkins[29] report use of the Delphi Technique in a study exploring generic, generalist, and advanced generalist practice with a panel of 42 authors and experts. The Delphi Technique is a method for collecting judgments without face-to-face interaction of participants. A set of questionnaires is designed and sent to participants. Subsequent questionnaires are designed to summarize information and feedback of opinions from earlier versions of the questionnaire. The first questionnaire presents a broad question and subsequent instruments are built on responses until sufficient information exchange has occurred.

The fourth approach, the focus group, is not a new development in data collection but has received widespread use in qualitative marketing research[30] and public relations.[31] Focus groups are a product of sociology, particularly Columbia University's Bureau of Applied Social Research.[32] Merton notes that as early as 1943 he, Paul Lazarsfeld, and their colleagues were using focused interviews with individuals and groups.[33] Merton, Fiske and Kendall, writing in 1955, note that "the advantages of the focused interview of groups more than offset its disadvantages when one seeks clues to diverse definitions of the situation by a numerous body of individuals."[34] Focus groups are a method of data collection in qualitative research.[35] The product of the group interaction consists of transcripts of the group discussion.[36] The advantages of focus groups as a data collection method include the opportunity to observe a large amount of interaction among participants in a limited period of time and the comparative ease of structuring the group approach compared with interviews of individuals.[37] The disadvantages of the focus group approach lie in the limitations of the unnatural social setting in which interaction takes place and uncertainty about the accuracy of what participants say, which can result in less control by the researcher over the data that is generated.[38] Merton notes that qualitative focus group interviews are a source of new ideas and hypotheses rather than evidence of "the extent and distribution of the provisionally identified qualitative patterns of response."[39]

Each of the four methods has advantages and disadvantages for data collection. The approaches vary in the degree to which they appear to meet standards of empirical verification of the roles and activities, knowledge, skills, and values necessary for social work practice. The task or job analysis used numerical measurement to represent everyday concepts. Statistical analysis can be performed using descriptive data analysis or higher order data reduction approaches such as factor analysis. Sampling procedures that produce representative cross-sectional responses are imperative if the data are to be useful in validating constructs of practice.

The nominal group method, the Delphi Technique, and the focus group are qualitative approaches that can serve exploratory or phenomenolog-ical purposes. The exploratory purpose is served when practice constructs are presented to group members. Validation of the constructs occurs through re-cording of the everyday experience of practitioners in the nominal group or through use of the Delphi Technique. The phenomenological purpose can probably best occur in the focused group. Group members are helped to share their common-sense conceptions of practice, and the reciprocity of perspec-tives of group members can take place. The data are thus in the language of the practitioner rather than the language of predetermined constructs of the researcher or social work educator.

The focus group approach was selected by the authors because of the exploratory-descriptive nature of the research, the desire of the researchers to have face-to-face contact with study participants, and the appropriateness of the phenomenological approach to data collection. The focus group can in-volve consumers of the curriculum of the school to solicit their oral presenta-tion of the content necessary for preparing advanced-level social work practi-tioners.

## EMPLOYING THE FOCUS GROUP
## IN CURRICULUM ASSESSMENT

In planning for the data collection, to serve as one source of information to guide faculty in a curriculum revision of the masters program at Virginia Com-monwealth University, the authors organized focus group sessions throughout the state. Fourteen group sessions were conducted. A series of questions to be posed to focus group participants was developed. The first question solicited data reported here. The question stated: What knowledge and skills are essential for a social worker entering practice in your setting? The question was addressed to group participants and response recorded by the group leader.

The groups were comprised of social workers in various parts of the state where the school has on- or off-campus MSW programs. Faculty were asked to nominate focus group participants. A letter of invitation was sent to potential participants for three of the focus groups. The response rate of those invited was 80%. In addition, 11 focus group sessions were conducted during field instruc-tion sessions in two locations. A total of 149 participants provided data for anal-ysis. The average number of members in each focus group session was nine.

The advantage of this approach is that it allowed the researchers to col-lect data from heterogeneous groups of social work practitioners who both practice and supervise advanced-level social workers in a wide variety of public and private settings throughout the state. As stated earlier, a further advantage is that responses were solicited in practitioners' own language versus a language that employs concepts directly from a conceptual model of social work education.

## REPRESENTATIVENESS OF THE RESPONSES

Virginia is a diverse state, reflecting the economic and cultural differences found in many parts of the nation. With a total population of over 6 million, 75.4% are white, 18.3% black, 2.5% Asian or Pacific Islanders, 2.5% Hispanic origin, 0.3% American Indian, Eskimo or Aleut, and 0.9% other racial origin.[40] The geographic and population density of the state ranges from the Washington beltway to the rural areas of the southwestern region. Five percent of the population are foreign born, and almost seven percent of the population speak a language other than English at home. Income in 1989 dollars indicates an average per capita income of $15,713, and 7.7% of families were below the poverty level according to the 1990 census.[41]

Practitioners, who were the respondents, work with clients from a wide range of cultural and racial origin and economic status. One limitation concerning the respondents should be noted. Many of the participants in the focus group discussions are graduates of the VCU School of Social Work. The language used may have been acquired in the professional socialization process that is an inherent part of social work educational experience.

## DATA ANALYSIS

Data were analyzed using content analysis strategies. A total of 1183 responses were recorded during the 14 focus group sessions. The responses were solicited from four questions posed during the focus group sessions. These questions were: (1) What knowledge and skills are essential for a social worker entering practice in your setting? (2) What are the strengths of the curriculum in preparing graduates to enter practice in your setting? (3) What changes do you think should be made in the curriculum to prepare graduates to enter practice in your setting? (4) What suggestions do you have for organizing the advanced (second) year of study—around populations, social problem areas, fields of practice?

Each comment recorded during a focus group session was used as a data element in a line-by-line analysis used in the open coding phase of data analysis.[42] This approach allowed the tabulation and grouping of duplicate responses by participants. Categories of responses were developed for the knowledge and skill areas. These categories are groupings of concepts and labeled to fit the content of each. Beginning categories of knowledge and skill statements were developed by sampling each seventh statement recorded in the focus group sessions. The phenomenon, knowledge, and skills necessary for social work practice were recorded along with the context within which the knowledge, skill, action, or value statement was proposed by participants, using the beginning categories.

## RESPONSES TO CHANGING PRACTICE NEEDS

Seventeen categories of responses were developed from the content analysis of the 623 responses to the question posed to focus group participants about the essential knowledge, skills, and values necessary for practice in their settings. These responses appear to represent a range of categories of knowledge and skill essential for social work practice. The categories of responses developed from the content analysis and from the representative statements of focus group participants are displayed in Diagram 9–1.

## WHAT IS ADVANCED GENERALIST IN THE PRACTICE OF SOCIAL WORK?

Evident in a review of the comments of focus group participants is that the practice of social work is both diverse and unified. This is in line with the problem focus, problem solving, and multilevel processes of advanced generalist practice noted in Chapter 1. There is a core of skills that are necessary for the practitioner in any setting. In many respects data from the focus group analysis are parallel to that of other studies employing task and content analysis strategies as well as nominal group and the Delphi Technique. Knowledge that there is a core of knowledge, skills, and values among practitioners does not necessarily lead to the conclusion that the advanced generalist model is an appropriate framework for organizing education for social work practice. According to the framework presented in Chapter 1, the advanced generalist must be able to practice independently, is heavily influenced by ethical decision making, respects multicultural practice, and draws from a variety of theories and intervention methods. Some of the distinguishing features of this conceptualization of practice taken from the focus group comments are discussed below.

## SETTINGS OF PRACTICE

The settings of practice of focus group participants were diverse. Respondents came from public, private, and proprietary settings. One emphasis in the comments of participants regardless of setting is the relevance of the multidisciplinary approach in practice. Participants emphasized the need for social workers to be knowledgeable of the roles and functions of other professional disciplines, possess skills necessary for multidisciplinary work, including skill in collaboration and negotiation, and yet be secure in their own professional role as a social worker. In the multidisciplinary practice, social workers must be knowledgeable of the language of other professions and the function of all agency services in the delivery network.

**DIAGRAM 9–1**    Categories of Responses from Focus Group Participants

| CATEGORY | EXEMPLAR STATEMENTS | N OF RESPONSES |
|---|---|---|
| Direct practice roles | Psychopathology and emotional disorders<br>Group dynamics<br>Family relationships and dynamics<br>Human development and behavior<br>Relationship building<br>Knowledge of medications<br>Skill in a wide range of interventions<br>Short-term treatment approaches<br>Empowerment<br>Referral skills<br>Knowledge and skill in documentation<br>Interviewing skills<br>Empathy<br>Ability to meet the client at his or her own<br>    level<br>Ability to join quickly with the client | 149 |
| Indirect practice roles | Knowledge of resources<br>Advocacy<br>Knowledge of how systems impact people<br>Knowledge of service delivery systems<br>Knowledge of entitlement programs<br>Knowledge to analyze and evaluate policy<br>Knowledge of how to effect change within a sys-<br>    tem<br>Progam management and development<br>Laws<br>Case management<br>Ability to lead meetings<br>How to use supervision | 113 |
| Multilevel assessment | Knowledge of biopsychosocial assessment<br>Assessment skills<br>DSM-III-R<br>Substance abuse<br>Socio-cultural evaluation<br>Ability to see the whole person in the<br>    situation<br>Family assessment | 51 |
| Problem focus of practice | Substance abuse<br>Sexual abuse<br>AIDS<br>Poverty<br>Medical knowledge<br>Homelessness | 40 |
| Social work role and the organization | Adapting to the agency's mission<br>Knowledge of the agency's interaction with other<br>    agencies<br>Ability to work with less supervision<br>Planning and implementing tasks | 40 |

**DIAGRAM 9–1** (Continued)

| CATEGORY | EXEMPLAR STATEMENTS | N OF RESPONSES |
|---|---|---|
| Skill in teamwork and collaboration | Skill in multidisciplinary work<br>Knowledge of how to work with people<br>Collaborative skills<br>Diplomacy<br>Ability to negotiate | 33 |
| Functioning as a professional | Ability to view social work from a broad perspective<br>Ability to identify with the profession<br>Feeling empowered and prepared as a social worker<br>Committment to the profession<br>Respect for other professionals | 30 |
| Populations as a focus for practice | AIDS victoms<br>Trauma victims<br>Elderly<br>People with health problems | 28 |
| Self awareness of the social work practitioner | Self awareness<br>Comfort with self<br>Awareness of gender issues | 26 |
| Skill in written and oral communication | Good writing skills<br>Good oral skills | 22 |
| Values and ethics | Commitment to social justice<br>Knowledge of social work values and ethics | 20 |
| Life-long learner | Self-directed learner<br>Ability to learn new approaches<br>Desire to grow and learn | 18 |
| Personal attributes | Creativity<br>Good judgement<br>Willingness to risk<br>Flexibility | 12 |
| Knowledge of human diversity | Multicultural sensitivity<br>Knowledge of working with culturally different people | 12 |
| Research | Knowledge of practice effectiveness research<br>Use of computer technology<br>Research as an underpinning of practice | 10 |
| Theory | Knowledge of systems theory<br>Beginning theoretical base | 8 |
| Skill in making presentations | Group presentation skills<br>Ability to report facts objectively | 5 |
| Skill in serving as an expert witness | Knowledge of expert witness role | 4 |
| Knowledge of the Profession | Knowledge of the economic realities of practice<br>Knowledge of social work as a business | 2 |

## KNOWLEDGE FOR DIRECT PRACTICE

Social work educators stress the importance of theory undergirding practice as the source of knowledge. Practitioners in this study emphasized self-awareness of the practitioner (e.g., comfort with self and the client, awareness of gender issues), personal attributes (e.g., creativity, good judgment, and flexibility), and the ongoing development of the social worker (e.g., ability to learn new approaches, desire to grow and learn) as major components of the knowledge base for social work practice.

The most striking responses about the theory that undergirds social work practice were systems theory, the biopsychosocial approach to understanding human development and behavior, and a multicultural view of the human experience and human diversity. This multicultural view was embraced by participants from larger urban centers of the state as well as social workers practicing in nonmetropolitan and rural settings. What was striking about the responses was the convergence of opinion that multicultural practice is essential. The modal response was that advanced practitioners need to be exposed to and be capable of applying (1) a range of theories for understanding human development and human behavior and (2) a range of intervention strategies based on more than one theoretical approach. Of theory, many participants noted that it is important for the practitioner to know how to learn and adapt to the changing needs of clients and the social problems confronting the social worker in practice. The ability to learn new approaches—or self-directed and life-long learning—was emphasized by respondents.

Respondents emphasized the need for skills in multilevel assessment and problem solving. These skills include knowledge of the components of a biopsychosocial assessment, diagnostic frameworks (e.g., DSM-III-R), family dynamics and family assessment tools, and assessment of substance abuse. Focus group respondents emphasized that advanced practitioners must have knowledge of psychopathology, group dynamics, family relationships and dynamics, substance abuse, human development and human behavior, the impact of physical illnesses on individuals and families, and psychotropic medications regardless of the setting of practice.

## THE SOCIAL WORKER AS PROGRAM PLANNER
## AND SERVICE MANAGER

Respondents noted the importance of educating advanced social workers to assume program planning, management, and administrative roles in organizations. The need for skills in program and service development, mediation, collaboration, networking, proposal writing, budgeting, and contracting was stressed by respondents. The need for knowledge of funding sources, policy and legislative processes, the components of supervision, administration, and program management, as well as knowledge of power, agency politics, and skill in handling competing needs was reported by respondents.

## DIRECT AND INDIRECT PRACTICE KNOWLEDGE AND SKILLS

A major theme evident in the focus group responses was the emphasis on the indirect practice roles as a core for both clinical or direct practice and administration and policy or indirect practice. Examples of indirect practice knowledge and skills necessary for the clinical or direct service practitioner and the program manager, supervisor, or administrator include knowledge of service delivery systems and entitlement programs, skill in analyzing and evaluating social policies and the impact of policies on clients and service delivery organizations, and knowledge of laws governing practice. The advanced practitioner must be knowledgeable about resources, legislative processes, research, organizational behavior, funding sources, and managed care systems, to note a few examples. Both clinical and management, planning and administrative personnel must have the ability to lead meetings and to use knowledge of group dynamics required by team and multidisciplinary approaches.

## THE PRACTITIONER AND AGENCY FUNCTION

Prominent in the responses was the need for the social worker to know the role of social work in the organization and have the ability to adapt to the agency's mission. In addition, the practitioner must have the ability to plan and implement tasks and carry out assignments. The ability to work with less supervision in a time of retrenchment and increasing demands for services was emphasized. Respondents also noted that the social worker must be prepared to implement short-term or brief models of intervention and understand the "business" of the agency—funding sources, accountability, and reimbursement policies. A recurring theme in the focus group responses was that the advanced practitioner must begin employment with the ability to "hit the ground running."

## THE VALUES AND ETHICS OF THE PRACTITIONER

Focus group participants emphasized the need for development of self-awareness among students as future practitioners. In support of the model presented in the third chapter of this text, comments from participants indicate the need for renewed emphasis in the curriculum on the specific teaching of social work values and ethics. A commitment to social justice was a theme evident in the focus group responses.

## THE ADVOCACY ROLE OF THE SOCIAL WORKER

A critical theme in the focus group responses was the advocacy role in social work practice. Advocacy was viewed as essential to both the direct (or clinical) and the indirect practice roles. One respondent captured statements about the advocacy role in stating that the social worker must be a "persistent advocate for clients."

## IMPLICATIONS OF THE STUDY FOR CHANGING PRACTICE NEEDS

Quantitative research is needed to examine the multiple roles and activities of social workers in the changing environment of social work practice. Clarification of the advanced generalist frame of reference is needed. Is this a new framework for practice or another label for "good old-fashioned" social work practice? What was called for by respondents is a practice model that integrates the essential direct and indirect practice roles of the social worker to adequately prepare them for agency practice. The categories identified in Diagram 9–1 comprise another perspective of advanced generalist practice. The responses of focus group participants may very well respond to the question presented in Chapter 1, "What should be included in an advanced generalist concentration?" by depicting what social work practitioners expect from MSW social workers as they begin post-MSW degree employment.

Empirical research on outcomes of practice comparing graduates of various advanced practice education models is called for. The model of education may not be the determining variable in the quality of services provided by the social worker. Several questions about the framework should be addressed: Is there a verifiable set of constructs that comprise advanced generalist practice? Does practice change as the social worker increases in practice experience? Does the framework apply to rural, nonmetropolitan, and urban settings?

## SUMMARY

A study using focus groups was employed by Virginia Commonwealth University to obtain responses from practitioners in a variety of practice settings throughout the state. The study used qualitative data analysis procedures to identify whether responses to the knowledge, skill, and values identified by social work practitioners fit the description of the advanced generalist model for social work practice.

The major themes of the responses of focus group participants were that social work practice requires a commitment to social work values and ethics, knowledge for multiple levels of assessment, and intervention that draws from a variety of theoretical approaches. Emphasis was placed on the need for direct service practitioners to be well-grounded in knowledge and skills that have traditionally been identified with planning and administrative practice roles. Study respondents stressed the importance of multidisciplinary practice, knowledge of the social work role in the organization, teamwork, and collaborative skills as essential to the practice of the advanced social worker. Knowledge of human diversity, a problem focus for practice, skill in multiple levels of assessment and intervention, and the need for the practitioner to engage in life-long learning were themes identified by respondents that are congruent with the advanced generalist model.

The authors recommend further research to define empirically the advanced generalist model and to distinguish the model from traditional frameworks for organizing social work education. The research should extend the qualitative approach used in this study for building a quantitative research approach for defining the advanced generalist model. The advanced generalist model appears to meet the changing needs of social work practice.

## NOTES

1. This framework was originally proposed by Bartlett and the NASW Commission on Practice as the essential nature of social work practice. Harriett M. Bartlett, "Toward Clarification and Improvement of Social Work Practice," *Social Work* 3 (May 1958): 3–9.

2. Harriett M. Bartlett, *Analyzing Social Work Practice by Fields* (New York: National Association of Social Workers, 1961), p. 9.

3. Emilia E. Martinez-Brawley, "Rural Social Work as a Contextual Specialty: Undergraduate Focus or Graduate Concentration?," *Journal of Social Work Education* 21, no. 3 (Fall 1985): 36–42.

4. This approach is based on grounded theory and the procedures of qualitative research. As described by Strauss and Corbin, grounded theory is inductively derived through systematic data collection and analysis: "one does not begin with a theory, then prove it. Rather, one begins with an area of study and what is relevant to that area is allowed to emerge." Anselm Strauss & Juliet Corbin, *Basics of Qualitative Research Grounded Theory Procedures and Techniques* (Beverly Hills: Sage Publications, 1990), p. 23.

5. Armando Morales, "Beyond Traditional Conceptual Frameworks," *Social Work* 22, no. 5 (September 1977): 387.

6. Curriculum Policy Statement for Master's Degree Programs in Social Work Education (Alexandria, Va.: Council on Social Work Education, July 19, 1922) and Curriculum Policy Statement for Baccalaureate Degree Programs in Social Work Education (Alexandria, Va.: Council on Social Work Education, July 19, 1992).

7. Harriett M. Bartlett, *The Common Base of Social Work Practice* (New York: National Association of Social Workers, 1970).

8. Bartlett, *Analyzing Social Work Practice*, 1988.

9. Paula A. Meares, "Educating Social Workers for Specialization," *Social Work in Education* 3, no. 2 (Summer 1981): 36–52.

10. National Association of Social Workers, *Social Case Work: Generic and Specific:*

*A Report on the Milford Conference* (Washington, D.C.: National Association of Social Workers, 1974, reprint of 1929 ed.).

11. Bartlett, *Analyzing Social Work Practice*.

12. Nancy Carroll, "Areas of Concentration in the Graduate Curriculum: A Three Dimensional Approach," *Journal of Education for Social Work* 11, no. 2 (Spring 1975): 3–10; Emilia E. Martinez-Brawley, "Rural Social Work as a Contextual Specialty: Undergraduate Focus or Graduate Concentration?" *Journal of Social Work Education* 21, no. 3 (Fall 1985): 36–42.

13. Mary Ann Jimenez, "Historical Evolution and Future Challenges of the Human Service Professions," *Families in Society: The Journal of Contemporary Human Services* 71, no. 1 (January 1990): 3–12.

14. Jimenez, "Historical Evolution"; and Mimi Abramovitz, "The Privatization of the Welfare State: A Review," *Social Work* 31, no. 4 (July/August 1986): 257–266.

15. Daniel Stoesz, "A Theory of Social Welfare," *Social Work* 34, no. 2 (March 1989): 101–109.

16. *Curriculum Policy Statement for Baccalaureate Degree Programs* and *Curriculum Policy Statement for Master's Degree Programs*.

17. For a discussion of the job analysis see: Ernest J. McCormick, *Job Analysis: Methods and Applications* (New York: AMACOM, 1979); Stephen E. Bemis, Ann Holt Belenky, and Dee Ann Soder, *Job Analysis An Effective Management Tool* (Washington, D.C.: The Bureau of National Affairs, Inc., 1983).

18. Sidney A. Fine and W. W. Wiley, *An Introduction to Functional Job Analysis: Methods for Manpower Analysis*. Monograph No. 4 (Kalamazoo, Mich.: W.E. Upjohn Institute for Employment Research, 1971); Robert J. Teare, "A Task Analysis for Public Welfare Practice and Educational Implications," in F. Clark, M. Arkava, and associates, eds. *The Pursuit of Competence in Social Work* (San Francisco: Jossey-Bass Publishers, 1979); Robert J. Teare, *Social Work Practice in a Public Welfare Setting: An Empirical Analysis* (New York: Praeger, 1981); Bradford W. Sheafor, Robert J. Teare, Mervyn W. Hancock, and Thomas P. Gauthier, "Curriculum Development through Content Analysis: A New Zealand Experience," *Journal of Social Work Education* 21, no. 3 (Fall 1985): 113–124; Marilyn Lamber, "A Taxonomy of Case Management Tasks in Community Mental Health Facilities," *Social Work Research and Abstracts* 28, no. 3 (September 1992): 3–10.

19. Marilyn A. Biggerstaff and Robin I. Eisenberg. *Summary Report: Job Verification Analysis Study* (Culpeper, Va.: American Association of State Social Work Boards, 1989).

20. Michael R. Daley and Martha Williams, "The Protective Services Questionnaire: Assessing Knowledge and Skills in Child Protective Services," *Social Work Research and Abstracts* 15, no. 3 (Fall 1979): 32–38; Betty L. Baer and Ronald Federico, *Educating the Baccalaureate Social Worker: Report of the Undergraduate Social Work Curriculum Development Project* (Cambridge, Mass.: Ballinger Publishing Co., 1978); Marilyn A. Biggerstaff and Michael S. Kolevzon, "Differential Use of Social Work Knowledge, Skills, and Techniques by MSW, BSW, and BA Level Practitioners," *Journal of Education for Social Work* 16, no. 3 (Fall 1980): 67–74

21. The nominal group technique (NGT) was developed by Delbecq and Van de Ven in 1968 as a planning tool. For detailed information on NGT procedures, see Andre L. Delbecq, Andrew, H. Van de Ven, and David H. Gustafson, *Group Techniques for Program Planning A Guide to Nominal Group and Delphi Process* (Glenview, Ill.: Scott, Foresman & Co., 1975).

22. Charles Zastrow and R. Navarre, "The Nominal Group: A New Tool for Making Social Work Education Relevant," *Journal of Education for Social Work* 13, no. 1 (Winter 1977): 113.

23. Paul A. Hare, *Handbook of Small Group Research* (New York: The Free Press, 1962).

24. Andrew L. Delbecq and Andrew Van de Ven, "A Group Process Model for Problem Identification and Program Planning," *Journal of Applied Behavioral Science* 7 (1971): 466–492.

25. Zastrow and Navarre, "The Nominal Group."

26. Zastrow and Navarre, *ibid.*

27. The Delphi Technique was developed by Dalkey at the Rand Corporation in the 1950s. For detailed information about these procedures, see Norman C. Dalkey, *Delphi* (Rand Corporation, 1967), Delbecq, Van de Ven & Gustafson, *Group Techniques for Program Planning;* and Harold A. Linstone and Murray Turoff, eds., *The Delphi Method: Techniques and Applications* (Reading, Mass.: Addison-Wesley Publishing Co., 1975).

28. Neil Griffin and Jerry Eure, "Toward a Definition of the Professional Foundation in Social Work Education," *Journal of Social Work Education* 21, no. 3 (Fall 1985): 73–91.

29. Mona Struhsaker Schatz and Lowell Jenkins, *Differentiating Generic Foundation, Generalist Social Work Perspective, and Advanced Generalist Practice in the Generalist Perspective: Final Report of a National Delphi Study* (Fort Collins, Colo.: Colorado State University, Department of Social Work, 1987).

30. Bobby J. Calder, "Focus Groups and the Nature of Qualitative Marketing Research," *Journal of Marketing Research* 14 (August 1977): 353–364.

31. Larissa A. Grunig, "Using Focus Group Research in Public Relations," *Public Relations Review* 16, no. 2 (Summer 1990): 36–49.

32. Robert K. Merton and Patricia L. Kendall, "The Focused Interview," *American Journal of Sociology,* 51 (1956): 541–557; Robert K. Merton, Marjorie Fiske, and Patricia L. Kendall, *The Focused Interview* (New York: The Free Press, 1956).

33. Robert K. Merton, "The Focussed Interview and Focus Groups Continuities and Discontinuities," *Public Opinion Quarterly* 51 (Winter 1987): 550–556.

34. Merton, Fiske, and Kendall, "The Focused Interview," p. 135.

35. Procedures for conducting focus groups are found in: Richard A. Krueger, *Focus Groups: A Practical Guide for Applied Research* (Newbury Park, Calif.: Sage 1988).

36. David L. Morgan, *Focus Groups as Qualitative Research.* (Newberry Park, Calif.: Sage Publications, 1988).

37. *Ibid.*

38. *Ibid.*

39. Merton, "The Focussed Interview and Focus Groups," p. 558.

40. U.S. Department of Commerce, Bureau of the Census, *1990 Census of Population and Housing. Summary Population and Housing Characteristics. Virginia* (Washington, D.C.: U.S. Government Printing Office, 1991).

41. *Ibid.*

42. Strauss and Corbin describe open coding as the naming and categorizing of phenomena, breaking down the data into discrete parts in preparation for analysis of similarities and differences. Strauss and Corbin, *Basics of Qualitative Research.*

# 10
# Advanced Generalist Practitioners: Responding to Changing Practice Needs

*INTRODUCTION*

In the Fall of 1992, an invitation was sent to each of the ten MSW programs in the United States offering concentrations in advanced generalist practice in 1990.[1] They were invited to participate in a follow-up study of advanced generalist graduates of accredited MSW programs. Five of the ten schools responded, and a questionnaire was sent to 161 practitioners from the participating programs who graduated between 1988 and 1991 with concentrations in advanced generalist practice.

The study was conducted in an effort to enhance the quality and relevance of advanced generalist social work education and practice. The questionnaire (see Appendix E) was designed to obtain information about the current practice of advanced generalists and their perceptions of the preparation they received in their advanced generalist concentrations. Central questions raised by the researcher were:

1. Where are advanced generalists practicing in the field of human services today? (Family service, health, judicial system, school, other?)
2. What are advanced generalists doing in the field? (Casework, group work, community organization, supervision, management, administration, policy development, program planning, family therapy, research, teaching, other?)
3. What are advanced generalists' perceptions of their current practice? (Holistic, problem solving, globally aware, advanced generalist, other?)
4. To what extent do graduates believe that their graduate programs prepared them for various dimensions of advanced generalist practice? (Direct practice, indirect practice, integrated practice, cross-cultural practice, multicultural practice, international social work, ethical decision making, teamwork, referrals, computer usage, open selection of theories for assessment and intervention, evaluation and comparison of social processes, programs, and policies?)
5. To what extent do advanced generalists perceive their practice as being impacted by international events or developments?
6. What theories are being used by advanced generalists for assessment and intervention in their practice?
7. What curriculum areas need to be introduced or strengthened in advanced generalist education programs?

In this chapter, the results of the study are presented with their implications for social work education and practice as the profession continues to grow and respond to changing practice needs.

## THE STUDY

### Study Sample

Of the 161 questionnaires sent, 19 were returned unopened and marked "no forwarding address." Of the remaining 142 questionnaires, 57 (40.13%) were completed and returned by advanced generalists. All except three of the respondents graduated with their MSW degree in 1990 and 1991 (Diagram 10–1). The respondents averaged 4.84 years of social work experience and 2.83 years of voluntary service prior to their entering graduate school (Diagram 10–2).

**DIAGRAM 10–1**  Year Respondents Graduated

| GRADUATION YEAR | NUMBER OF RESPONDENTS |
|---|---|
| 1991 | 11 |
| 1990 | 43 |
| 1989 | 2 |
| 1988 | 1 |

**DIAGRAM 10–2**   Experience

| TYPE OF EXPERIENCE | AVERAGE YEARS | STANDARD DEVIATION |
|---|---|---|
| Social work | 4.84 | 5.70 |
| Volunteer | 2.83 | 4.62 |

### Findings

Location: Over half of the graduates (57.9%, $n = 33$) indicated that they were working in the fields of health (31.58%, $n = 18$) or mental health (26.31%, $n = 15$). The two other main work environments identified were family service (21.05%, $n = 12$) and schools (8.77%, $n = 5$) (Diagrams 10–3 and 10–4).

*Practice Modalities:*  In response to the inquiry of how their time was spent in the field (Diagrams 10–5 and 10–6), Casework (41.47%) and agency administration (9.56%) averaged the highest percent of time spent in the field for the total 57 respondents. An average of 60.23% of the 57 respondents' time was given to the direct practice modalities of casework, group work, family therapy, or community organization. An average of 26.09% of their time was given to the indirect practice modalities of supervision, management, administration, policy development, program planning, research, and/or teaching. Other activities, such as consulting, case reviewing, attending in-services, making referrals, and offering psychotherapy, were identified for an average of 11.3% of the time spent by the 57 respondents.

It is of relevance to this text that 68.4% ($n = 39$) of the respondents indicated that they were *concurrently* engaged in direct and indirect practice modalities (called "integrated practice"). Fourteen (24.56%) participants selected only direct practice modalities, and four (7%) selected only indirect practice modalities. Only three of the fourteen indicating direct practice modalities said that 100% of their time was spent doing casework. Only three of the four

**DIAGRAM 10–3**   Work Environment

| TYPE OF ENVIRONMENT | PERCENTAGE OF RESPONDENTS | NUMBER OF RESPONDENTS |
|---|---|---|
| Health* | 31.58 | 18 |
| Mental health | 26.31 | 15 |
| Family | 21.05 | 12 |
| School | 8.77 | 5 |
| Other[†] | 10.53 | 6 |
| No response | 1.75 | 1 |

*Health includes health, home health, and hospital
[†]Other includes victim advocacy, county SS, residential treatment, prison, homeless shelter, training center

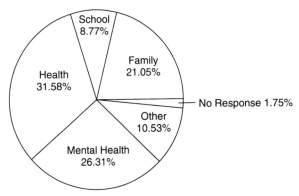

**DIAGRAM 10–4** Work Environment

indicating indirect practice modalities said that 100% of their time was spent doing agency administration.

*Practice Descriptions* Participants were asked to indicate the degree to which they saw their current practice reflecting some of the concepts presented in this text. As found in Diagram 10–7, to a large or total degree, the graduates saw their practice as problem solving (86%, $n = 49$), holistic (79%, $n = 45$), and advanced generalist (65%, $n = 37$). It is interesting to note that although 30% ($n = 17$) of the graduates said that their practice has been impacted by international events or developments (question #8 on questionnaire), only 18% ($n = 10$) described their practice as globally aware to a large or total extent. When asked in question #8 to describe how their practice was

**DIAGRAM 10–5** How Time Is Spent

| TYPE OF WORK | PERCENTAGE OF TIME |
| --- | --- |
| Casework | 41.47 |
| Family therapy | 8.35 |
| Group work | 6.88 |
| Community organization | 3.53 |
| Other* | 11.30 |
| Research | 0.70 |
| Teaching | 2.09 |
| Policy development | 2.09 |
| Management | 3.07 |
| Program planning | 4.05 |
| Supervision | 4.53 |
| Agency administration | 9.56 |
| (Unaccounted time) | 2.39 |

*Other includes community referrals, inservices, psychotherapy, consulting, advising, and reviewing cases for permanency options.

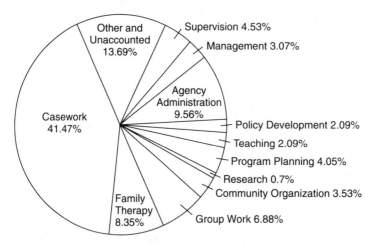

**DIAGRAM 10–6**    How Time Is Spent

impacted, responses included the Persian Gulf War, the restructuring of Russia, Germany, Yugoslavia, changes in international adoption policies, influx of migrants, medical technology, world economy, and global economic slowdown. Forty- four percent ($n = 25$) of the graduates saw their practice as "built on an ecological systems perspective" to a total or large degree. Other ways they described their practice (question #6) included rural, androgogical, team oriented, interdisciplinary, clinical, having a focus on client advocacy and empowerment, social learning, or characterized by early intervention. Additional words used by individual graduates were "Christian," a "300 caseload," and "repressed by administrative red tape."

*Perceptions of Proficiency*    The graduates were asked how proficient they thought they were in various components of advanced generalist practice (Diagram 10–8). All of the respondents indicated that they saw themselves as

**DIAGRAM 10–7**    Description of Practice

| QUESTION | TOTALLY, NO., (%) | LARGE DEGREE, NO., (%) | MODERATELY NO., (%) | SMALL DEGREE, NO., (%) | NOT PRESENT, NO., (%) |
|---|---|---|---|---|---|
| Holistic | 8 (14) | 37 (65) | 5 ( 9) | 5 ( 9) | 2 ( 4) |
| Problem solving | 7 (12) | 42 (74) | 8 (14) | 0 ( 0) | 0 ( 0) |
| Eco systems perspective | 1 ( 2) | 24 (42) | 20 (35) | 8 (14) | 2 ( 4) |
| Advanced generalist | 10 (18) | 27 (47) | 14 (25) | 4 ( 7) | 0 ( 0) |
| Globally aware | 1 ( 2) | 9 (16) | 21 (37) | 18 (32) | 6 (11) |
| Other* | 4 ( 7) | 7 (12) | 0 ( 0) | 0 ( 0) | 0 ( 0) |

*Other includes advocacy, client empowerment, social learning, christian, early intervention, and team oriented.

**DIAGRAM 10–8** Perception of Proficiency

| QUESTION | VERY PROFICIENT (%) | SOMEWHAT PROFICIENT (%) | NOT VERY PROFICIENT (%) | NOT AT ALL PROFICIENT (%) |
|---|---|---|---|---|
| Direct practice | 43 (75) | 14 (25) | 0 ( 0) | 0 ( 0) |
| Indirect practice | 20 (35) | 28 (49) | 8 (14) | 1 ( 2) |
| Integrated practice | 25 (44) | 27 (47) | 4 ( 7) | 0 ( 0) |
| Diverse theories for assessment | 29 (51) | 21 (37) | 7 (12) | 0 ( 0) |
| Diverse theories for intervention | 29 (51) | 20 (35) | 8 (14) | 0 ( 0) |
| Program and policy evaluation | 14 (25) | 30 (53) | 11 (19) | 2 ( 4) |
| Computer research skills | 10 (18) | 10 (18) | 19 (33) | 17 (30) |

"somewhat proficient" or "very proficient" in "direct practice" (100%, $n = 57$). Ninety-one percent ($n = 52$) thought that they were "somewhat" or "very proficient" in "integrated practice," and 84% ($n = 48$) perceived themselves as "very" or "somewhat" proficient in "indirect practice." Eighty-six to 88% ($n = 50$, $n = 49$) thought that they were "very" or "somewhat" proficient in using an "open selection of diverse theories (models, tools, techniques, concepts)" for assessment and intervention, and 78% ($n = 44$) thought that they were "very" or "somewhat" proficient in evaluating and comparing social process, programs, and policies. A much smaller percent (36%, $n = 20$) perceived themselves as proficient in the use of computer skills in social work research.

*Practice Involvement* The graduates were asked to what extent they thought that they engaged in cross-cultural, multicultural, and international practice (question #14), (Diagram 10–9). Seventy-five percent ($n = 43$) indicated "some" or "great" involvement in cross-cultural practice, 60% ($n = 34$) in multicultural practice, and 11% ($n = 6$) in international practice. Practitioners were asked also to what extent they engaged in referrals and teamwork. Ninety-three percent ($n = 53$) indicated "some" or "great" involvement with referrals and 96% ($n = 45$) with teamwork.

Of pertinence to Chapter 3 of this text, findings indicated 90% ($n = 51$) of the graduates said that they engaged in "ethical decision making," and 84%

**DIAGRAM 10–9** Perceived Involvement

| QUESTION | GREAT (%) | SOME (%) | LITTLE (%) | NOT AT ALL (%) |
|---|---|---|---|---|
| International S/W | 1 ( 2) | 5 ( 9) | 14 (25) | 37 (65) |
| Multicultural practice | 14 (25) | 20 (35) | 13 (23) | 10 (18) |
| Cross-cultural practice | 16 (28) | 27 (47) | 9 (16) | 5 ( 9) |
| Dealing with ethical dilemmas | 25 (44) | 23 (40) | 7 (12) | 2 ( 4) |
| Ethical decision making | 33 (58) | 18 (32) | 5 ( 9) | 1 ( 2) |
| Making referrals | 37 (65) | 16 (28) | 3 ( 5) | 0 ( 0) |
| Teamwork | 43 (75) | 12 (21) | 2 ( 4) | 0 ( 0) |

(*n* = 48) found themselves "dealing with ethical dilemmas" to a "great" or "some" extent. When asked to indicate what factors they would consider before making professional judgments in ethical dilemmas (question #7), more than half of the graduates agreed on the factors of "circumstances" (91%, *n* = 52), "person" (89.5%, *n* = 51), "outcome" (77.2%, *n* = 44), and "environment" (63.2%, *n* = 36). Less than half agreed on the factors of "norms" (49.1%, *n* = 28), "means" (43.9%, *n* = 25), and "ends" (43.9%, *n* = 25). Four respondents added the factor of "law" or "legal risks." One stated "morals," and one said "least harmful to others."

*Perception of Preparation* Diagram 10–10 reflects the participants' response to questions regarding their perceptions of the preparation they received in their graduate programs (question #14, a,b,c). When considering only the "great" extent of preparation option for practice preparation, the largest number of respondents (*n* = 19, 33%) identified "direct practice" as the priority area. When combining "great" with the next option, to "some" extent, however, it was "indirect practice" that received the highest priority (88%, *n* = 16 + 34 = 50). "Integated practice" preparation received the second highest total, assessed to a "great" extent by 30% (*n* = 17) and to "some" extent by 54% (*n* = 31), totaling 84% (*n* = 48). "Direct practice" received a total of 70% (*n* = 19 + 21 = 40).

*Major Theories* Graduates were asked to identify the major theories (models, tools, techniques) they used when making asessments (question #11). Systems theory, behavioral theory, and developmental theories, particularly Erikson's psychosocial theory, were the most frequently cited (Diagram 10–11). Inquiry extended to the identification of major theories (models, tools, techniques) used by participants for intervention (question #12). Systems theory, behavioral theory, cognitive theory, and problem-solving were the most frequently cited (Diagram 10–12). Twenty-three (40.35%) of the study participants left the question unanswered, or they listed only one theory (model, tool, technique) used by them in making assessments. Twenty (35.09%) did not indicate any theory, or they listed only one theory (model, tool, technique) used for intervention.

*Resulting Questions* The preceding data raised pertinent questions that led to further analysis. Why did 100% of the graduates perceive that they were

**DIAGRAM 10–10**  Perception of Preparation

| QUESTION | GREAT (%) | SOME (%) | LITTLE (%) | NOT AT ALL (%) |
|---|---|---|---|---|
| Direct practice | 19 (33) | 21 (37) | 14 (25) | 3 (5) |
| Indirect practice | 16 (28) | 34 (60) | 6 (11) | 1 (2) |
| Integrated practice | 17 (30) | 31 (54) | 8 (14) | 1 (2) |

**DIAGRAM 10–11** Major Theories (Models, Tools, Techniques) Used in Assessments Chosen by Three or More Respondents

| ASSESSMENT THEORY | PERCENTAGE OF RESPONDENTS | NUMBER OF RESPONDENTS |
|---|---|---|
| Systems Theory | 40.35 | 23 |
| Behavioral | 17.54 | 10 |
| Developmental | 12.28 | 7 |
| Erikson | 12.28 | 7 |
| Psychosocial | 12.28 | 7 |
| Eco Environmental | 8.77 | 5 |
| Cognitive | 8.77 | 5 |
| Interview Techniques | 8.77 | 5 |
| Problem Solving | 8.77 | 5 |
| Role | 7.01 | 4 |
| Family Treatment | 7.01 | 4 |
| Various Instruments | 7.01 | 4 |
| Reality | 5.26 | 3 |
| Crisis Intervention | 5.26 | 3 |
| Psychoanalytic | 5.26 | 3 |

"very" or "somewhat" proficient in direct practice and only 70% perceive that their graduate programs prepared them for direct practice to a "great" or "some" extent? Is there a significant relationship between perception of proficiency in practice (direct, indirect, integrated) and perception of graduate program preparation for practice (direct, indirect, integrated)? Is there a correlation between years of social work experience or voluntary experience prior to graduate school and perception of proficiency in direct, indirect, or integrated practice? Does the amount of time one currently spends doing direct,

**DIAGRAM 10–12** Major Theories (Tools, Techniques, Models) Used for Intervention Chosen by Three or More Respondents

| INTERVENTION THEORY | PERCENTAGE OF RESPONDENTS | NUMBER OF RESPONDENTS |
|---|---|---|
| Systems | 38.60 | 22 |
| Behavioral | 31.58 | 18 |
| Cognitive | 22.81 | 13 |
| Problem Solving | 15.79 | 9 |
| Family Oriented | 12.28 | 7 |
| Reality | 12.28 | 7 |
| Crisis | 10.53 | 6 |
| Eco Environmental | 8.77 | 5 |
| Objective Relation | 7.02 | 4 |
| Erikson | 7.02 | 4 |
| Gestalt | 7.02 | 4 |
| Social Learning | 5.26 | 3 |
| Rogerian | 5.26 | 3 |
| Rational Emotive | 5.26 | 3 |

indirect, or integrated practice correlate with one's perception of proficiency in, or graduate school preparation for, direct, indirect, or integrated practice? Did the responses of the graduates differ according to the school attended? For example, did all of the graduates who perceived that they were "very" proficient in direct (indirect or integrated) practice come from the same graduate program? Did all of the graduates who thought that their graduate programs prepared them for indirect (direct or integrated) practice to a "great" extent come from the same school?

Statistical analyses to identify significant relationships or differences among the variables were conducted. A significant relationship was found between the graduates' years of social work experience prior to graduate school and their perceived proficiency in direct practice (rho = .42, $p$ = .04). Years of prior experience was not significantly related to their perception of proficiency in indirect or integrated practice.

There was a high correlation between their perceived proficiency in indirect practice and the extent of time currently spent in indirect practice in the field (rho = .47, $p$ = .0002). There was not a significant relationship between their perceived proficiency in direct or integrated practice and their current time spent in direct or integrated practice.

There was a significant inverse correlation between the amount of time currently spent in direct practice and perceived proficiency in indirect practice (rho = -.46, $p$ = .0002). The more time graduates spent doing direct practice, the less proficient they thought they were in indirect practice.

The respondents' perception of their proficiency in indirect practice was significantly related to their perception of proficiency in integrated practice (rho = .59, $p$ = .0001). There was not a significant relationship between their perception of being proficient in direct practice and their perception of proficiency in indirect or integrated practice.

There was a significant relationship between their perceived preparation for direct practice in their graduate schools and their perceived proficiency in direct practice (rho = .34, $p$ = .0007). There was also a significant relationship between their perceived preparation for integrated practice and proficiency in integrated practice (rho = .26, $p$ = .05). There was not a significant relationship between their perceived preparation for indirect practice and their perceived proficiency in indirect practice.

There were significant relationships among the variables indicating the graduates' perceptions of preparation they received for direct, indirect, and integrated practice. The more preparation they perceived in one area, the more they perceived in the others (direct with indirect: rho = .42, $p$ = .001; direct with integrated: rho = .54, $p$ = .0001; indirect with integrated: rho = .75, $p$ = .0001).

The year of graduation from their MSW programs did not relate significantly to the graduates' perceptions of their proficiency, or with preparation for practice, or with the amount of time they spent in direct, indirect, or inte-

**DIAGRAM 10–13**   Respondents' Mean Perception of Proficiency in Indirect Practice According to Work Environments

| WORK ENVIRONMENT | N | MEAN | SD |
|---|---|---|---|
| Family | 12 | 3.4166 | .6685 |
| Health | 18 | 2.8888 | .8323 |
| School | 5 | 3.2000 | .8366 |
| Mental Health | 15 | 3.0666 | .5936 |
| Other | 6 | 3.8333 | .4082 |

grated practice. The particular school attended did not make any significant difference in the responses of the graduates. There was, however, a significant difference ($F = 2.5$, $p = .05$, DF = 4) in the graduates' perception of proficiency in indirect practice (scale of 0 to 4, Diagram 10–8) according to their current work environment (family, health, mental health, school, other). As found in Diagram 10–13, those in the field of "health" averaged the lowest perception of proficiency in indirect practice ($M = 2.8$, $n = 18$).

### Study Implications

This study raised a number of additional questions in need of further consideration. Why, for example, did only 49% of the graduates indicate a consideration of norms, morals, or values in making professional judgments concerning ethical dilemmas? Why did 63% of the sample see themselves as not very proficient or not at all proficient in the use of computer skills for social work research? Why did 43% of the practitioners indicate that being globally aware was either not present or only to a small degree present in their practice? As brought out in this text, the areas of (1) ethical decision making (Chapter 3), (2) computer technology (Chapter 7), and (3) international awareness (Chapter 2) are curriculum areas in need of attention and development in graduate social work programs to prepare students for current and future realities.

Another question raised by the study is: Why did not more graduates indicate a greater use of theories (tools, techniques, models) for assessment or intervention? The results reflect the possibility that the participants are unclear and limited in their use of theories (models, tools, techniques) in practice. Although systems theory appears to be the most commonly used theory by the advanced generalists, there was only 40% concurrence in this response. As brought out in Chapter 4 of this text, advanced generalists are expected to have a pool or range of theories, tools, models, or techniques at their disposal as they are called upon to work with multiple problems and populations.

In addition, it was not apparent in their responses that the participants saw the relationship between systems theory and ecological systems theory. It was not clear also that respondents saw a relationship between development,

Erikson, and psychosocial theory. The ability to recognize the common characteristics or "points of agreement" of different theoretical perspectives is increasingly emphasized in the social sciences and in the human services.[2] This ability to compare and integrate is a major challenge and expectation for advanced generalists.

The responses of the graduates, therefore, appear to reflect some confusion regarding the meaning of (1) theory for assessment (understanding), (2) theory for intervention (to guide actions) and (3) the interrelationships among and between theories. Graduate social work programs, particularly those offering advanced generalist concentrations where there is an inherent "open selection of theories," may find these implications helpful to curriculum development.

Although this study is limited because of the small sample size ($n = 57$), it provides a picture of the current practice of advanced generalists today. Clearly, their activities are congruent with the emerging practice needs described by the 149 practicing social workers identified in Chapter 9. The results of the study highlight areas in need of strengthening and further development by educational programs for advanced generalist practice.

### THE ADVANCED GENERALIST—A PRACTITIONER FOR ALL SEASONS

The identity of the advanced generalist is complex and multifaceted. Within the boundaries of the model practitioner presented in this text, there are several systemic identities of self. The advanced generalist may be described as a holistic practitioner, a pre-present-post modern theoretical practitioner, a policy practitioner, an internationalized practitioner, and a covenant practitioner. In other words, the advanced generalist is a practitioner for all seasons.

As developed in Chapter 5, holistic practice is actualized as the practitioner uses a problem focus and responds directly or indirectly to a problem (or problems) as needed at any given time. Holistic practitioners see the whole and partialize, select, and intervene at different levels. The advanced generalist, as pointed out in Chapter 4, calls upon diverse theories for assessment and intervention. The worker is aware of the traditional concepts, theories, tools, and processes that are intrinsic to the nature of social work. The concept of "person in environment," for example, has always served as a primary concept for distinguishing social work from other professions. At the same time, practitioners remain open to learning contemporary and emerging theories, modern and post modern, in their life-long process of knowledge development. They are able to see the interrelationship of theories and the value of integrating related theories in practice. They contribute to professional knowledge, as brought out in Chapter 7, by using quantitative, qualitative, or combined research methods, depending on the nature of the problem selected for study. Advanced generalists are holistic, pre-present-post modern theoretical practitioners.

If policy or program development is found to be needed to solve a problem, as pointed out in Chapter 8, advanced generalists recognize and respond to this need. They are frequently working in geographic areas where there are extensive and diverse unmet needs requiring the initiation or changing of social programs or policies. They may be involved in complex political situations that require advanced skill for evaluating, revising, or formulating effective policy. In addition to researching and documenting need and to advocating and obtaining funding, they are often expected to assume leadership in proposing relevant policy for program implementation and distribution of resources.

Advanced generalists may become involved with social policy at the local, national, foreign, or international level. They see the interrelatedness among social problems, issues, policies, and programs of different countries and populations. They are aware of global interdependence as it affects social welfare, recognizing, for example, the impact of U.S. policy on social welfare conditions in other countries. Building on a knowledge of the history and development of social welfare in their own country, they broaden their understanding by studying the philosophies, perspectives, policies, and practices used in other countries to address welfare needs and issues. In addition to descriptive studies of cross-national policy analysis, they conduct comparative process analysis in which decision-making processes among nations are studied in the light of various discrete and common influential factors.[3] Advanced generalists are policy practitioners[4] and internationalized practitioners.[5]

As advanced generalists come face-to-face repeatedly with ethical dilemmas, they reflect a professional commitment that endures throughout the stresses and challenges of conflicting situations. They demonstrate a way of life that entails entering the world of the oppressed or needy and standing with them in solidarity. This type of ethical practice has been described as a "covenant model."[6] Professionals in this model promise to return the gifts they have received in being prepared for human service. They are committed to serve and stand by clients and community as they work together in partnership to find appropriate ways to relieve distress and achieve social justice and development. Advanced generalists are "covenant" practitioners.

Many other practitioner identities are emerging in the profession that can be used to describe the advanced social work generalist. The studies cited in Chapters 9 and 10 point to the need for social workers who can be many things to many people at different places and times. Advanced generalists as put forth in this text are practitioners for all seasons.

## CONCLUSION

The human environment that consumes the services of advanced generalists throughout the world is constantly changing with emerging diverse problems and populations. The practitioners and their fields of practice, therefore, are called to be attentive and dynamically responsive to changing human needs. In his book *The Saturated Self,* Kenneth Gergen describes an emerging postmodern culture in which traditional disciplines lose their boundaries and cultural life forms blend and merge. As categories cease to be sacred and that which was securely identifiable becomes ever shifting, there will be, according to Gergen, a change in emerging conceptions of individual selves. He sees the individual moving into a stage called the "relational self." In this state, "One's sense of individual autonomy gives way to a reality of immersed interdependence, in which it is relationship that constructs the self."[7] Advanced generalist practitioners are at the cutting edge of this futuristic movement. Throughout their professional socialization, the reality of human interdependence and the need for adaptive, constructive use of self are persistently emphasized.

The curriculum of a professional social work education program involves a learning process and growth opportunities that, because of language limitations, cannot be fully explained in words. The nature and purpose of the program require a pedagogy that goes beyond cognition. Epistemology ("knowing") and ontology ("being") need to be united in a critically reflective and dialogical process within a community of discourse for self-reflection and professional development. Students in social work, particularly in advanced generalist concentrations, do not learn only knowledge, values, and skills. They are formed, informed, and transformed as they become aware of their being as subject and servant, as well as objective provider. Through an integrative learning process, they come to know that each relationship with clients, teachers, colleagues, or others leaves both changed, and that each exposure or interaction with human difference is an opportunity for growth into holism in their process of becoming. E. T. Hall writes: "The task is far from simple, yet understanding ourselves and the world we have created—and which in turn creates us—is perhaps the single most important task facing mankind today."[8] This statement may be seen as particularly applicable to social workers. Almost imperceptibly, forces from within and outside of the profession are calling for the creation of a new generation of social workers who can respond to changing and increasing human needs without constraints due to national boundaries or specialization limitations. Advanced generalist practice is in the process of becoming a model that will reflect and respond to emerging trends and needs. As today's expanding communication technologies force our world to become smaller with globally identifiable human problems, the profession of social work will continue to be called to serve as the voice and touch for the poor, the oppressed, and others in need.

The meta-approach to social work practice offered in this text is an overreaching perspective and mode for proceeding that can be adapted to a multiplicity of problems and environments. Advanced generalist practice is an emerging model of global awareness and integrated methodology that promotes commitment, confidence, and competence for social workers to face emerging issues and problems as we move into the year 2000 and beyond.

## *NOTES*

1. Schools identified in the Council on Social Work Education's *Summary Information on Master of Social Work Education Programs* (Alexandria, Va.: Council on Social Work Education, 1990).

2. Klaus Hurrelmann, *Social Structure and Personality Development* (New York: Cambridge University Press, 1988), p. 6.

3. Martin B. Tracy, "Cross-National Social Welfare Policy Analysis in the Graduate Curriculum: A Comparative Process Model," *Journal of Social Work Education* 28, no. 3 (Fall 1992): 341–352.

4. Bruce Jansson, *Social Welfare Policy: From Theory to Practice* (Belmont, Calif.: Wadsworth Publishing Co., 1990).

5. Richard J. Estes, Ed., *Internationalizing Social Work Education: A Guide to Resources for a New Century* (Philadelphia: University of Pennsylvania, 1992).

6. Pamela Miller, "Covenant Model for Professional Relationships: An Alternative to the Contract Model," *Social Work* 35, no. 2 (March 1990): 121–125.

7. Kenneth J. Gergen, *The Saturated Self* (New York: Basic Books, 1991), p. 147.

8. Edward T. Hall, *Beyond Culture* (Garden City, N.Y.: Anchor Press/Doubleday, 1976), p. 195.

# Appendixes

# International Social Work Questionnaire

**INTERNATIONAL SOCIAL WORK QUESTIONNAIRE**
**CUESTINARIO INTERNACIONAL**
**QUESTIONNAIRE INTERNATIONAL SUR L'AIDE SOCIALE**
**INTERNATIONALER SOZIALARBEIT FRAGEBOGEN**

1) What is social work in your country (a recognized profession, volunteer work serving the poor, social service delivery, etc.)?

1) Que es servicio social en su pais (profession reconosida, trabajo voluntario, auxilio a los pobres, reparto de servicios sociales, etc.)?

1) En quoi consiste l'aide sociale dans votre pays (Est-ce une profession reconnue, un travail effectue par des benevoles dans le but d'aider les personnes dans le besoin, etc. . .)?

1) Was ist Sozialarbeit in Ihrem Land (ein anerkannter Beruf, den Armen dienender Freiwilligendienst, Verteilung von Sozialunterstuetzung, etc.)?

2) What educational background or training do practicing social workers have in your country?

2) Que fondo de educacion o instruccion tienen los trabajadores de servicios sociales en su pais?

2) Quelles sont les etudes exigees et quelles sortes d'experiences sont requises pour travailler en tant qu'assistant(e) social(e)?

2) Welche Schulung, Lehre und Praktikum haben praktizierende Sozialarbeiter in Ihrem Land?

3) What types of education and training programs are available to prepare social workers to work in your country (degrees, years of education, schools)?

3) Que clase de educacion o programas de instruccion hay disponible para preparar a trabajadores de servicios sociales en su pais (licencia, anos de educacion, escuelas)?

3) Quelles genre d'etudes et quels genres de stages sont mis a la disposition de personnes s'engageant dans cette voie en votre pays (diplomes, nombres d'annees d'etudes, ecoles)?

3) Welche Art Schulen und Lehrprogramme stehen in Ihrem Land zur Verfuegung um Sozialarbeiter auf ihre Arbeit vorzubereiten (Abschluesse, Schulungsjahre, Schulen)?

4) Where do social workers work in your country (public/private types of agencies, private practice)?

4) Donde trabajan los trabajadores de servicios sociales en su pais (publico/privado tipo de agencias, practica privada)?

4) Ou exercent les assistants sociaux (agences privees ou publiques, cabinet personnel)?

4) Wo arbeiten Sozialarbeiter in Ihrem Land (oeffentliche/private Arten von Dienststellen, private Praxis)?

5) What activities and duties do social workers perform in your country (counseling, family therapy, home visits, community organization, administration, policy development, etc.)?

5) Que ocupaciones y obligaciones tienen los trabajadores de servicios sociales en su pais (consejar, terapeutica de familia, visitador de casa, organizacion de comunidad, administracion)?

5) En quoi consiste leur travail? Sous quelles formes l'aide sociale est-elle exercee (therapie familiale, visite a domicile, associations communautaires)?

5) Welche Aktivitaeten und Dienste leisten Sozialerbeiter in Ihrem Land (Beratung, Familientherapie, Hausbesuche, Gemeindeorganisationen, Verwaltung, Politik)?

6) a)  Is there a public social welfare program in your country?
6) a)  Tienen asistencia publica social en su pais?
6) a)  Votre pays a-t-il un systeme officiel d'aide sociale?
6) a)  Gibt es oeffentliche Sozialfuersorge in Ihrem Land?

    b)  What services does it offer?
    b)  Que servicios ofrecen?
    b)  Quels genres de services sont offerts par ce programme?
    b)  Welche Dienste bietet sie?

    c)  Who delivers these services?
    c)  Quien desempeña estos servicios?
    c)  Qui est en charge de l'organisation de ces services?
    c)  Wer leistet diese Dienste?

7) What other social services are available in your country (private agencies, religious agencies, private practice, etc.)?
7) Que otros servicios sociales hay disponibles en su pais (agencias publicas/privadas, agencias religiosos)?

7) Quelles sont les autres agences ou organisations existantes qui offrent le meme genre de service (privees, publiques, religieuses)?

7) Welch andere Dienste stehen in Ihrem Land zur Verfuegung (private Dienststellen, religioese Einrichtungen, Privatpraxen, etc.)?

8) What is the average workload of a social worker in a public agency in your country (types and numbers)?

8) Cuáles son las obligaciones normales (casos) de trabajadores de servicios sociales en una agencia publica en su pais (tipos y numeros)?

8) Quel est, en moyenne, le temps de travail d'un(e) assistant(e) social(e) en votre pays, et plus particulierement dans une agence du secteur publique (genre de travail et nombre d'heures)?

8) Was ist die durchschnittliche Arbeitslast von einem Sozialarbeiter in oeffentlicher Sozialarbeit in Ihrem Land (Arten und Zahlen)?

9) What are four of the major problems of people receiving help from social workers in your country today?

9) Que son los quatro problemas mayores de la gente que recibe ayuda de trabajadores sociales en su pais, hoy?

9) Quels sont les quatre plus grands problemes auxquels vous avez'eu a faire face en votre pays aujourd'hui?

9) Was sind die vier groessten Probleme fuer Leute die Sozialhilfe erhalten?

10) Please identify two social service agencies where social workers practice in your country (name, address, telephone, and contact person):

10) Por favor indica dos agencias de servicios sociales donde trabajadores sociales practican en su pais (nombre, direccion, telefono, intermediario):

10) Pourriez-vous nommer deux agences d'aide sociale dans lesquelles exercent des assistant(e)s sociaux (nom, adresse, telephone, personne a contacter):

10) Bitte nennen Sie zwei Sozialhilfestellen wo Sozialarbeiter praktizieren in Ihrem Land (name, adresse, telefon, kontakt person):

11) What would be two typical case examples assigned to social workers in your country? (Use the back of this page if necessary.)

11) Que serian dos ejemplos de casos tipicos asignados a un trabajador de servicios sociales en su pais? (Si es necesario puede usar el reverso de esta pajina.)

11) Donnez deux examples de situations typiques que vous avez-eu a resoudre en tant qu'assistant(e) social(e), en votre pays?

11) Was waeren zwei typische Exemplarfaelle, die Sozialarbeitern zugewiesen werden? (Benutzen Sie die Rueckseite wenn noetig.)

　拝　啓
　　　　寒冷の候、ますますご清栄の事とお慶び申し上げます。突然のお手紙で
失礼いたします。私はアメリカ合衆国ノースカロライナ州に於きまして、いろい
ろな国の社会事業について研究している者です。お手数とは存じますが、貴国の
社会事業の現状について、以下のアンケートにお答えいただき、同封の封筒に入
れ返送していただければ幸いです。ご協力に感謝いたします。

　　　　　　　　　　　　　　　　　　　　　　　　　　敬　具

　　　　　　　　　　　　　　　　イースト・カロライナ大学大学院
　　　　　　　　　　　　　　　　社会事業研究科教授
　　　　　　　　　　　　　　　　マリア・オニール・マクマホン


　　　　　　　国際的社会事業に関するアンケート


１）社会事業（ソーシャルワーク）の現状についてお答ください。
（専門職として確立したものにはどのようなものがあるか、生活困窮者に対する
ボランティア活動、社会的サービスは直接には誰が担当しているかなど）




２）実際に活動しているソーシャルワーカーはどうのような教育や、トレーニン
グを受けていますか？




３）ソーシャルワーカーとして働くためにはどのような教育やトレーニングの機
会、機関がありますか？（学校、学位、教育年限など）

４）ソーシャルワーカーはどのような場で働いていますか？
（私的／公的施設や、私的（個人的）活動の状況など）

５）ソーシャルワーカーはどのような活動や、役目を担っているますか？
（カウンセリング、家庭療法、個別訪問、コミュニティ活動の組織化、行政管理、
意識改革など）

６）ａ）貴国には公的な社会福祉のプログラムがありますか？

　　ｂ）どのようなサービスが行われていますか？

　　ｃ）誰がそのサービスを直接に担当していますか？

７）その他にはどのような社会サービスがありますか？
（私的機関、宗教的機関、個人的活動など）

８）ソーシャルワーカーの平均的な仕事量についてお答ください。（形式や数等）

９）社会奉仕活動を受ける側の、今日に於ける問題点の主なものを４つ挙げてください。

１０）ソーシャルワーカーが活動している社会事業機関を２つ挙げてください。
１機関名：

　住所：

　電話番号：

　担当者名：

２機関名：

　住所：

　電話番号：

　担当者名：

１１）ソーシャルワーカーの活動の典型的な例を具体的に２つ挙げてください。

## APPENDIX B

# The NASW Code of Ethics
# International Federation of Social Workers: International Code of Ethics for the Professional Social Worker
# Universal Declaration of Human Rights

### THE NASW CODE OF ETHICS[1]

I. **The Social Worker's Conduct and Comportment as a Social Worker**

A. **Propriety—The social worker should maintain high standards of personal conduct in the capacity or identity as social worker.**

1. The private conduct of the social worker is a personal matter to the same degree as is any other person's, except when such conduct compromises the fulfillment of professional responsibilities.

2. The social worker should not participate in, condone, or be associated with dishonesty, fraud, deceit, or misrepresentation.

3. The social worker should distinguish clearly between statements and actions made as a private individual and as a representative of the social work profession or an organization or group.

B. **Competence and Professional Development—The social worker should strive to become and remain proficient in professional practice and the performance of professional functions.**

1. The social worker should accept responsibility or employment only on the basis of existing competence or the intention to acquire the necessary competence.

2. The social worker should not misrepresent professional qualifications, education, experience, or affiliations.

**C. Service—The social worker should regard as primary the service obligation of the social work profession.**

1. The social worker should retain ultimate responsibility for the quality and extent of the service that individual assumes, assigns, or performs.

2. The social worker should act to prevent practices that are inhumane or discriminatory against any person or group of persons.

**D. Integrity—The social worker should act in accordance with the highest standards of professional integrity and impartiality.**

1. The social worker should be alert to and resist the influences and pressures that interfere with the exercise of professional discretion and impartial judgement required for the performance of professional functions.

2. The social worker should not exploit professional relationships for personal gain.

**E. Scholarship and Research—The social worker engaged in study and research should be guided by the conventions of scholarly inquiry.**

1. The social worker engaged in research should consider carefully its possible consequences for human beings.

2. The social worker engaged in research should ascertain that the consent of participants in the research is voluntary and informed, without any implied deprivation or penalty for refusal to participate, and with due regard for participants' privacy and dignity.

3. The social worker engaged in research should protect participants from unwarranted physical or mental discomfort, distress, harm, danger, or deprivation.

4. The social worker who engages in the evaluation of services or cases should discuss them only for the professional purposes and only with persons directly and professionally concerned with them.

5. Information obtained about participants in research should be treated as confidential.

6. The social worker should take credit only for work actually done in connection with scholarly and research endeavors and credit contributions made by others.

## II. The Social Worker's Ethical Responsibility to Clients

**F. Primacy of Clients' Interests—The social worker's primary responsibility is to clients.**

1. The social worker should serve clients with devotion, loyalty, determination, and the maximum application of professional skill and competence.

2. The social worker should not exploit relationships with clients for personal advantage, or solicit the clients of one's agency for private practice.

3. The social worker should not practice, condone, facilitate or collaborate with any form of discrimination on the basis of race, color, sex, sexual orientation, age, religion, national origin, marital status, politi-

cal belief, mental or physical handicap, or any other preference or personal characteristic, condition or status.

4. The social worker should avoid relationships or commitments that conflict with the interests of clients.

5. The social worker should under no circumstances engage in sexual activities with clients.

6. The social worker should provide clients with accurate and complete information regarding the extent and nature of the services available to them.

7. The social worker should apprise clients of their risks, rights, opportunities, and obligations associated with social service to them.

8. The social worker should seek advice and counsel of colleagues and supervisors whenever such consultation is in the best interest of clients.

9. The social worker should terminate service to clients, and professional relationships with them, when such service and relationships are no longer required or no longer serve the clients' needs or interests.

10. The social worker should withdraw services precipitously only under unusual circumstances, giving careful consideration to all factors in the situation and taking care to minimize possible adverse effects.

11. The social worker who anticipates the termination or interruption of service to clients should notify clients promptly and seek the transfer, referral, or continuation of service in relation to the clients' needs and preferences.

G. **Rights and Prerogatives of Clients—The social worker should make every effort to foster maximum self-determination on the part of clients.**

1. When the social worker must act on behalf of a client who has been adjudged legally incompetent, the social worker should safeguard the interests and rights of that client.

2. When another individual has been legally authorized to act in behalf of a client, the social worker should deal with that person always with the client's best interest in mind.

3. The social worker should not engage in any action that violates or diminishes the civil or legal rights of clients.

H. **Confidentiality and Privacy—The social worker should respect the privacy of clients and hold in confidence all information obtained in the course of professional service.**

1. The social worker should share with others confidences revealed by clients, without their consent, only for compelling professional reasons.

2. The social worker should inform clients fully about the limits of confidentiality in a given situation, the purposes for which information is obtained, and how it may be used.

3. The social worker should afford clients reasonable access to any official social work records concerning them.

4. When providing clients with access to records, the social worker should take due care to protect the confidences of others contained in those records.

5. The social worker should obtain informed consent of clients before taping, recording, or permitting third party observation of their activities.

I.  **Fees—When setting fees, the social worker should ensure that they are fair, reasonable, considerate, and commensurate with the service performed and with due regard for the clients' ability to pay.**

   1. The social worker should not divide a fee or accept or give anything of value for receiving or making a referral.

III. **The Social Worker's Ethical Responsibility to Colleagues**

   J.  **Respect, Fairness, and Courtesy—The social worker should treat colleagues with respect, courtesy, fairness, and good faith.**

   1. The social worker should cooperate with colleagues to promote professional interests and concerns.

   2. The social worker should respect confidences shared by colleagues in the course of their professional relationships and transactions.

   3. The social worker should create and maintain conditions of practice that facilitate ethical and competent professional performance by colleagues.

   4. The social worker should treat with respect, and represent accurately and fairly, the qualifications, views, and findings of colleagues and use appropriate channels to express judgements on these matters.

   5. The social worker who replaces or is replaced by a colleague in professional practice should act with consideration for the interest, character, and reputation of that colleague.

   6. The social worker should not exploit a dispute between a colleague and employers to obtain a position or otherwise advance the social worker's interest.

   7. The social worker should seek arbitration or mediation when conflicts with colleagues require resolution for compelling professional reasons.

   8. The social worker should extend to colleagues of other professions the same respect and cooperation that is extended to social work colleagues.

   9. The social worker who serves as an employer, supervisor, or mentor to colleagues should make orderly and explicit arrangements regarding the conditions of their continuing professional relationship.

   10. The social worker who has the responsibility for employing and evaluating the performance of other staff members, should fulfill such responsibility in a fair, considerate, and equitable manner, on the basis of clearly enunciated criteria.

   11. The social worker who has the responsibility for evaluating the performance of employees, supervisees, or students should share evaluations with them.

   K.  **Dealing with Colleagues' Clients—The social worker has the responsibility to relate to the clients of colleagues with full professional consideration.**

   1. The social worker should not solicit the clients of colleagues.

   2. The social worker should not assume professional responsibility for the clients of another agency or a colleague without appropriate communication with that agency or colleague.

   3. The social worker who serves the clients of colleagues, during a temporary absence or emergency, should serve those clients with the same consideration as that afforded any client.

**IV. The Social Worker's Ethical Responsibility to Employers and Employing Organizations**

    **L. Commitments to Employing Organization—The social worker should adhere to commitments made to the employing organization.**

      1. The social worker should work to improve the employing agency's policies and procedures, and the efficiency and effectiveness of its services.

      2. The social worker should not accept employment or arrange student field placements in an organization which is currently under public sanction by NASW for violating personnel standards, or imposing limitations on or penalties for professional actions on behalf of clients.

      3. The social worker should act to prevent and eliminate discrimination in the employing organization's work assignments and in its employment policies and practices.

      4. The social worker should use with scrupulous regard, and only for the purpose for which they are intended, the resources of the employing organization.

**V. The Social Worker's Ethical Responsibility to the Social Work Profession**

    **M. Maintaining the Integrity of the Profession—The social worker should uphold and advance the values, ethics, knowledge, and mission of the profession.**

      1. The social worker should protect and enhance the dignity and integrity of the profession and should be responsible and vigorous in discussion and criticism of the profession.

      2. The social worker should take action through appropriate channels against unethical conduct by any other member of the profession.

      3. The social worker should act to prevent the unauthorized and unqualified practice of social work.

      4. The social worker should make no misrepresentation in advertising as to qualifications, competence, service, or results to be achieved.

    **N. Community Service—The social worker should assist the profession in making social services available to the general public.**

      1. The social worker should contribute time and professional expertise to activities that promote respect for the utility, the integrity, and the competence of the social work profession.

      2. The social worker should support the formulation, development, enactment and implementation of social policies of concern to the profession.

    **O. Development of Knowledge—The social worker should take responsibility for identifying, developing, and fully utilizing knowledge for professional practice.**

      1. The social worker should base practice upon recognized knowledge relevant to social work.

      2. The social worker should critically examine, and keep current with, emerging knowledge relevant to social work.

      3. The social worker should contribute to the knowledge base of social work and share research knowledge and practice wisdom with colleagues.

VI. **The Social Worker's Ethical Responsibility to Society**

   P.  **Promoting the General Welfare—The social worker should promote the general welfare of society.**

   1. The social worker should act to prevent and eliminate discrimination against any person or group on the basis of race, color, sex, sexual orientation, age, religion, national origin, marital status, political belief, mental or physical handicap, or any other preference or personal characteristic, condition, or status.

   2. The social worker should act to ensure that all persons have access to the resources, services, and opportunities which they require.

   3. The social worker should act to expand choice and opportunity for all persons, with special regard for disadvantaged or oppressed groups and persons.

   4. The social worker should promote conditions that encourage respect for the diversity of cultures which constitute American society.

   5. The social worker should provide appropriate professional services in public emergencies.

   6. The social worker should advocate changes in policy and legislation to improve social conditions and to promote social justice.

   7. The social worker should encourage informed participation by the public in shaping social policies and institutions.

---

*INTERNATIONAL FEDERATION OF SOCIAL WORKERS:* [2]
*INTERNATIONAL CODE OF ETHICS*
*FOR THE PROFESSIONAL SOCIAL WORKER\**

Social work originates variously from humanitarian, religious and democratic ideals and philosophies and has universal application to meet human needs arising from personal-societal interactions and to develop human potential. Professional Social Workers are dedicated to service for the welfare and self-fulfillment of human beings; to the development and disciplined use of scientific knowledge regarding human and societal behaviors; to the development of resources to meet individual, group, national and international needs and aspirations; and to the achievement of social justice.

### Principles

1. Every human being has a unique value, irrespective of origin, ethnicity, sex, age, beliefs, social and economic status or contribution to society.

2. Each individual has the right of self-fulfillment to the degree that it does not encroach upon the same right of others.

\*Adopted by the International Federation of Social Workers General Meeting, San Juan, Puerto Rico, July 10, 1976.

3. Each society, regardless of its form, should function to provide the maximum benefits for all of its members.

4. The professional Social Worker has the responsibility to devote objective and disciplined knowledge and skill to aid individuals, groups, communities, and societies in their development and resolution of personal-societal conflicts and their consequences.

5. The professional Social Worker has a primary obligation to the objective of service, which must take precedence over self-interest, aims or views.

### Standards of Ethical Conduct

1. Seek and understand the worth of each individual and the elements which condition behavior and the service required.

2. Uphold and advance the values, knowledge and methodology of the profession, refraining from any behavior which damages the functioning of the profession.

3. Clarify all public statements or action whether on an individual basis or as a representative of a professional association, agency or organization.

4. Recognize professional and personal limitations, encourage the utilization for all relevant knowledge and skills and apply scientific methods of inquiry.

5. Contribute professional expertise to the development of sound policies and programmes to better the quality of life in each society.

6. Identify and interpret the social needs, the basis and nature of individual, group, community, national and international social problems, and the work of the social profession.

#### Relative to Clients

1. Maintain the client's right to a relationship of mutual trust, to privacy and confidentiality, and to responsible use of information. The collection and sharing of information or data shall only be related to the professional service function to be performed with the client informed as to its necessity and use. No information shall be released without prior knowledge and informed consent of the client, except where the client cannot be responsible or others may be seriously jeopardized.

2. Recognize and respect the individual goals, responsibilities, and differences of clients. Within the scope of the agency and the clients' social milieu, the professional service shall assist clients to take responsibility for personal actions and to help all clients with equal willingness. Where the professional service cannot be provided under such conditions the client shall be so informed in such a way as to leave the client free to act.

3. Help the client-individual, group, community, or society to achieve self-fulfillment and maximum potential within the limits of the equal rights of others. The service shall be based on helping the client to understand and use the professional relationship, in furtherance of the clients legitimate desires and interests.

#### Relative to Agencies and Organizations

1. Work or co-operate with those agencies and organizations whose policies, procedures, and operations are directed toward adequate service delivery and encouragement of professional practice consistent with the Code of Ethics.

2. Responsibly execute the stated aims and functions of the agency or organization, contributing to the development of sound policies, procedures, and practice in order to obtain the best possible standard of service.
3. Sustain ultimate responsibility to the client, initiating desirable alterations of policy, procedures, and practice through appropriate agency and organizational channels. If necessary remedies are not achieved after channels have been exhausted, initiate appropriate appeals to higher authorities or the wider community of interest.
4. Insure professional accountability to client and community for efficiency and effectiveness through periodic review of client, agency and organizational problems and self-performance.

### Relative to Colleagues
1. Respect the training and performance of colleagues and other professionals extending all necessary co-operation that will enhance effective services.
2. Respect differences of opinion and practice of colleagues and other professionals, expressing criticism through appropriate channels in a responsible manner.
3. Promote and share opportunities for knowledge, experience, and ideas with all professional colleagues, other professionals and volunteers for the purpose of mutual improvement and validation.
4. Bring any violations of client interest or professional ethics and standards to the attention of the appropriate bodies and defend colleagues against unjust actions.

### Relative to the Profession
1. Maintain the values, knowledge and methodology of the profession and contribute to their clarification and improvement.
2. Uphold the professional standards of practice and work for their advancement.
3. Defend the profession against unjust criticism and work to increase confidence in the necessity for professional practice.
4. Encourage new approaches and methodologies needed to meet new and existing needs.

---

## UNIVERSAL DECLARATION OF HUMAN RIGHTS[3]

### Preamble

**Whereas** recognition of the inherent dignity and of the equal and inalienable rights of all members of the human family is the foundation of freedom, justice, and peace in the world.

**Whereas** disregard and contempt for human rights have resulted in barbarous acts which have outraged the conscience of mankind, and the advent of a world in which human beings shall enjoy freedom from speech and belief and freedom from fear and want has been proclaimed as the highest aspiration of the common people.

**Whereas** it is essential, if man is not to be compelled to have recourse, as a last resort, to rebellion against tyranny and oppression, that human rights should be protected by the rule of law.

**Whereas** it is essential to promote the development of friendly relations between States.

**Whereas** the Peoples of the United Nations have in the Charter reaffirmed their faith in fundamental human rights, in the dignity and the worth of the human person and in the equal rights of men and women and have determined to promote social progress and better standards of life in larger freedom.

**Whereas** Member States have pledged themselves to achieve, in co-operation with the United Nations, the promotion of universal respect for and observance of human rights and fundamental freedom.

**Whereas** a common understanding of these rights and freedoms is of the greatest importance for the full realization of this pledge.

**Now, therefore,**

**The General Assembly,**

**Proclaims** this Universal Declaration of Human Rights as a common standard of achievement for all peoples and all nations, to the end that every individual and every organ of society, keeping this Declaration constantly in mind, shall strive by teaching and education to promote respect for these rights and freedoms and by progressive measures, national and international, to secure their universal and effective recognition and observance, both among the peoples of Member States themselves and among the peoples of territories under their jurisdiction.

### Article 1

All human beings are born free and equal in dignity and rights. They are endowed with reason and conscience and should act towards one another in a spirit of brotherhood.

### Article 2

Everyone is entitled to all the rights and freedoms set forth in this Declaration, without distinction of any kind, such as race, colour, sex, language, religion, political or other opinion, national or social origin, property, birth or other status.

Furthermore, no distinction shall be made on the basis of the political, jurisdictional or international status of the country or territory to which a person belongs, whether it be independent, trust, non-self-governing or under any other limitation of sovereignty.

### Article 3

Everyone has the right to life, liberty and the security of the person.

### Article 4

No one shall be held in slavery or servitude; slavery and the slave trade shall be prohibited in all their forms.

### Article 5

No one shall be subjected to torture or to cruel, inhuman or degrading treatment or punishment.

### Article 6

law.
Everyone has the right to recognition everywhere as a person before the

### Article 7

All are equal before the law and are entitled without any discrimination to equal protection of the law. All are entitled to equal protection against any discrimination in violation of this Declaration and against any incitement to such discrimination.

### Article 8

Everyone has the right to an effective remedy by the competent national tribunals for acts violating the fundamental rights granted him by the constitution or by law.

### Article 9

No one shall be subjected to arbitrary arrest, detention or exile.

### Article 10

Everyone is entitled in full equality to a fair and public hearing by an independent and impartial tribunal, in the determination of his rights and obligations and of any criminal charge against him.

### Article 11

1. Everyone charged with a penal offence has the rights to be presumed innocent until proven guilty according to law in a public trial at which he has had all the guarantees necessary for his defence.

2. No one shall be held guilty of any penal offence on account of any act or omission which did not constitute a penal offence, under national or international law, at the time when it was committed. Nor shall a heavier penalty be imposed than the one that was applicable at the time the penal offence was committed.

### Article 12

No one shall be subjected to arbitrary interference with his privacy, family, home or correspondence, nor to attacks upon his honour and reputation. Everyone has the right to the protection of the law against such interference or attacks.

### Article 13

1. Everyone has the right to freedom of movement and residence within the borders of each State.

2. Everyone has the right to leave any country, including his own, and to return to his country.

### Article 14

1. Everyone has the right to seek and to enjoy in other countries asylum from persecution.

2. This right may not be invoked in the case of prosecutions genuinely arising from non-political crimes or from acts contrary to the purposes and principles of the United Nations.

### Article 15

1. Everyone has the right to a nationality.

2. No one shall be arbitrarily deprived of his nationality nor denied the right to change his nationality.

### Article 16

1. Men and women of full age, without any limitation due to race, nationality or religion, have the right to marry and to found a family. They are entitled to equal rights as to marriage, during marriage and at its dissolution.

2. Marriage shall be entered into only with the free and full consent of the intending spouses.

3. The family is the natural and fundamental group unit of society and is entitled to protection by society and the State.

### Article 17

1. Everyone has the right to own property alone as well as in association with others.

2. No one shall be arbitrarily deprived of his property.

### Article 18

Everyone has the right to freedom of thought, conscience and religion; this right includes freedom to change his religion or belief, and freedom, either alone or in community with others and in public or private, to manifest his religion or belief in teaching, practice, worship and observance.

### Article 19

Everyone has the right to freedom of opinion and expression; this right includes freedom to hold opinions without interference and to seek, receive and impart information and ideas through any media and regardless of frontiers.

### Article 20

1. Everyone has the right to freedom of peaceful assembly and association.

2. No one may be compelled to belong to an association.

### Article 21

1. Everyone has the right to take part in the government of his country, directly or through freely chosen representatives.

2. Everyone has the right of equal access to public service in his country.

3. The will of the people shall be the basis of the authority of government; this will shall be expressed in periodic and genuine elections which shall be by universal and equal suffrage and shall be held by secret vote or by equivalent free voting procedures.

### Article 22

Everyone, as a member of society, has the right to social security and is entitled to realization, through national effort and international cooperation and in accordance with the organization and resources of the State, of the economic, social and cultural rights indispensable for his dignity and the free development of his personality.

### Article 23

1. Everyone has the right to work, to free choice of employment, to just and favourable conditions of work and to protection against unemployment.

2. Everyone, without any discrimination, has the right to equal pay for equal work.

3. Everyone who works has the right to just and favourable remuneration ensuring for himself and his family an existence worthy of human dignity, and supplemented, if necessary, by other means of social protection.

4. Everyone has the right to form and to join trade unions for the protection of his interest.

### Article 24

Everyone has the right to rest and leisure, including reasonable limitation of working hours and periodic holidays with pay.

### Article 25

1. Everyone has the right to a standard of living adequate for the wealth and well-being of himself and of his family, including food, clothing, housing and medical care and necessary social services, and the right to security in the event of unemployment, sickness, disability, widowhood, old age or other lack of livelihood in circumstances beyond his control.

2. Motherhood and childhood are entitled to special care and assistance. All children, whether born in or out of wedlock, shall enjoy the same social protection.

### Article 26

1. Everyone has the right to education. Education shall be free, at least in the elementary and fundamental stages. Elementary education shall be compulsory. Technical and professional education shall be made generally available and higher education shall be equally accessible to all on the basis of merit.

2. Education shall be directed to the full development of the human personality and to the strengthening of respect for human rights and fundamental freedoms. It shall promote understanding, tolerance and friendship among all nations, racial or religious groups, and shall further the activities of the United Nations for the maintenance of peace.

3. Parents have a prior right to choose the kind of education that shall be given to their children.

### Article 27

1. Everyone has the right to freely participate in the cultural life of the community, to enjoy the arts and to share in scientific advancement and its benefits.

2. Everyone has the right to the protection of the moral and material interests resulting from any scientific, literary or artistic production of which he is the author.

### Article 28

Everyone is entitled to a social and international order in which the rights and freedoms set forth in this declaration can be fully realized.

### Article 29

1. Everyone has duties to the community in which alone the free and full development of his personality is possible.

2. In the exercise of rights and freedoms, everyone shall be subject only to such limitations as are determined by law solely for the purpose of securing due recognition and respect for the rights and freedoms of others and of meeting the just requirements of morality, public order and the general welfare in a democratic society.

3. These rights and freedoms may in no case be exercised contrary to the purposes and principles of the United Nations.

### Article 30

Nothing in this Declaration may be interpreted as implying for any State, group or person any right to engage in any activity or to perform any act aimed at the destruction of any of the rights and freedoms set forth herein.

### NOTES

1. "The NASW Code of Ethics," Adopted by the 1979 NASW Delegate Assembly, effective 1980, found in *Code of Ethics: Professional Standards,* NASW Policy Statements 1 (Silver Springs, Md.: National Association of Social Workers, Inc., 1979), pp. 3–9.

2. "International Federation of Social Workers International Code of Ethics for the Professional Social Worker," Adopted by the International Federation of Social Workers General Meeting, San Juan, Puerto Rico, July 10, 1976, currently under revision.

3. "Universal Declaration of Human Rights," Adopted by the United Nations General Assembly, 1948, found in *Teaching and Learning About Human Rights: A Manual for Schools of Social Work and the Social Work Profession* (New York: United Nations, 1992), pp. 101–104.

# Regional Office Functions
# Regional Director—Duties and Responsibilities
# Director of Social Services—Duties and Responsibilities

## REGIONAL OFFICE FUNCTIONS*

Assure uniform implementation of statutes, rules, and policy

Provide technical assistance, consultation, and management guidance to county departments of social services

Advise county boards of social services in matters such as developing goals to meet social needs of community, planning budgets, helping boards to understand their responsibilities and identifying those areas where they do not have responsibility (such as operations), helping boards to develop evaluation plans for Directors

Advise Boards of County Commissioners on funding from Federal and State levels and on the level of local funding needed to provide adequate service to their citizens

Work with County Finance Officer to help reconcile DSS expenditures and reimbursements to county general ledger

*North Carolina Department of Human Resources Division of Social Services

Advise County Director in budget management; assist counties in maximizing Federal funds for purchase, lease, or rental of building space, monitor expenditures to assure spending within allocation; provide recommendations for fiscal improvements relating to audits or fiscal monitoring.

In the Public Assistance programs, assist counties with error reduction through a variety of means such as direct evaluations of the Food Stamp Program, helping implement unit management, use of Regional Quality Control staff and error reports to identify specific problem areas and to plan with IM staff for corrective action, use of clerical staff to review completed forms, implementation of special projects and incentives

Help county departments of social services establish fraud units, or identify staff to handle fraud, to assist with fraud prevention and to provide information on prosecution when fraud is identified

Monitor the services program and assist counties in developing corrective action plans to improve services programs and to assure adherence to statutes, rules, and policies

Orient new County Directors by providing them with a complete assessment of the status of the county department of social services, including organization, work flow, income maintenance programs, services programs, their strengths and weaknesses

Provide training to county staff on all Federal and State changes in program policies and procedures

Provide closer and more direct supervision for field staff and help prevent isolation of out-stationed staff

Provide a focal point where responses can be provided to counties more quickly and more efficiently

Perform inspection of county facilities to assure compliance with Federal standards

Assist counties in understanding and complying with the requirements of Titles VI and VII of the Civil Rights Act; monitor compliance; maintain records of compliance in office of Assistant Director for Federal review and audit

Provide direct service to eligible refugees under the Refugee Assistance Program

## REGIONAL DIRECTOR—DUTIES AND RESPONSIBILITIES*

1. Has delegated authority to insure that all federal and state social services policies are followed in the county social services departments within a specific geographic region.
2. Manages and directs all field program consultants and other administrative personnel assigned to the region with responsibilities for program and policy interpretation, technical assistance, training, and policy compliance.
3. Maintains direct contact with the Assistant Director for Regional Administration for guidance and direction in the execution of regional operations.

*North Carolina Department of Human Resources, Division of Social Services

4. Participates in regularly scheduled and special meetings with the Assistant Director for Regional Administration, other regional directors, and Division program managers to keep abreast of policy changes, development of new programs, engage in policy formulation, and make suggestions for change in policy, as well as participating in agency planning, goal setting, and the definition of statewide priorities.

5. Works through the field staff or directly with leaders of the counties including county commissioners, social services board members, county managers, and local agency directors to resolve local program and administrative problems and to insure compliance with established policies.

6. Performs all administrative duties relative to programs and personnel in the region including supervision of staff activities; evaluating the performance of field personnel in accordance with state personnel policies; employment and discharge of all regional personnel in accordance with state personnel policies and after consultation with Division management; coordination and approval of itineraries of field staff; provide leadership in developing and executing regional plans, goals, and priorities in accordance with Division goals and objectives.

7. Advises county social services directors on administrative and budget matters and provides management orientation and assistance to new directors.

8. Holds regular joint and special meetings with Directors of County Social Services Department as needed to discuss common problems, advise directors of policy and program changes, and to seek local participation in development of program enhancements.

## DIRECTOR OF SOCIAL SERVICES—DUTIES AND RESPONSIBILITIES* [GS 108-A-14 specifies 14 duties and responsibilities]

1. To serve as executive officer of the county social services board and act as its secretary.

2. To appoint departmental staff under the merit system rules.

3. To administer public assistance and social services programs under applicable regulations.

4. To administer funds provided by the Board of Commissioners for the care of indigent persons in the county under policies approved by the social services board.

5. To act as the agent of the State Social Services Commission and DHR in relation to work they require in the county.

6. To investigate adoption cases and supervise adoptive placements [see GS Chapter 48].

7. To issue employment certificates to children under regulations of the State Department of Labor [GS 95-25.5].

8. To supervise domiciliary homes for the aged or disabled persons under the Social Services Commission's rules and regulations [GS Chapter 131D and 131D, Article 3].

*North Carolina Division of Social Services, 1992.

9. To assist and cooperate with the Department of Correction and its representatives [GS 148-33.1(f) and GS 148-4(7)].

10. To act in conformity with the law regarding the sterilization of mentally ill and mentally retarded persons [GS Chapter 35].

11. To investigate reports of child abuse and neglect, as well as take appropriate action to protect children found to be abused or neglected [the Juvenile Code (GS Chapter 7A, Subchapter XI)].

12. To accept children for placement in foster homes and supervise each placement for as long as foster care is needed [Juvenile Code].

13. To investigate the proposed placement of a child under age twelve (12), when notified of the proposed placement by the prospective adoptive parents, to determine whether the placement is contrary to the child's welfare [see also GS 48-3].

14. To receive and evaluate reports of abuse, neglect, or exploitation of disabled adults as well as to take appropriate action to protect them.

There are a number of statutes that address the director's duties or authority. Some examples are: guardianship of adults [GS 35A]; services to the blind [GS Chapter III]; consent for a pregnant minor to marry [GS 51-2; and unclaimed bodies [GS 130A-415].

# Research Glossary of Terms

**Bias:** that quality of a measurement device that tends to result in a misrepresentation of what is being measured in a particular direction, e.g., the questionnaire item "Don't you agree that the supervisor is doing a good job?" would be biased in that it would generally encourage more favorable responses.[1] "Any effect that systematically distorts the outcome of a research study so that the results are not representative of the phenomenon under investigation."[2]

**Central tendency:** summary averages (arithmetic mean, median, mode).

**Construct:** an abstraction that social scientists discuss in their theories, such as power, intelligence, social status, income. Variables serve as concrete representation of constructs. No single variable can totally represent a construct.

**Control group:** group of targets that does not receive treatment.

**Experimental group:** group of targets to which treatment or aid or condition is applied/supplied. "The group in which the independent variable is manipulated."[3]

**External validity:** the extent to which a researcher can generalize the findings of a study to settings and populations beyond the study conditions.

**Hypothesis:** a conjecture about reality. It is a statement that the researcher has reason to believe is true for which there is no proof. Most hypotheses are concerned with relationships among different aspects of phenomena and require at least two variables. The types of relational hypotheses are causal, associative, and multivariate.

**Internal validity:** determination that the intervention did or did not cause the desired change among the studied targets.

**Measure of association:** computing the strength of a relationship between two variables.

**Operationalizing:** a sequence of steps taken by researchers to obtain a measurement that involve generating a scale or a set of categories; concrete empirical procedures are specified that will result in measurements of variables; specifying; moving from the abstract to the specific.

**Random selection:** a systematic process which ensures that every element and every combination of elements in a population have a specifiable chance of being chosen for a study; each element has an equal chance of selection independent of any other event in the selection process.

**Reliability:** ". . . a matter of whether a particular technique, applied repeatedly to the same object, would yield the same result each time."[4]

**Sampling:** an activity used by researchers to select representative units from a study population. From data gathered from these units, researchers draw inferences about the nature of the entire population, i.e., they generalize that what is true of the sample will be true of the population. Sample size ranges from 10–20 percent of the population in descriptive research to 30 subjects in experimental research.[5] There are two types of samples:

    A. *Non-probability:* A sample selected in some fashion other than randomly, e.g., judgmental, quota, snowball samples.

    B. *Probability:* Selection of a sample involving some random selection mechanism, e.g., systematic sample, stratified random sample, cluster sample, etc.

**Study population:** "the theoretically specified aggregation of study elements . . . from which the sample is actually selected."[6]

**Test of statistical significance:** a class of statistical computations that indicate the likelihood that the relationship observed between variables in a sample can be attributed to sampling error only.[7] "A determination of whether a difference between conditions or a relationship is so large that the possibility of its happening by chance is minimal."[8]

**Validity:** the extent to which an empirical measure adequately reflects the real meaning of the concept being investigated; determining whether the research measures what it was designed to measure. Although the ultimate validity of a measure can never be proven, relative validity is accepted on the basis of face validity, criterion validity, content validity, construct validity, internal validation, and external validation.[9]

**Variable:**   a set of mutually exclusive attributes; an entity expected to change or to take on different values in the investigation. These values may be qualitative (sex) or quantitative (age). Babbie cites five types of variables which appear regularly in research:

A. *Independent variables* are presumed to be causal factors, to bring about the change.

B. *Dependent variables* are factors to be explained or those presumed to be effects of the intervention.

C. *Antecedent variables* operate prior in time to the independent variable and the dependent variable. It is of particular interest if it explains the relationship between the independent and dependent variables.

D. *Intervening variable:* the relationship between the independent variable and the dependent variable is influenced by a variable that occurs between them in time.

E. *Attribute variable* is a measurement imposed on a phenomenon the researcher wishes changed or needs to take into account in his change efforts.[10]

### NOTES

1. Allen Rubin and Earl R. Babbie, *Research Methods for Social Work* (Belmont, CA: Wadsworth Publishing Co., 1993), p. 695.

2. Robert W. Weinbach and Richard M. Grinnell, *Statistics for Social Workers,* 2nd ed. (New York: Longman Publishing, 1991), p. 194.

3. Ibid., p. 199.

4. Rubin and Babbie, *Research Methods for Social Work,* p. 168.

5. Ibid., pp. 219–238.

6. Ibid., p. 225.

7. Ibid., p. 704.

8. Weinbach and Grinnell, *Statistics for Social Workers,* p. 210.

9. Rubin and Babbie, *Research Methods for Social Work,* p. 704.

10. Earl A. Babbie, *Survey Research Methods* (Belmont, CA: Wadsworth Publishing Co., 1973), pp. 244–245, 304–306.

# Advanced Generalist Questionnaire

October 20, 1992

Dear Advanced Generalist:

I am conducting a study of graduates from schools offering concentrations in advanced generalist practice ("advanced generic," "advanced practice in the generalist perspective," or "integrated methods"). I would like to describe the current practice of advanced generalists in the book I am writing called, *Advanced Generalist Practice, With an International Perspective.* It will be a sequel to the book I wrote called, *The General Method of Social Work Practice: A Problem Solving Approach.* I hope it will serve to enhance quality education for advanced generalist practice.

Would you kindly complete the enclosed questionnaire and return it in the self-addressed stamped envelope by November 11, 1992. Responses from graduates will not be identified according to name. Your participation in this study is greatly needed. Thank you for your assistance.

Sincerely,

*Maria O'Neil McMahon*

Dr. Maria O'Neil McMahon,
Professor
East Carolina University
School of Social Work
Ragsdale Hall—Rm. 214A
Greenville, N.C. 27858

## Advanced Generalist Practice Questionnaire

1. How would you generally describe your work environment (i.e. school, Judicial System, Family Service, Health, etc.)?_____

2. Advanced generalists may work with various systems such as individuals, families, groups, or communities. With what systems and for approximately what % of time do you work?

Individuals_____% Families_____% Groups_____% Communities_____%

Other_____% . . . please specify_____

3. In your present practice, what do you do for approximately what % of time?

Casework_____% Community Organization_____% Supervision_____%

Management_____% Group Work_____% Agency Administration_____%

Policy Development_____% Program Planning_____% Family Therapy_____%

Research_____% Teaching_____% Other, please specify: _____

---

4. Please answer by placing a check in the appropriate column.

| How **PROFICIENT** do you think you are in: | Very | Somewhat | Not very | Not at all |
|---|---|---|---|---|
| a. Direct practice (client work)...................... | | | | |
| b. Indirect practice (research, administrative, supervisory, etc.).............. | | | | |
| c. Integrated practice (both direct & indirect)...................................... | | | | |
| d. Using an "open selection" of diverse theories (models, concepts, tools, techniques) for assessment ................... | | | | |
| e. Using an "open selection" of diverse theories (tools, techniques, concepts, and models) for intervention..................... | | | | |
| f. Evaluating and comparing social process, programs, and policies.............. | | | | |
| g. Using computer skills in social work research................................................ | | | | |

5. Please place a check in the appropriate column indicating the **DEGREE** to which you see your current practice described in the following ways:

| | Totally | Large degree | Moderately | Small degree | Not present |
|---|---|---|---|---|---|
| a. Holistic................................ | | | | | |
| b. Problem solving.................... | | | | | |
| c. Built on an ecological systems perspective............. | | | | | |
| d. Advanced generalist............. | | | | | |
| e. Globally aware...................... | | | | | |
| f. Other (Please descibe in #6 below)................................. | | | | | |

6. Is there any other way you might describe your current practice?_____

_____

_____

7. When faced with an ethical dilemma, what factors do you consider before making your professional judgement? Please check all that apply:

norms_____ circumstances_____ outcomes_____ means_____ ends_____ person_____

environment_____ other_____, please specify_____

8. Has your practice been impacted in any way by international events or developments?

yes_____ no_____ If yes, please describe_____

_____

_____

9. Please list the racial/ethnic backgrounds of your clients that are different from your own: ___

_____

10. Do you engage in international social work (working with people, programs, laws, policies of other countries)? Please describe: _____

_____

_____

11. Please identify some of the major theories (models, tools, techniques, concepts) you use in making assessments:_____

_____

_____

12. Please identify some of the major theories (concepts, tools, techniques, models) you use for intervention:_____

_____

_____

13. Additional Information: Prior to your MSW program did you have:

    a. Social Work Experience? Years_____ Months_____

    b. Voluntary experience in human services? Years_____ Months_____

    In what year did you graduate with your MSW degree?_____

14. Please answer by placing a check in the appropriate column.

To what **EXTENT** do you think:

| | Great | Some | Little | Not at all |
|---|---|---|---|---|
| a. Your graduate social work program prepared you for direct practice.............. | | | | |
| b. Your graduate social work program prepared you for integrated practice........ | | | | |
| c. Your graduate social work program prepared you for indirect practice ............ | | | | |
| d. You engage in cross-cultural practice (clients of racial/ethnic background different from yours)................................ | | | | |
| e. You engage in multi-cultural practice (working with clients of several different racial/ethnic backgrounds)...................... | | | | |
| f. You engage in international social work... | | | | |
| g. You engage in ethical decision making.... | | | | |
| h. You find yourself dealing with ethical dilemmas................................................. | | | | |
| i. You engage in teamwork.......................... | | | | |
| j. You engage in making referrals................ | | | | |

Thank you for completing and returning this questionnaire.

# Index